THE LIBRARIES OF LONDON

THE LIBRARIES OF LONDON

Second, revised edition

Edited by
RAYMOND IRWIN
and
RONALD STAVELEY

THE LIBRARY ASSOCIATION
CHAUCER HOUSE, MALET PLACE
LONDON
1961

First edition, 1949

© R. Irwin and R. Staveley, 1961

Made and printed in England by
STAPLES PRINTERS LIMITED
at their Rochester, Kent, establishment

CONTENTS

INTRODUCTION

IT is now over fifty years since Reginald Arthur Rye published his *Students' guide to the libraries of London*. A second edition appeared in 1910, and a third edition revised and enlarged in 1927. This great work of nearly six hundred pages quickly established itself as one of the fundamental textbooks of librarianship, but it has been out of print for many years.

The original edition of this present work was published in 1949. It was based on a series of seventeen lectures delivered during a week's vacation course at the School of Librarianship and Archives, University College London. Each of its chapters described the history and purpose of an individual library, or a group of related libraries, and was written by a librarian who knew his subject from the inside. This also is now out of print, and the opportunity has been taken to publish a revised edition covering a much wider and more representative selection of London's libraries.

The introduction to the first edition emphasised two points. First, that although *The libraries of London* would supplement Rye's book and bring it up to date in some respects, there was no thought that it could replace Rye. The historical material in Rye's *Students' guide*, both in its long and important introductory chapter and in the accounts of many individual libraries, will render it a valuable source book for many years to come; and it will always serve a useful purpose as a directory of our libraries in the early decades of this century. Since Rye's book was written, however, much has happened to change the face of London. New libraries have appeared; old libraries have changed; services are expanding to meet wider demands. There is room therefore for a new survey of the work of our libraries which can be shelved alongside Rye's great volume. Even in the last ten years there have been many important developments in the character and extent of the services which a reader can obtain from the libraries of this city, so that the first edition of *The libraries of London* is itself largely out of date.

Secondly, it was explained that there was no intention of providing a complete guide to all the available libraries. There are other reference works[1] which supply at least brief details of all English libraries of any note, and there is no need to repeat them here. In this new edition, however, it has seemed right to widen the field considerably, so as to present a much fuller picture of the library resources of London. All of the chapters have been carefully revised, and most have been largely re-written. An entirely new chapter has been devoted to the large and important library at University College London; the University of London Library is given a chapter to itself; the chapter on the British Library of Political and Economic Science has been fully revised; and the other university libraries are discussed in a separate chapter. Additional chapters are also included on certain important groups of libraries which received inadequate treatment in the first edition, notably the music libraries, the ecclesiastical libraries, the industrial libraries, and technical and professional libraries and the libraries of the learned societies and of the London County Council. One chapter in the first edition has been omitted, namely, that dealing with the Public Record Office. Important as this chapter was, it nevertheless describes a different kind of institution, and is not strictly comparable with the others; it would belong more appropriately perhaps to a survey of archival rather than library resources. In his original chapter on this, Sir Hilary Jenkinson looked forward to the possibility of a course of lectures on the archives of the London area. This ideal is still in front of us, and the need for such a survey grows apace. It is our hope that we shall be able to publish in due time a parallel study not only of the Public Record Office but also of the many other record collections in and around London.

It should be noted here that in neither the first edition nor in this has any attempt been made to describe the commercial and subscription libraries (other than the London Library). These have formed an important feature of the literary and social life of London since the middle of the eighteenth century. For the most part, however, their history, their purposes and their problems are so different from those of other libraries that they tend to form a distinct class by themselves. A separate and well-documented study of their fortunes and misfortunes could make a valuable contribution to London history, but this again is an

---

[1] e.g. The Aslib directory: a guide to sources of information in Great Britain and Ireland, ed. by Miriam Alman, 2 vols., 1958, and *The Libraries, Museums and Art Galleries Year Book, 1954–55.*

ideal for the future. [2] Another class of library omitted is that associated with the offices of the great national newspapers; active and highly efficient their libraries are, but not generally accessible to the student or research worker. [3]

The introduction to the first edition drew attention to the fact that University College (where the original lectures on which these chapters are based were delivered) lay in the bibliographical heart of London, with a score of great libraries almost within the proverbial stone's throw. The School of Librarianship and Archives was established at this College in 1919, the first Director being Dr. E. A. Baker. He was succeeded by J. D. Cowley in 1934. The School was closed on the outbreak of war in 1939, and towards the end of the war Cowley resigned his post on receiving appointment as Goldsmiths' Librarian to the University of London. Shortly afterwards, by a cruel stroke of fate, he was killed while on active service with the R.A.F. Those of us who are left to carry on in their place know how much we owe to the inspiration and wisdom of both J. D. Cowley and E. A. Baker. The School, which re-opened in 1945, now offers courses for the academic postgraduate diplomas in librarianship and archive administration, and many hundreds of senior librarians, both in this country and overseas, and an increasing number of archivists too, owe their initial training to the School. There are two other full-time library schools in London, at the North-Western Polytechnic and at Ealing Technical College; both of these offer courses for the Library Association's examinations.

It is appropriate to add here that the area in which University College London is situated is particularly rich in special collections devoted to the subject of bibliography, which must always occupy a central place in library studies. The libraries of the University (especially the Middlesex North Library) and of University College are of special importance to the student of this subject. The resources of the British Museum in this connection need no comment. The neighbourhood of the Museum, however, has become a natural focus for literary activities of all kinds: for publishing houses and booksellers, whose centre of gravity has tended to move from St. Paul's Churchyard to Bloomsbury; for bibliographical research of all kinds; and for co-operative library agencies such as the National Central Library and the

[2] On these libraries see:

HAMLYN, H. M. Eighteenth-century circulating libraries in England. *Library*. Fifth series (4) 1947, 197–222.

[3] LEWIS, J. Newspaper libraries. Library Assocn., 1952.

British National Bibliography. There are in fact three centres of special bibliographical importance today in London. The first is Bloomsbury; the second, Burlington House, where can be found the libraries of many learned societies; the third is in South Kensington, where are the libraries of the Science Museum, the Natural History Museum and the Victoria and Albert Museum.

It will be appropriate to mention here two organisations of importance to librarians which are our near neighbours at University College, and are not described elsewhere in this book. The *British National Bibliography* is a co-operative venture sponsored authoritatively by the British Museum, the Library Association, the Publishers' Association, the Booksellers' Association, the National Book League, the British Council, the Royal Society, the National Central Library, the Unesco Co-operating Body for Libraries, and Aslib. It could scarcely have had a more imposing array of godparents, and their confidence has been justified by its steadily expanding circulation during ten years of vigorous activity. In this period it has gained a world-wide reputation as a model for the printed national bibliographies which Unesco is seeking to encourage in every country. Since 1950 the *B.N.B.* (as it is familiarly known) has been published weekly, giving in subject order the new publications of the week together with an author and title list. The last issue each month contains an author, title and subject index, and cumulations are issued every three, six, nine and twelve months. A cumulation for the years 1951–54 has been published; further, five-yearly, cumulations are planned. In addition a service of printed entries on cards and slips is provided; and the *British Catalogue of Music* was launched in 1958, with quarterly and annual volumes. The architect behind this very complicated structure has from the start been Mr. A. J. Wells, and the credit for its success must be given largely to his enthusiasm and initiative. The authoritative character of this great reference work should be emphasised; it is compiled in conjunction with the Copyright Office of the British Museum, and its publication has a distinguished record of regularity, punctuality and comprehensiveness.

Another co-operative reference work whose editorial office is at the British Museum is the *British union – catalogue of periodicals.* The four volumes of this work, edited by J. D. Stewart, were completed in 1958; after the issue of a supplementary volume, its continuation will be taken over by the National Central Library. On the other hand, the *World list of scientific periodicals published in the years 1900–1950*, edited by William Allan Smith and Francis L. Kent, with the assistance of

G. B. Stratton, is based on the library of the Zoological Society; and the *Subject Index to Periodicals* is published quarterly, with an annual cumulation by the Library Association, which also issues *Library Science Abstracts* quarterly and *The Library Association Record* monthly.

The National Central Library (to which a chapter of the present work is devoted) and Chaucer House have for many years been next-door neighbours of University College. The rapid expansion of the College since the war has made it necessary for these premises to be absorbed by the University, which is providing a new building for them in Store Street not far away. Chaucer House is the headquarters of the Library Association, the professional body uniting libraries and library authorities under its Royal Charter, and maintaining a system of qualifying examinations and a register of chartered librarians. It can be fittingly mentioned here because it possesses an important library and information service in the special subject of librarianship. The Association was founded in 1877, but its library, though it grew steadily through the years, was not established on a secure and per-manent basis till 1934. The aim has been to build up a comprehensive collection of books on librarianship in every language, and it now claims to have one of the largest collections in the world devoted to librarianship and bibliography, with nearly 25,000 books, pamphlets and periodicals. A printed catalogue of its holdings in March 1956 was published in 1958; this was edited by D. C. Henrik Jones, who was its distinguished librarian for twenty-five years till his retirement in 1959. This library provides an invaluable professional service, and is in continuous use by countless librarians and students.

Mention should be made here of one other association of pro-fessional interest, namely Aslib, whose offices are at 3 Belgrave Square, S.W.1. This exists particularly to serve the interests of those working in scientific and industrial libraries and information bureaux. It has an excellent library, and its many publications include the *Journal of Documentation*, a quarterly devoted to the "recording, organisation and dissemination of specialised knowledge", and an annual *Index to theses accepted for higher degrees in the universities of Great Britain and Ireland*.

There are of course many other societies of interest to the librarian, especially in the literary and bibliographical sphere. It will be sufficient if only two of these are mentioned here. The office of the Biblio-graphical Society is at the British Academy in Burlington Gardens. Its quarterly, *The Library*, and its many separate publications, have main-tained a scholarly tradition in the field of critical and historical bibliography for seventy years. Not far from Burlington Gardens, at 7 Albemarle Street, are the offices of the National Book League, founded in 1925 to foster a wider and more discriminating interest in books. The N.B.L. has a useful library of some 5,000 'books on books', and its exhibitions and reading lists have established a wide reputation, while its Book Information Bureau is in constant use for telephone and postal inquiries.

This preliminary glance at the contemporary background of London's libraries will indicate something of the wealth of literary and scientific resources to which the chapters of this book may serve as signposts. The libraries described are of every kind and size, and the chapters are arranged so far as possible in a logical order. The first six chapters are concerned with those having a definitely national status, beginning of course with the British Museum itself. Two chapters follow describing the libraries of Parliament and the Government Departments, and then three dealing with those maintained by the City of London, the London County Council and the London boroughs. Next there are four chapters studying the many academic libraries of the University of London. The London Library and the libraries of the various learned societies come next, followed by chapters on technical, professional and industrial libraries. Finally there are four chapters concerned with groups of libraries serving the special interests of the Church, Law, Medicine and Music.

It has been thought advisable to omit the bibliography which was printed in the original edition, and to concentrate the references at the foot of the various chapters.

We must close this introduction by acknowledging our debts to the many good friends who have helped us in the production of this book, especially of course to the contributors who have so readily given their services in writing and revising the various chapters. We have in addition received willing assistance from the staff of the Library Association at Chaucer House. Finally we would express our thanks to Miss Mary Piggott, who has willingly undertaken the laborious task of compiling the index.

RAYMOND IRWIN

RONALD STAVELEY

CHAPTER I

THE BRITISH MUSEUM

By Sir Frank Francis, K.C.B.

Director and Principal Librarian

FOUR departments of the British Museum might justly be considered to constitute the British National Library. These are the Departments of Printed Books, Manuscripts, Oriental Printed Books and Manuscripts and Prints and Drawings. If I concentrate in this chapter largely on the work of one only of these departments, the Department of Printed Books, I do so because space does not allow of a full description of the work and activities of all four and because the work of the Printed Books falls more closely into the theme of this series of studies. Readers of this book will not need to be reminded of the quality of the manuscript record material in the British Museum, ranging from its extensive collections of early Egyptian papyri and the cuneiform library of Ashurbanipal to the papers of modern statesmen and the manuscripts of modern authors, and including manuscript music and maps from all parts of the world and prints and drawings as remarkable for their documentary as for their artistic interest.

The British Museum is the national deposit library. That is to say, it receives and preserves for public record, and endeavours to produce on demand, a copy of every piece of printed matter published in the United Kingdom. It is also a public reference library, having as its objectives first the acquisition of all books in all languages likely to be required for reference and research by the scholars who use it, and second the production of catalogues and the arrangement of exhibitions to make the collections known.

It is not necessary to say anything of the history of the Museum. This is sufficiently well known to most librarians, and it has in any case been successfully dealt with by Dr. Arundell Esdaile, Secretary of the Museum from 1926 to 1940, in *The British Museum Library* (Library Association and Allen & Unwin, 1946). This work should also be referred to for a detailed account of the Museum collections. It is proposed in this chapter to give an account of the services which the Museum offers to the public and of its internal organisation.

The collections of the Museum have been built up by gifts, by purchase and, most important of all, by the books acquired under the provisions of the Copyright Acts. The copyright privilege came to the Museum with the Royal Library in 1757, which had enjoyed the right to a copy of every book published since 1662, but it was only after the middle of the nineteenth century that the rights of the Museum were energetically enforced. Since the time of the great Principal Librarian, Sir Anthony Panizzi, acquisitions from this source have been progressively more complete. The Museum officials, moreover, have made great efforts to make good the gaps caused by imperfect observance of the Copyright Acts and to increase the resources of the library by wise purchases and by attracting gifts. One of the main principles of the buying policy has been, and is still, to acquire all English books and periodicals which are not represented in the collections.

The collection of English printed books is thus very large indeed. It includes some notable special collections: the Thomason collection of Civil War and Commonwealth publications; the collection of plays bequeathed by David Garrick in 1779; the Burney collection of seventeenth- and eighteenth-century newspapers; the King's Library, the library of George III, rich in English literature; and the Wise collection of English literature. Its main feature is its comprehensiveness. This should not be lost sight of, for it means that not only the standard works, which are available in many places, but vast numbers of secondary and minor books which are far from being so common, are available for consultation.

It was at one time the declared policy of the library to attempt to make itself all-inclusive in all subjects and in all languages. In more recent times, various considerations have led to the adoption of a more limited policy, so far as the *purchase* of books is concerned, and the Museum has tended, in the case of foreign books, to specialise on subjects which might be roughly grouped as humanistic. This is due in part to the existence in London of 'national special' libraries such as the Science Library, the Patent Office Library, and the Natural History Museum Library which specialise in the subjects with which the British Museum has found it most difficult to deal. It should not be inferred, however, that the collections as a whole betray this bias. The foundation collections of Sir Hans Sloane included his library of 40,000 volumes rich in natural history and medicine, and later accessions have included such collections as the very fine natural history library of Sir Joseph Banks. The Museum's purchases, moreover, for many years were made on a wide and inclusive scale so as to preserve the catholicity of the early collections. It is the present practice of the Museum to attempt to acquire 'English' books printed abroad and also to buy books by outstanding authors and important books likely to be of historical importance in every field of knowledge. It is also a fact that many most important scientific works are published in the proceedings of learned societies and academies and as dissertations. These the library is very rich in.

Besides the special collections I have mentioned, the Museum is rich in incunabula, and in the early printed literature of European countries. It has extensive collections of the pamphlet literature of the Reformation and of the French Revolution. In music it has large collections, supplemented by the purchase in 1947 of the Hirsch Library and the magnificent gift by Her Majesty the Queen in 1957 of the Royal Music Library which had been on permanent loan to the Museum since 1911. The Grenville Library bequeathed to the Museum by the Rt. Hon. Thomas Grenville in 1846 has fine examples of early printing, literature, history and travel.

The manuscripts include the Cotton collection of books from the libraries of the monasteries dispersed at the Reformation, and of political papers, the Harleian, rich in political history, the Sloane, rich, like Sloane's printed books, in botany and zoology, the Royal collection, which incorporates the books of Thomas Cranmer, Lord Lumley and the Earl of Arundel, and many others. The collections number over 60,000 volumes of manuscripts, besides large numbers of charters and seals, and 2,500 papyri.

The volumes in the Department of Oriental Printed Books now number approximately: printed books 250,000, manuscripts 50,000.

In all there are upwards of 6,000,000 books on all subjects and in all languages available for consultation in the Museum.

ADMISSION

It has been found impossible, in practice, to grant admission to these collections indiscriminately. Situated as it is in the centre of London and attached to a world-famous collection of antiquities, the danger of being completely overrun by chance inquiries of a trivial nature is so great that admission has had to be restricted to those who need to consult books not elsewhere available. This condition is interpreted with insight and understanding, and no genuine inquirer whose requirements cannot be met elsewhere, need fear that his request for admission will be refused. Admission to all the reading rooms – the great domed Reading Room, the Manuscript Students' Room, the Oriental Students' Room, and the Print Room – is by ticket, obtained on application in writing to the Director and Principal Librarian. Tickets are valid, as a rule, for six months and may be renewed at the end of that time, again by written application. Objection is frequently taken to this requirement, but a moment's reflection will show that it is not unreasonable in view of the great demands on the available accommodation. Temporary tickets of admission are issued in the Director's office in cases where application is made to see a particular book or to carry out a small piece of research. Such tickets are valid for the day of issue or for periods up to a week. Special tickets are issued for each of the reading rooms.

The main reading room of the Department of Printed Books is, of course, the domed Reading Room, built in 1857 at the instance of Sir Anthony Panizzi. The administrative staff is accommodated at the centre, behind a circular counter. In front of this counter are two others arranged concentrically, which contain the General Catalogue and a number of reference books. Readers are accommodated at long desks, radiating like spokes of a wheel from the outer of the two catalogue desks. The reader in search of a book of which he knows the author and title, will find it in the General Catalogue under the author's name. This catalogue, which consists of over 1,500 volumes, is a complete record of all printed books in Western languages in the library, with the exception of newspapers, music and maps, for which there are separate catalogues.

Requests for books are made on tickets with a carbon attached, on which the prospective reader enters the heading under which the book is entered in the General Catalogue, a brief title, the date and the press-mark, adding his own name, the letter and number of his seat in the Reading Room, and the date. This ticket is dispatched by pneumatic tube to one of a number of receiving stations in the bookstacks. On receipt, the duplicate ticket is detached and inserted in the pocket of a cardboard strip known as a shelf-board. This is taken, together with the reader's ticket, to the place where the book is stored and is left on the shelf in place of the book. The ticket is placed in the book and this, with others being dispatched at the same time, is placed in a box and delivered by means of a mechanical conveyor to a central delivery station adjoining the Reading Room. Here books are sorted and sent into the Reading Room for delivery to the readers by the Reading Room staff. The entire operation, it is found, takes up to one hour. The reader can avoid this delay by asking for books in advance. Such requests should contain full details of the books asked for: the Reading Room staff is not large enough to undertake to look up books in the General Catalogue.

The walls of the Reading Room on the ground floor contain a library of reference books comprising some 25,000 volumes to which readers have open access. These volumes are arranged in convenient groups each clearly labelled. Sets of certain learned periodicals in frequent demand for scholarly research are also included. The reference books in the Reading Room are kept under review and, wherever necessary, new books are substituted for those which are superseded. A catalogue of books in the Reading Room on cards is placed in a cabinet located at the inner end of seat K14. This card catalogue replaces the fourth edition (1910) of a printed catalogue which was first published in 1859.

When the reader has finished his reading, he returns his books to the central desk and receives in exchange his original application slips. Should he wish to consult the same books on the following day, they can be reserved for him and they are issued to him when next required, on the production of the original slips. Books are reserved for readers for two days and if not applied for are returned to the shelves on the morning of the third day. Should a reader wish to have books reserved for a longer period than this, permission must be obtained from the Superintendent of the Reading Room, but it is unusual for permission to be withheld. Readers' tickets which for any reason are not claimed by the end of the day, are retained and checked against the books the following day. When the books are returned they are sorted immediately and distributed to the various sections of the library and are replaced on the shelves, the shelf-boards which had been left in their place being removed.

Certain books may be read only in the North Library. This is a special reading room with seats for about one hundred, set aside for the consultation of rare and valuable books, specially large books, collections of unbound parts of serials and any other books which it is desired to keep under close supervision. Where it is necessary for a reader's work, books can be transferred from the main Reading Room into the North Library, on application to the Superintendent. Arrangements are also made, on occasion, for large numbers of books to be made available in this room. The North Library contains a small reference library, mainly bibliographical. A series of microfilm readers is provided in the gallery of this room.

Applications for music and maps are made in the same way as applications for ordinary books, except that they are made on special coloured slips. Music and maps are consulted in the two reading rooms, rare and valuable items being reserved for consultation in the North Library. The need for separate, adequate, reading rooms for music and maps is felt very severely. There is little doubt that the Museum collections, which are very large, would be better appreciated, and even more widely used, if such special reading rooms were provided. As it is, consultations in the Music Department are limited to those who wish to consult the rough, pre-1800 subject index and the manuscript index to the opera librettos, or to look through large standard sets of music, and to those who require special information not ascertainable from the catalogues or from the reference books provided.

Special rooms are provided for the consultation of the Department's very extensive collection of official publications of the United Kingdom and of many countries from many parts of the world and for the consultation of current numbers of periodicals and serials from the countries of Eastern Europe.

The Reading Room is staffed by a Superintendent and his deputy, and a number of assistants of the Civil Service executive and clerical officer grades, whose services are at the disposal of the readers. The function of this staff is to man an Enquiry Desk situated at the entrance to the Reading Room, to maintain the service of books to readers, to assist in finding books and to give advice on problems of research or bibliography. The Reading Room, in common with other sections of the library, is the recipient of very many requests, by post and telephone, for bibliographical information of all degrees of complexity, from all quarters of the globe. Except in cases where an answer would involve lengthy research, these inquiries are dealt with on the spot. Where detailed research is involved, the Superintendent is often able to recommend the services of a private researcher who is willing to undertake such work for a fee in a private capacity.

The photographic service of the Museum supplies photographs, photostats and microfilms of printed books and manuscripts to order.

Application is made on an official form obtainable in the reading rooms, or by post. A rapid photocopy service is available in the Reading Room by which photocopies can be supplied within a few hours.

CATALOGUES[1]

The General Author Catalogue of Printed Books is in volume form.[2] Its basis is the printed catalogue of 1880–1905, which was cut up, mounted and interleaved. It was kept up to date up to the end of 1955 by the insertion of entries from printed monthly Lists of Accessions. Additions to the library since 1955 are entered separately in a card index, pending the completion of the lithographic reprint of the author catalogue which is at present in progress. This reprint will provide in one alphabetic sequence in some 250 to 300 volumes the complete catalogue of all books in the library up to the end of 1955. It is hoped to supplement this with annual volumes of accessions and to cumulate these annual volumes into volumes covering periods of five or ten years. The General Author Catalogue is supplemented, for books published since 1880, by the series of Subject Indexes. These are published every five years; the first four issues were cumulated in 1900, but there has been no cumulation since that time.

The subject index of the modern works added to the library of the British Museum is an important reference book. It has from the beginning combined a number of class headings with more strictly subject headings; it is claimed that this method, based on actual experience of readers' wants in the Reading Room itself, meets the day-to-day requirements quite successfully. Novels, plays and poetry are excluded, but books in all other fields, in all languages, except Oriental, are included. Pending the publication of the quinquennial volume, a Temporary Subject Index is maintained for the use of the readers. This was formerly prepared by pasting entries from the printed Accessions Lists, arranged by subjects, into volumes of the same size as those of the

---

[1] A series of guides to the catalogues of the library was published in *J. Doc.* 4 (1) June 1948, 7 (1) March 1951, and 7 (3) Sept. 1951. These guides are available separately. Detailed descriptions are also given in ESDAILE, A. The British Museum Library, 1946, pp. 175–321.

[2] But, as Esdaile remarks (The British Museum Library, p. 366), such a statement conceals the fact that every leaf, every column and every individual entry is movable. He likens the catalogue to a sheaf catalogue. See further on this question on p. 26 below.

General Catalogue; since 1955 the temporary Subject Index is maintained on cards. Beginning with the volume covering the years 1946–50, the Subject Index is printed by photo-offset lithography from the printed entries in the monthly Lists of Accessions.

Besides the Author Catalogue of books there are also the catalogues of music, maps and newspapers. There are two main catalogues of music: that of "Old Music", printed before 1800 and "Modern Music", printed since that date. They are similar to the General Catalogue in the manner in which they are kept up to date, but only in the case of the "Old Music" was a separately published volume the basis of the catalogue: this was the *Catalogue of printed music published between the years 1487 and 1800 now in the British Museum*, compiled by W. Barclay Squire and published in 1912. The catalogue of "Modern Music" has been built up largely from a series of Accessions Lists which have appeared annually since 1884, but it still contains many of the manuscript entries, which were usual before 1880. There is also a printed *Catalogue of the King's Music Library*, which was presented to the British Museum, to mark the two hundredth anniversary of the gift of the old Royal Library, in 1957. Music is entered in these catalogues under the names of the composers, but additional entries are given for editors and others connected with individual works and also, in the case of vocal works, for the name of the composition. Modern sheet music, however, is not catalogued; it is stored in ten-yearly groups, and classified within each group under composers' names. A manuscript card index of this music is kept in the Music Room. Sheet music is available on application to the Superintendent of the Reading Room: applicants are asked to give the composer's name and, in the case of vocal works, the exact title, together with the approximate date of publication. This provision applies also to recently published music which has not appeared in the catalogue.

The Catalogue of Maps is also uniform with the General Catalogue. It is made up of an original *Catalogue of printed maps, plans, and charts*, 1885, and annual Accessions Lists, the whole being cut up and mounted in over one hundred folio volumes. The Map Catalogue is a subject catalogue, the main entry for each map being the place concerned. Additional entries are given for cartographers, editors and contributors of all kinds.

A catalogue on cards of the collections of 'State papers', i.e. official publications, is being built up, and is available for consultation, in the State Paper Room.

Finally the newspapers. All the newspapers published after 1800 are now stored at the British Museum Newspaper Repository at Colindale (a suburb on the north-west side of London). Newspapers printed before 1801 are entered in the General Catalogue; those printed after that date have a special catalogue, maintained in the same way as the remainder of the Museum catalogues. This catalogue is divided into: (1) London and Surburban, (2) Provincial, (3) Foreign. It should be added that a complete file of *The Times* is maintained at the British Museum proper, as well as at the Newspaper Library, and that in the very near future it is planned to microfilm a large part of the newspapers in the collection, thus making them available in the Museum in microfilm as well as at Colindale in the original.

Besides these catalogues, which are the main tools at the reader's disposal in the main Reading Room, there are the catalogues of manuscripts, of Oriental printed books and manuscripts and also a number of specialised catalogues of the printed books.

INTERNAL ADMINISTRATION

English books are available to readers through the General Catalogue about two months after receipt in the Museum, though in cases of urgent need they can be made available, on special application, at any time after receipt. In the case of foreign books, the delay is, of course, much longer, though books are ordered from abroad as soon as they appear in the publishers' lists. Let us now examine the means by which books are acquired, catalogued and made available.

Books enter the British Museum through one of the following channels: by copyright deposit, by purchase, by gift or by international exchange.

(1) *Copyright.* Under the Copyright Act of 1911 publishers of books and periodicals published in the United Kingdom are required to deposit, in the British Museum, within one month of the date of publication, a copy of every book or periodical so published. Modifications introduced by Acts passed in 1915 and 1932 exclude certain publications wholly or mainly in the nature of trade advertisements, railway time-tables, books consisting of blank sheets and one or two other similar categories: these need not be supplied except on written application from the Trustees. Orders in Council have extended the application of the Copyright Act to the Crown Colonies and, by the Act of Separation of Southern Ireland from the United

Kingdom in 1921, the obligation of deposit for books printed in Eire was retained and was further confirmed by the Eire Industrial and Commercial Property (Protection) Act of 1927. The number of books and periodicals received by copyright is roughly 36,000–40,000 separate works, 90,000–100,000 serials or parts, 1,500–1,600 maps, 8,000–9,000 separate pieces of music, 225,000 newspapers and about 5,000 odd items.

Books printed in the United Kingdom are received in the Copyright Office, a section of the Department of Printed Books staffed by a Superintendent and clerical officers. A signed receipt is given by the Copyright Office for every book received: in the case of newspapers receipts are given only when asked for. Books and periodicals received are entered in registers under the names of the publishers making the deposit, as well as under the names of the authors. Books are not retained in the Copyright Office more than two days, but before being sent to the library the British Museum stamp is impressed in indelible blue ink, showing the date on which the book was deposited. As soon as the books have been stamped, they are taken to the office of the *British National Bibliography* for cataloguing and are sent on without delay to the office of the Principal Keeper of Printed Books for entry in the General Catalogue of the British Museum. While awaiting this process they are stored in order of receipt and can be traced by reference to the Copyright Office register or the *British National Bibliography* entry. Periodicals which are shelved in the Newspaper Library at Colindale are kept in pigeon-holes in the Copyright Office for twelve months; except for certain newspapers for which there is a public demand; these are sent to Colindale each month. To ensure that the provisions of the Copyright Act are fully carried out, current published lists, such as *The Publishers' circular*, *The Bookseller* and *The Times literary supplement* are searched and checked against the receipts, and application is made for any books which have not been received. Should it appear, at some later stage, as for example when a book is being catalogued, that other publications of the author have not been received in the library, it is customary to inform the Superintendent of the Copyright Office who then takes steps to acquire the volumes. Copyright registers are retained permanently for record purposes: existing registers date back to 1850.

(2) *Acquisition by Purchase*. The provisions of the Copyright Act apply broadly speaking to books published in the United Kingdom and the colonies. Foreign books of all kinds, except such as are presented to the Museum or acquired by exchange, and such American books –

fortunately a considerable number – as are copyrighted in this country, are purchased. A sum of money for this purpose is included in the grant voted annually for the maintenance of the Museum; in 1960–61 it is something over £50,000. Foreign books are selected from current publishers' lists, which are searched, on publication, by officers of the Department specially qualified in the various languages. Sir Anthony Panizzi, perhaps the greatest Principal Librarian in the history of the Museum, is said to have expressed the view that the British Museum should aim at possessing the best library of the literature of any country outside that country itself. It becomes increasingly doubtful, in view of the great increase in the literary production of every country, if Panizzi's ideal could be maintained today, but purchases are made on an extensive scale from all the countries of Europe and the United States, and, on a less extensive scale, from the South American countries and the countries of Asia and Africa. A genuine attempt is made to acquire all important books in 'humane' subjects. Books on literary, historical, archaeological, sociological, artistic, economic, philosophical and theological subjects are bought, and in the non-humane subjects attempts are made to ensure that books of historical importance, as well as books treating of the history of those subjects, are bought. The range of the Museum's purchases of books and periodicals will be considerably extended when the Trustees assume responsibility for the new library of Science and Invention. Reviews are read, and suggestions for particular purchases are welcomed from any quarter. The actual purchase is made through booksellers in the various countries, and these booksellers are encouraged to take a personal interest in the Museum's work and to make suggestions for purchases and to comment when desirable on books chosen for the Museum. Where, as frequently happens at the present time, there are no current lists of publications, efforts are made to make good the deficiency by any available means.

The purchase of antiquarian books goes on continually, but the funds for this purpose are naturally limited. (It is right to add here that the Museum has had, and happily still has, generous friends, who are often ready to aid in an important purchase. Since 1931 one of the most fruitful sources of this sort has been the Friends of the National Libraries, an organisation to which not only the British Museum but libraries all over the country have great cause to be grateful.) Detailed search through all antiquarian catalogues, when they arrive in such quantities as they do in the Museum, involves a great expenditure of time and labour, and, in the case of a library with very extensive

collections on all subjects, is really uneconomic. Special search is therefore usually limited, in the Museum, to the catalogues of auction sales
and of the more important booksellers. Many books are offered to the
Museum either by private individuals or by booksellers. Readers and
individual members of the staff are encouraged to make suggestions for
acquisitions in the fields within which they specialise.

All orders for books are dispatched through the Purchasing Section
of the Department. Here a card catalogue is maintained of all books
ordered: on receipt, books are checked against the index and against
the invoices, which are then certified as correct.

During the last years of the war and since the end of the war, this
section has had the additional task of organising the replacement of
books lost in the bombing of 1941. Duplicated lists of missing books,
'broken down' by languages, by subjects and by publishers were
circulated and booksellers' catalogues were also searched and their
stocks carefully examined. A number of replacements also came from
books rescued from 'salvage drives', lists of which were sent to the
Museum for examination. Large numbers of books were freely sent
from abroad as a result of the lists of losses: notable donors were
Canada, Denmark and Sweden. The number of books replaced is in
the neighbourhood of 30 or 40 per cent of the 150,000–200,000
destroyed, but in a number of cases the replacements have been later
editions or more up-to-date texts which were not previously in the
collections.

From the Purchasing Section books are dispatched to the office of
the Principal Keeper to await stamping. Purchased books are stamped
in red ink, with the date of the meeting of the Trustees at which their
purchase was approved. The invoices are kept permanently, being
bound up into volumes year by year. They form a very useful record
of the source of interesting copies.

(3) *Acquisition by Donation.* The British Museum has received, and
continues to receive, large donations from every part of the world,
especially from learned institutions whose publications form one of the
most valuable sections of any large learned library. Many publications
are received by gift, which could never be acquired in any other way;
these include private printings in small numbers of copies, annotated
and association copies, grangerised copies and many foreign books,
including theses, which would otherwise be passed over. Gifts must
always remain one of the most profitable sources of strength in the
Museum collections, and the officials of the Museum look upon it as a

public duty to maintain contact with potential donors in all countries. It is pleasing to be assured, as frequently happens, that the donor feels honoured at having his gift associated with the Museum collections.

Donations are as a rule acknowledged by the Principal Keeper; specially valuable gifts, however, are reported individually to the Trustees and are acknowledged by them. Serial publications which are donated are carefully checked and indexed, so that defects are speedily detected.

When acknowledged and reported to the Trustees, donations are stamped with the Museum stamp, this time in green ink (yellow was previously used), and are assembled for cataloguing with copyright and purchased books.

(4) *Acquisition by International Exchange.* The basis of international exchange is an arrangement between governments for the exchange of official publications. The exchange, so far as this country is concerned, takes place through H.M. Stationery Office. Since the last war, however, direct exchanges between libraries have been extensively developed. This is due partly to international currency problems, but partly also to the desire of academic institutions to utilise their own publications as a means of increasing their holdings of foreign literature.

The importance of complete or comprehensive collections of the official publications of foreign governments need not be stressed, but it would be idle to suppose that the building up of such collections, whatever agreements are in force, is an easy or straightforward matter. Not only is the bulk of them so great as to be beyond the scope of most libraries, however large, but they call for the utmost vigilance, almost inhuman patience and persistence, a knowledge of what is being published officially in all quarters of the globe, and, what is perhaps most important of all, a really keen collaborator on the spot!

The maintenance of the State Paper collections is the direct responsibility of the Superintendent of the State Paper Room. The Museum has good collections, apart of course from our own English state papers, of the state papers of the Dominions, the Colonies and the United States. The collections of the state papers of other countries vary in comprehensiveness; most countries are represented and every effort is made to make each collection as comprehensive as possible, and there is a good collection of the proceedings of the various state legislatures.

Direct exchanges between the British Museum and other institutions are conducted by the Acquisitions Division on the advice of the language specialists about the books offered. It is arguable that this method of acquisition is not really economic, involving as it does, when conducted on a large scale, complicated comparisons of valuations. Such operations can be carried on more easily by booksellers. Circumstances, however, have made it necessary to acquiesce in it.

Cataloguing. As they are acquired and stamped with the British Museum stamp, books are assembled in the office of the Principal Keeper. Hence they are distributed as required to the cataloguing staff, a record being kept of the books sent to each individual. The cataloguing staff is made up of officers of the Assistant Keeper and Executive Officer grades.

The British Museum Catalogue was published in volume form between 1880 and 1905. The current General Catalogue of the library is made up from copies of the 1881–1905 Catalogue, cut up, mounted and interleaved, with entries from the monthly Accessions Lists inserted at the appropriate places. The alphabetical order of the Accessions is rigidly maintained and, whenever necessary, slips already pasted into the volumes are moved to accommodate new entries. The original 'column' is retained as long as possible, and when looking out a book it is necessary for the reader to search the 'column' as well as the Accessions. Where the retention of the 'column', however, impedes easy reference, the 'column' itself is taken up and the individual entries cut out and mounted separately. In this way great flexibility is maintained and the entries are kept under constant observation and revision. When, because of the insertion of large numbers of Accessions, a volume becomes too bulky for easy handling, it is split up into two or more volumes. The whole catalogue now occupies about 1,500 volumes. There are three copies of the General Catalogue; one is kept in the Catalogue Room as the working copy, one is kept in the Reading Room and the third is used to supplement the Reading Room copy when volumes are removed each month for the insertion of new entries. A revised edition of the complete General Catalogue was begun in 1930 and work on it continued up to 1954, by which time fifty-one volumes set up and printed by letterpress printing had been issued. After this the method of production was completely changed, and whereas before, the volumes were set up afresh and printed by letterpress printing, now they are reproduced by photo-offset lithography from copy made up from the current General Catalogue in the

Reading Room. This change is designed to simplify and speed up production and it is hoped that the whole catalogue in 250 or 300 volumes will be completed in five or six years depending on the number of volumes.

This photo-offset edition of the General Catalogue will be complete up to the year 1955. For books acquired after 1955 a card catalogue of current acquisitions is provided. This will be maintained until the printing of the new edition has been completed. As volumes of the new edition are available, they are treated in the same way as the old catalogue and copies are cut up mounted and interleaved and substituted for the corresponding volumes of the old catalogues for the use of readers in the Reading Room.

Catalogue entries are written on oblong blue slips made of tough paper. When catalogued the book, with all the catalogue entries (main and added entries), passes to a reviser who checks the entries for accuracy and examines the heading to ensure that the correct one has been chosen. The book, still with the catalogue slips, next passes to the 'placer' or classifier who places it in the appropriate place on the shelves within the Museum's broad system of classification. Each book is given a fixed press-mark which is written inside the book and on each of the catalogue slips, the book being subsequently labelled on the spine with a printed label. The catalogue slips are collected, sorted into alphabetical order, numbered and sent off to the printer each month. These are printed on cards, but a few copies are printed on long paper slips suitable for cutting up and mounting. On their return from the printer the cards are inserted in the card catalogue of current acquisitions and the long slips kept ready for the insertion of entries in the volumes of the new General Catalogue as soon as these are ready for this process. The official in charge of this operation is known as the Incorporator. His work consists in indicating the correct place in each volume for the new entries to be inserted, in deciding whether re-arrangement is necessary, and in keeping a watch on the general correctness of the choice of heading. The actual physical insertion of the slips into the various copies of the General Catalogue is entrusted to a special staff trained for the purpose. The slips are pasted into the catalogue carefully by the top and bottom edges and can be readily removed if desired by the insertion of a paper-knife. This section of the bindery staff is also responsible for inserting new leaves in the General Catalogue where necessary and for dividing volumes as they become too bulky. The process of incorporation is completed each month so that there is a minimum of delay between the printing of the lists and their availability in the General Catalogue.

The manuscript catalogue slips are retained permanently and are filed chronologically under the catalogue headings. They are used for all subsequent alteration and, as they contain notes by the original cataloguer, are a useful record of research. A separate set of the Accessions entries is cut up, mounted on cards and filed by press-mark, thus providing a complete shelf-catalogue.

The Subject Index is compiled from the Monthly Lists of Accessions. Subject headings are indicated by hand on each entry in the Accessions (excluding, of course, cross-references) and these are inserted in the Temporary Subject Index in the Reading Room; a second set, similarly marked, is retained in preparation for the complete five-yearly Subject Index. Before the war, it was customary for the five-yearly volume to be printed and published at the latest two years after the five-yearly period. Unfortunately, owing to the war, the work has fallen considerably behind. Here again, by the introduction of photo-offset methods it should be possible to speed up the printing. The Subject Index is now being compiled from printed cards and produced by photo-offset lithography, thus reducing the work of preparation and proof-reading to the minimum.

Once the books are on the shelves, they are available to readers. The staff engaged on the work of procuring books for readers is distributed at various points in the bookstacks. The readers' application forms are sent to these points, as has already been indicated, by means of pneumatic tubes. Each book is taken from the shelf by its press-mark and its title checked with the reader's description. When it is taken away, the shelf-board with the duplicate book ticket inserted is substituted and remains until the book is replaced. The books, with the readers' application forms in them, are then sent by means of the mechanical conveyor to the central distributing point, where they are sorted and sent into the Reading Room.

The Museum has its own bindery on the premises. The binding is let out by contract for a period of years. The contract has now been held for a number of years by H.M. Stationery Office, and it seems likely that this arrangement will continue. The number of books bound in the course of a year is over 15,000 with over 1,000 repairs and 'rebinds', and, in addition to this, some 19,000 books are put into temporary casing. It is the practice of the library not to allow any books to be placed on the shelves without some form of casing. The Newspaper

Library at Colindale has its own binding shop on the spot; over 6,000 volumes are bound annually, with some 2,000 put into temporary bindings.

Staff. A word now about the general administration and the staffing of the library. The overall control of all the departments of the British Museum is in the hands of the Director and Principal Librarian, whose function it is to administer the Museum in accordance with the policies laid down by the Trustees. The organisation and day-to-day control of the Department of Printed Books is the responsibility of the Principal Keeper of Printed Books; under him there are two Keepers (whose rank is the equivalent of that of the heads of the remaining departments of the Museum), one being the Principal Keeper's deputy, and the other being responsible for relations with the public, the reading rooms and the information service. Under the three senior officers of the department there are six Deputy Keepers each responsible for divisions of the department: the main Reading Room, the Map Room, the Music Room, the State Paper Room, the Cataloguing Division, and the Acquisitions Division; there is a seventh Deputy Keeper responsible for binding and also for the supervision of the North Library. Under these officers senior Assistant Keepers direct special sections such as that devoted to Slavonic and East European languages, the Subject Index and the Placing. Junior Assistant Keepers serve their professional apprenticeship, so to speak, by work on the General Catalogue and by assisting the seniors in the administration of the sections to which I have just referred. Assistant Keepers are roughly equivalent in qualifications and pay to the Administrative grade of the Civil Service. They are recruited on academic record – they are normally required to have a good honours degree, preferably in classics, with a sound knowledge of two modern foreign languages – and after an interview by the Civil Service Commission. No professional library qualifications are required in candidates, though, of course, some of them have such qualifications. Assistant Keepers are expected to specialise in a language or languages or in a subject likely to be of value to the Museum service. In normal times, they have experience of the work in all branches of the department. The grade of Assistant Cataloguers, roughly equivalent to the Executive grade of the Civil Service, is playing an increasingly important part in the routine work of cataloguing and of dealing with public inquiries.

Apart from these the library employs a large staff of the Civil Service Clerical Officer, Library Assistant and Paper Keeper grades whose function is to perform all routine duties for the public service and for the various sections of the department.

The British Museum suffered severely during the war. It lost many books; it lost a great deal of storage space; many most useful members of the staff who were taken for military service or other employment did not return. Its recovery and rehabilitation coincided with a time when demands were being made for the development and extension of library services. This difficult period is over and the services which the library is able to offer are greater than they were before the war. More important than this, plans are being made to build a separate British Museum Library building, to the south of the present Museum building, which will house all the library departments, Printed Books, Manuscripts, Oriental Printed Books and Manuscripts and Prints and Drawings. Here it will be possible to develop the use of the collections by the provision of specialised reading rooms, reference rooms and exhibition galleries. But it should not be forgotten that the system which owes its origins to Panizzi has done pretty well for over one hundred years.

CHAPTER II

THE LIBRARY OF
THE BRITISH MUSEUM (NATURAL HISTORY)
AND SOME OTHER LIBRARIES OF NATURAL HISTORY

By A. C. Townsend
Librarian, British Museum (Natural History)

AT first glance it may seem paradoxical that natural history, which depends in the first place upon field work in natural surroundings, should have accumulated around it a vast literature which is steadily growing and involving more and more bibliographical work as the sources of this literature become more various and differentiated.

Upon further reflection, however, it will be seen that the study of natural history implies observation, description, and revision of knowledge about natural history collections, and that without large and comprehensive libraries, the research work of museums and other biological institutions would be inadequate, not to say nugatory. Taxonomy, or classification of plants and animals, in particular demands much bibliographical research, and in an institution where taxonomy and the proper identification of species is carried out, it is essential to have a library which should contain well-nigh every book and periodical in which descriptions of new species of plants and animals, recent or fossil, have been published. It is only by means of a complete coverage of the literature, for example, that the principles of scientific nomenclature can be observed, to ensure, for one thing, that the same name is not given to different species.

The literature to be consulted in any branch of natural history bulks vastly – upwards of 2,500 journals are searched for the purpose of the *Zoological Record* alone, but London is fortunate in possessing vast resources which are at the disposal of the student of natural history, and although no library is ever entirely complete, the chances of getting what one requires in London are, in most fields, probably greater than anywhere else in the world.

For books on natural history, as on anything else, the national library at the British Museum, Bloomsbury, must first be mentioned before we pass on to a consideration of the specialist libraries, and we should call to mind that one of the foundation collections of the Museum was the library of Sir Hans Sloane (1660–1753), rich in botanical literature and scientific journals.

Of still greater importance to the naturalist is the library of Sir Joseph Banks (1743–1820), which came into the possession of the Museum in 1827. This collection was catalogued by Banks's librarian, the Swede, Jonas Dryander, who compiled the five octavo volumes (1798–1800), still considered as a catalogue of great utility and exemplary accuracy. In these days of minute analysis in classification, it is of some interest to note that in the botanical section of Dryander's catalogue there are 833 subdivisions. Small wonder that his friend Sir J. E. Smith said that no other science possessed anything similar.

But in spite of Sloane and Banks and the Copyright Acts, the serious student of natural history will sooner or later have to make his way to the scientific collections – and library – of the natural history branch of the British Museum, or, to give it its official and somewhat cumbersome title, the British Museum (Natural History), which was first opened to the public in 1881.

Now it is not generally known that the elaborate Romanesque building in Cromwell Road contains, in addition to what are perhaps the finest collections of natural history specimens in the world, a library of paramount importance to those working on those collections, as well as to all advanced students of systematic natural history.

The library of the British Museum (Natural History), which at the present time contains about 300,000 volumes, may be said to have developed from the nucleus formed by the fifteen volumes of manuscript catalogues of Sir Hans Sloane's collections, an annotated copy of Sloane's *Voyage to the islands Madeira, Barbados . . . Jamaica* (1707–25) with the original drawings from which the plates to that work were made, and a copy of Ray's *Historia plantarum* (1686–1704) used by Sloane in connection with his herbarium. These were all kept with the Sloane collections instead of being incorporated into the Department of Printed Books.[1]

[1] For the history of the collections and library of the British Museum (Natural History) the following should be consulted:

    (a) The history of the collections contained in the natural history departments of the British Museum. 2 vols. and appendix. London. The Trustees of the British Museum, 1904–12.

    (b) A short history of the collections. British Museum (Natural History)

The first step towards the formation of a separate natural history library was taken in 1827, when the Banksian collections and library were transferred to the Trustees, and it was agreed that the Keeper of the Banksian Botanical Collections should also have exclusive care and management of the manuscripts and drawings. Furthermore, 148 volumes, that were either duplicates or had manuscript notes in them, remained in what afterwards became the Department of Botany.

From this time until the period immediately preceding the removal of the natural history collections to South Kensington, the several departments all had their own working libraries, but relied for their further requirements upon the Department of Printed Books.

The flow of accessions into the departmental libraries went on steadily between 1835 and 1879, and in 1880 a special vote was obtained from Parliament for the building up of a new library to serve the departments at South Kensington. It was decided at this time that the several departments should continue to purchase and hold works relating to their special subjects, while a fifth library, the 'General Library', was formed to contain works, the subject matter of which concerned two or more of the departments.

At the present time the library of the British Museum (Natural History) consists of a General Library and five sections corresponding to the Departments of Zoology, Entomology, Palaeontology, Botany and Mineralogy. There is also a small, but growing sectional library of Anthropology. As has been indicated, these Departmental Sections contain books and serial publications which treat exclusively of the particular branch of the subject with which the department in question is concerned. In the General Library, however, are found works on general biology and natural history, travel, topography, biography, general scientific magazines and the serial publications of scientific academies, societies, and those issued by universities and governments.

The General Library of the Museum is housed in pleasant, roomy quarters in the new North Block of the Museum which was opened to the public in October 1959. There is a well-furnished Reading Room, a Map or Atlas Room, and a Catalogue Room, in addition to the staff

Special Guide No. 9. London. The Trustees of the British Museum, 1931.

(c) TOWNSEND, A. C., and STRATTON, G. B. Zoological libraries. Library Resources in the Greater London Area, No. 6. London. The Library Association, 1957.

and working rooms. The Map Room contains, in addition to a collection of maps and gazetteers, the large folios and double folios (the latter are stored horizontally) which cannot be accommodated on the shelves with the other books. The Catalogue Room contains the card-catalogue for the whole Museum library, and a collection of library catalogues, general bibliographies and indexes which it is hoped to build up into a valuable reference collection for bibliographers. In the General Library are also found certain special collections about which more will be said later.

Additions to the Museum library are made by purchase, donation and exchange, and it should perhaps be recalled that the Museum does not enjoy any privileges under the Copyright Acts, though it has much material to offer in exchange in the form of its guides, monographs, natural history catalogues, and more especially in its *Bulletin*, issued since 1950 in six separate series.

During its comparatively brief history, the Museum library has received such major gifts as the splendid ornithological library of the ninth Marquess of Tweeddale, presented in 1887, and the fine entomological library of Lord Walsingham, presented in 1910. In more recent times Sir John Murray gave his valuable library of books and pamphlets on oceanography to the Museum in 1921, and these are kept as a special collection with some relics of the famous voyage of the 'Challenger'. In 1939, the library was further enriched by the extensive and finely bound library of some 40,000 volumes at Tring Museum which the late Lord Rothschild bequeathed to the Trustees, together with the Museum itself. It may perhaps be mentioned here that the Tring library contains a number of works which are not available at South Kensington, including such rarities as William Turner's *Avium praecipuarum . . . historia* (1544), the rare volume on birds and mammals by T. R. Peale published in 1848 as Vol. 8 of the *United States Wilkes Expedition* (1838–42), and some collections of original drawings, among which we may give as examples, a volume of drawings of the birds of Georgia, attributed to John Abbot, and notes and drawings for the *Aurelian* by Moses Harris (1766). The Tring library is particularly strong in ornithology and entomology.

Although the field which the Museum library attempts to cover is a wide one – it is now thought necessary to subscribe to such journals as the *Journal of Immunology* and the *Journal of Chromatography* – the ever elusive ideal of completeness is kept before those whose task it is to build up the collection and who must, in the course of their work, often ponder upon a saying of the late Dr. C. Davies Sherborn, the eminent bibliographer and compiler of *Index Animalium*. Sherborn, in the Epilogue to his *Index*, wrote as follows:

"In any well-appointed Natural History Library there should be found every book and every edition of every book dealing in the remotest way with the subjects concerned. One never knows wherein one edition differs from or supplements the other, and unless these are on the same table at the same time, it is not possible to collate them properly. Moreover, for accurate work it is necessary for the student to verify every reference he may find; it is not enough to copy from a previous author; he must verify each reference itself from the original."

Sherborn worked for over forty years at the British Museum (Natural History) and claimed to have acquired over 1,000 volumes for the library there, though, in his own words, "gaps still remain to be filled".

Sherborn's vast bibliographical knowledge was freely placed at the disposal of the successive editors of the Museum Library Catalogue, published in five quarto volumes between 1903 and 1915, and in three supplementary volumes issued during the period 1921–40.[2] The first five volumes of the Main Catalogue, and the first supplementary volume were prepared by B. B. Woodward, the first librarian of the Museum, a first-class librarian and a meticulous bibliographer, who was transferred from the Department of Printed Books to South Kensington in 1881. The catalogue is an author catalogue with full collations and what are now called 'analyticals'. It is of the greatest value to naturalists, librarians, bibliographers and booksellers, particularly on account of the many notes which accompany many of the entries.

Indeed, as has been indicated, much bibliographical work goes on in the Museum during the course of the daily work of classification and research. This ranges from compilation of the lists of references with which most scientific articles and monographs are equipped, to the preparation of such major works of reference as the *Zoological Record*. During these operations, problems of correct dates of publication and editions continually arise, and the printed catalogue of the Museum library and the card catalogue of recent additions are in constant con-

[2] Catalogue of the books, manuscripts, maps and drawings in the British Museum (Natural History). 5 vols., Supplement 3 vols. London. The Trustees, 1903–40.

sultation. It should perhaps be mentioned here, that although the books are split up among the General Library and the five Departmental Sectional Libraries, all purchases of books are made, and all cataloguing is carried out for the whole Museum in the General Library, which also has supervision of the binding programme for the whole Museum. When books are sent to the Departmental Libraries, duplicate catalogue slips are sent with them for the sectional library catalogues. There is no general subject index, but since 1955 a *List of Accessions to the Museum Library* has been issued, arranged according to the Universal Decimal Classification, and accompanied every six months with a name and subject index. It is hoped to issue this *List* nine or ten times during the year, and it can be sent to those libraries or institutions which may wish to apply for a copy. In addition to this, a Hand-list of Periodicals for the whole Museum library is in course of preparation, and the Zoological, Entomological and Mineralogical sections are already available.

The books in the General, Zoological and Palaeontological Libraries are classified according to a scheme drawn up by B. B. Woodward, whereas the Botanical and Mineralogical Sections employ the U.D.C. Serial publications are arranged according to the country of origin.

As well as being especially rich in the earlier scientific periodicals, the Museum library possesses a large number of original drawings of considerable interest. To mention only some of these, in the Botanical and Zoological Libraries are drawings by the brothers Franz and Ferdinand Bauer, of whom the former was employed by Sir Joseph Banks in making drawings of the plants at Kew Gardens. Franz Bauer was probably the finest botanical draughtsman of all time, and the Museum has a large collection of his beautiful drawings. Ferdinand Bauer accompanied Robert Brown as botanical and zoological artist on Flinder's voyage to Australia in the 'Investigator' (1801–03) and brought back a series of drawings of the plants and animals observed during that voyage. In the Botanical Library are the original drawings for Sowerby's *English botany*, over 2,500 in number, a collection of drawings by Georg Dionysius Ehret, the originals for the plates of James Bolton's *Filices Britannicae*, and nineteen volumes of water-colour drawings by Sydney Parkinson (d. 1771) and pencil sketches of plants and animals made on Cook's first voyage (1768–71), when Parkinson accompanied Banks as draughtsman. There are many other collections of scientific and historical interest in the Botanical Library. More recently (1948) the Museum received as a bequest from the late Miss

B. D. Corfe some 218 water-colour drawings of plants and 89 pencil drawings of flower sections. The Museum already possessed a number of Miss Corfe's original drawings of flowering plants, including those made for the Museum's series of picture postcards.

In the General Library are a number of collections of drawings, including those painted by P. C. de Bevere for J. G. Loten, Dutch Governor of Ceylon (1752–57). These drawings depict the fauna and flora of Ceylon and the Malay Archipelago, and were used by Peter Brown, Sydney Parkinson, George Edwards, Thomas Pennant, and others, for their illustrated books on natural history. Also in the General Library is a large volume of water-colour and pencil sketches made by the explorer Thomas Baines (1822–75) during an expedition to the goldfields of Mashonaland. Some of these sketches have been used to illustrate Baines's *Northern goldfields diaries* published for the Government of Southern Rhodesia. [3]

Other collections include the drawings of plants and fish from the Eocene of Monte Bolca, the work of an eighteenth-century artist, which were originally in the Banksian Library, and the large collection of drawings formed by Hugh Falconer (1808–65) in connection with a work on the Siválik beds. This collection, which, like the Monte Bolca drawings mentioned above, is in the Palaeontological Department, includes water-colours and pen-and-ink drawings of Indian fossils and a set of various fossil mammalia drawn by J. Dinkel, J. J. Kaup and others.

The Zoological Department houses, among other sets of drawings, the Parkinson, Forster and Ellis drawings made on Cook's first, second, and third voyages respectively, the Hardwicke collection of illustrations of Asiatic Zoology, some of which were used for J. E. Gray's *Illustrations of Indian zoology* and Jardine and Selby's *Illustrations of ornithology*, and the so-called *Watling* drawings of natives, animals and plants from the neighbourhood of Port Jackson. Some of the latter drawings are the originals of the plates for J. White's *Journal of a voyage to New South Wales* (1790). In the Zoological Department are the four volumes of original pencil drawings of fishes of the Rio Negro, made by Alfred Russel Wallace between 1850 and 1852, and six volumes of original drawings, some of them signed by A. Latham, T. Davies, Lord Stanley and J. Abbot and used to illustrate John Latham's *General history of birds* (1821–24) and other of his works.

[3] BAINES, THOMAS. The northern goldfields diaries of Thomas Baines, ed. by J. P. R. Wallis. 3 vols. 1946.

In the Entomological Department, which was set up as an independent department, with its own sectional library, in 1935, there is much historical material of importance, including nine volumes of original water-colour drawings done upon vellum for Godart and Duponchel's *Histoire naturelle des lépidoptères de France* (1820–43) and a collection of original drawings, plates and manuscripts representing the work of Jacob Hübner (1761–1826) and other Austrian and Bavarian entomologists who, with him, laid the foundations of the classification of the Lepidoptera from 1770 to 1850.

In fact, the original drawings and manuscripts are perhaps the most surprising, and certainly the least known to the public of the Museum library's treasures, and though they are indeed recorded in the Library Catalogue, it is much to be hoped that a separate, annotated catalogue of these drawings and manuscripts will be prepared for publication, especially as many additions have been made since the printed volumes of the Library Catalogue were issued.

With regard to manuscripts, in addition to the important Sloane and Banksian items already mentioned, there is a collection of manuscripts relating to the three voyages of Captain Cook, and, to mention only one other collection of outstanding interest, there are the twenty-one volumes of the transcripts of Sir Joseph Banks's correspondence, made by the daughters of the banker-naturalist and antiquary Dawson Turner (1775–1858), and covering the period 1766–1820. These transcripts formed the basis of the Calendar of Sir Joseph Banks's Correspondence, published by the Trustees in 1958.[4] The Dawson Turner transcripts, and the correspondence of Robert Brown in three volumes, are kept in the Botanical Library.

In the General Library is a series of manuscripts of Sir Richard Owen, first Superintendent of the Natural History Departments of the British Museum, among which is a valuable collection of letters, mostly addressed to Owen, on scientific subjects (1792–1867) in twenty-one volumes.

Other manuscripts in the Museum library include the letter-book (1761–83) of Dru Drury, the eighteenth-century entomologist; seven volumes of the scientific correspondence of the Northumbrian zoologist Joshua Alder (1792–1867), and of Canon A. M. Norman (1831–1918); the notebooks of A. R. Wallace, giving localities for his collection of birds from the Malay Archipelago (1856–61); the MS. diary

---

[4] The Banks letters, etc., ed. by W. R. Dawson. London. The Trustees, 1958.

of R. B. Hinds, naturalist accompanying H.M.S. 'Sulphur' in 1836–42; and the original MS. journal of botanical and zoological observations made by H. N. Moseley during the voyage of the 'Challenger' (1873–75).

As befits a museum of natural history, its library contains a fine collection of Linnaeana, which owes much to the enthusiasm and generosity of Mr. Basil H. Soulsby, Woodward's successor as Librarian of the Museum. A special catalogue of the works of Linnaeus and of Linnaeana was published by the Trustees in 1933.[5] This work, compiled by Soulsby, who unfortunately did not live to see its publication, is that section of the Museum Library Catalogue which relates to Linnaeus, systematically arranged, and with the titles of additional items in the library at Bloomsbury. It forms a revised and enlarged second edition of a catalogue compiled by B. B. Woodward and W. R. Wilson, which was originally issued by the Trustees to commemorate the bicentenary of the birth of Linnaeus in 1907. This first edition has 27 pages, but the second edition runs to 246, with 65 pages of Addenda and Corrigenda. An index to this work was compiled by Dr. C. Davies Sherborn and published by the Trustees in 1936.

This collection of some 1,226 volumes contains many Linnaean items of great interest and rarity, ranging from the fundamental treatises, such as the various editions of the *Systema naturae* and the *Species plantarum*, to such hors d'oeuvres as the rare poem in Latin, French and English, written by the eccentric Frederick Calvert, seventh Baron Baltimore, in honour of Linnaeus, and published in an edition of ten copies at Augsburg in 1770 under the title of *Gaudia poetica*.

As an example of the exhaustive manner in which this second edition of the Linnaean catalogue was compiled, we may instance the treatment of the various sets and editions of the *Amoenitates academicae*, a hard nut for any bibliographer to crack. In Soulsby's catalogue, an analytical account of the ten sets of the *Amoenitates* in the Museum library is followed by a catalogue of the original separate editions with translations and adaptations.

Before concluding this brief account of the Museum library, it

[5] A catalogue of the works of Linnaeus (and publications more immediately relating thereto) preserved in the libraries of the British Museum (Bloomsbury) and the British Museum (Natural History) (South Kensington). 2nd edition. London. The Trustees, 1933.

should perhaps be emphasised that the library is not a public library in the sense that it is open to all who may wish to read therein. It is primarily for the use of the Museum staff in connection with their work of identifying, classifying and preserving for students the specimens acquired by the Museum. The library is, however, available to accredited students who have applied for and obtained the authorisation of the Director of the Museum. In addition, a large number of postal inquiries are dealt with in the course of a year, as well as those received by telephone or in the course of personal visits. Moreover, it should not be forgotten that the Natural History Museum is a part of the British Museum, and endeavours to live up to the scholarly standards and hospitable traditions of that great institution.

Going on to consider some of the other London libraries which deal wholly, or almost wholly, with natural history, we begin with a brief account of the library of the **Zoological Society of London** at Regent's Park.

This collection, which was started in 1836, contains at present an estimated stock of some 100,000 volumes, with about 500 current periodicals. A list of the periodicals in the library was published in 1949. The Society issued a printed catalogue of its library in 1854 – a modest volume of 44 pages, and the fifth edition of 856 pages appeared in 1902 – a most useful reference book. In 1949 a card-catalogue of subjects was begun, based on the Bliss classification, and including all book accessions and periodical articles of 20 pages or more in length.

The Society also publishes the *Zoological Record*, now edited by the Society's librarian, which is the principal work of reference to zoological literature.

Besides containing a number of rare works, the Society's library contains several special collections of original drawings and photographs, some of which it may be useful to note here. There are, first of all, the drawings and manuscript notes by Bryan Hodgson on the mammals and birds of India, eight folio volumes in all, and we may recall here that the British Museum (Natural History) also possesses over 1,000 drawings of vertebrata, presented to the Museum by Hodgson in 1845 and 1858.

Other collections in the Society's library include Colonel S. R. Tickell's illustrated manuscript notes on the Indian fauna, C. F. Sharpe's fine water-colours of Indian birds, and the drawings of mammals, birds and reptiles by the famous animal painter Joseph

Wolf. The library also maintains a collection of photographic prints, and has some 11,000 negatives, mainly of vertebrate animals but including some invertebrates as well.

The principal function of the library is to provide zoological literature for the Society's Fellows and Associates, who may borrow books from the library. About 4,000 books are lent annually to Fellows, and some 750 to other libraries and institutions. [6]

An important collection of books on botany and zoology is to be found in the library of the **Linnean Society of London** at Burlington House. The Society was founded in 1788, and its library grew rapidly, containing at the present time about 70,000 volumes and about 400 current periodicals. The library also contains Linnaeus's own library of about 1,500 volumes, many of them annotated either by Linnaeus himself or by his contemporaries. The printed library catalogue, the fourth of a series, published in 1925, indicates the Linnaean items with a special distinguishing mark. There are numerous important manuscripts in this library, and a catalogue of these has begun to be published, the fourth part having been issued in 1948. In this work, the correspondence of Sir James Edward Smith, the first president of the Society, and the correspondence of John Ellis are among the material now catalogued. The library is a private one, for the use of the Fellows of the Society. [7]

Also in Burlington House is the library of the **Geological Society of London,** containing about 92,000 volumes and, like the library of the Linnean Society, for the use of Fellows of the Society. The library includes those of G. B. Greenhough and Sir Joseph Prestwich, and it is interesting to note that the Society treasures the original drawings of J. L. R. Agassiz's *Recherches sur les poissons fossiles* (1833–34), the MS. of James Hutton's *Theory of the earth* (1795), and a number of the original maps of William Smith, the "father of British geology" (1769–1839). There are about 800 current periodicals taken by the library. Books are lent to kindred societies and to Government departments.

Another important library, open to the public for reference, is that of the **Geological Survey and Museum of Practical Geology,** situated since 1934 in Exhibition Road, South Kensington.

---

[6] I am indebted to the kindness of Mr. G. B. Stratton, M.B.E., Librarian of the Society, who has given me details as to the library under his care.

[7] Catalogue of the manuscripts in the library of the Linnean Society of London. Parts 1–4, 1934–48 (in progress).

The Survey is the oldest national survey in the world, and its working library contains about 70,000 books, 28,000 maps and 1,000 current periodicals. The collection originated with the library of Sir H. T. De La Beche (1796–1855), and includes a number of rare and ancient books on geological science. There is also a large collection of photographs taken by Survey officers in the course of their duties. Prints of these photographs, which cover the geological features of those areas of the British Isles now under survey, can be obtained by members of the public. The Survey is now an 'outstation' of the Department of Scientific and Industrial Research.

South Kensington is, indeed, a centre of scientific activity, and the libraries in the district include those of the Museums, the Commonwealth Institute of Entomology, the Science Library, and if these institutions do not provide an answer, the research worker can also approach the libraries of the Royal Entomological Society of London and of the Royal Geographical Society.

The library of the **Royal Entomological Society** has been built up steadily since the foundation of the Society in 1833, and now contains an estimated total of 13,000 volumes and 34,000 reprints. In his *History of the Entomological Society of London* (1933), Dr. S. A. Neave tells us (p. 75) that "it is no exaggeration to say that today there are few libraries in existence in which entomological literature is better presented. Its great strength lies in its very complete collection of the old systematic works as well as of the many large and expensive monographs that Entomological Science has produced in such a profusion." Among the many valuable donations made to the Society's library we can mention the rich collection of rare illustrated works which came from the library of W. W. Bromfield in 1852, and, most important of all, the entomological library of H. T. Stainton (1822–92), a famous collection much used by H. A. Hagen in the compilation of his well-known *Bibliotheca entomologica* (1862–63) and containing the whole of the library of James F. Stephens (1792–1852).

The first edition of the catalogue of the Society's library appeared in 1836, in the first volume of the Society's *Transactions*. A second edition was published in 1861, and the third in 1893, this last being a substantial volume of 291 pages with some 6,000 entries. A supplement was issued in 1900 giving some further 4,000 entries. Lists of additions to the library now appear in the Society's *Proceedings* (Series C). A list of the serial publications in the library was published in 1951. Although the library is for the use of Fellows of the Society only, since 1929 it has been an outlier of the National Central Library, and non-Fellows may be permitted to consult the books upon application.

A few doors away, in Queen's Gate, are the publication office and library of the **Commonwealth Institute of Entomology,** founded in 1913, and now the senior organisation in the system of Commonwealth Agricultural Bureaux which exist to provide information and abstracting services in the agricultural field.

The work of the Institute's library is closely connected with its abstract journal, the *Review of Applied Entomology*, and the collection consists of books, periodicals and reprints in a wide field which covers economic entomology, agriculture, horticulture, forestry, zoology, medicine, etc. The Institute works in close collaboration with the Entomological Department of the British Museum (Natural History), and thus has access to library facilities of an unrivalled kind in the field of general and economic entomology. Furthermore, the Institute compiles every year the Insecta portion of the *Zoological Record*, utilising its own resources and those of the British Museum (Natural History) and other libraries.

There are at present about 14,243 bound volumes and some 47,063 reprints in the library, which receives periodicals in exchange for the *Review of Applied Entomology* and for the quarterly *Bulletin of Entomological Research*. There are about 720 serial publications in the library, including bulletins and annual reports. There is a main author-catalogue and a small subject-index to the monographs, useful for answering general inquiries. Work is also proceeding on the author-catalogue of articles in periodicals.[8]

We may now consider the most recent addition to London's libraries of natural history, the library of the **Nature Conservancy,** with headquarters in Belgrave Square, and branches in Edinburgh and elsewhere.

The Conservancy was set up in 1949 by Royal Charter, and its library covers all aspects of natural history, with particular emphasis on works relating to the British fauna and flora. A special effort is being made to build up a comprehensive collection of literature on conservation, and the library receives over 500 current periodicals from all over the world. An accessions list of the more important additions

[8] For much of this information I am indebted to B. A. Trott, Librarian of the Institute. Cf. also SCHEFFAUER, F. F. The Library of the Commonwealth Institute of Entomology. *Lib. Assn. Rec.* 53 1951, 193–195.

to the library is produced monthly, and this is available to interested libraries. The book collections at the research stations are related to the scientific work being carried out at those stations, and stock can be moved from one station to another should the need arise. The Conservancy library is primarily for the use of the scientific staff, but loans are made through the National Central Library and the Science Library Supplementary Lending scheme.

Let us now consider two libraries situated at some distance from the centre of London, but which, none the less, play an important part in the library activities of the metropolitan area. The first of these libraries is the Horniman Museum and Library at Forest Hill, administered by the London County Council, and the second is the library of the Royal Botanic Gardens at Kew.

The **Horniman Library** contains about 23,000 volumes, and is open to the public, although books may only be borrowed through the National Central Library. The library is designed to illustrate the natural science collections of the Museum, with particular stress on Zoology and Anthropology. The Museum has one of the largest collections of musical instruments in the country, and the library has recently received a bequest from Adam Carse of books, illustrations and manuscripts dealing with music and old musical instruments. The bequest includes about 300 books in all languages, many of them rare and unobtainable. There are about 150 periodicals in this library, many rare pamphlets, some MSS. and drawings, a large collection of illustrations and lantern slides. About 300 volumes are added to the library every year. There is accommodation for about twenty-four readers, and among those making use of this excellent working library are students from training colleges, schoolchildren and members of local societies, as, for example, the London Natural History Society.[9]

Also at a considerable distance from the scientific concentration at South Kensington and the learned bustle of Burlington House, are the **Royal Botanic Gardens** at Kew, with the famous Herbarium and Library attached thereto.[10]

[9] Mr. L. J. P. Gaskin, Librarian of the Horniman Museum, has very kindly supplied me with these details.

[10] For this account of the library at Kew, I would like to acknowledge the kind help of Mr. H. S. Marshall, the Librarian, who has given me many notes on the rich and important collections in his charge.

The library at Kew, founded in 1853, developed in the early days *pari passu* with the Herbarium, and is closely associated with the descriptive and classificatory work of the latter. At the present moment (1959) the library consists of over 50,000 volumes and includes a collection of more than 1,000 books on travel relating in a greater or a lesser degree to botany.[11] The early writers on botany are also well represented at Kew, and there is a valuable auxiliary to the library in the collection of prints and drawings of plants, mounted on sheets of paper and preserved in portfolios.

The library is classified by subjects, and also by geographical considerations, as the various floras are arranged first by continents, and then by countries or groups of countries, following the arrangement adopted for the Herbarium. The periodicals are arranged by continents, and then subdivided by countries.

There are also special sections for the general works of reference, the pre-Linnaean books and Herbals, books on certain special subjects, travel books, special groups of plants, and a collection of over 80,000 reprints and pamphlets.

Among the manuscripts in the Kew library are some Banksian and Bentham items, including the latter's diary from 1807 to 1883, and a number of letters from Charles Darwin to Sir W. Thiselton-Dyer (1873–81) and Professor Henslow (1831–37) respectively. There is also the botanical correspondence of Sir J. D. and W. J. Hooker, including the latter's journal of a tour in Switzerland, 1814.

In addition, there are two branch libraries at Kew: (1) the 'Gardeners' Library', containing books on gardening for the most part, and (2) the Museum library in Museum No. 4, containing books on economic botany.

At Kew is prepared the *Index Kewensis* – an alphabetical list of every plant name published, with an exact reference to the work and the page of that work on which the name first appeared. The first two volumes, which include all names up to 1885, were prepared by B. D. Jackson under the direction of Sir J. D. Hooker, and were published in 1893–95. The work is still being carried on, and twelve supplements to this work have now appeared. Its connection with the library and its bibliographical implications are obvious.

[11] Printed catalogues of the Kew library were issued first of all in 1899 (as *Bulletin of miscellaneous information, additional series 3*), also in 1919 as a Supplement to the 1899 edition.

Passing from botany to horticulture, there is little doubt that to the serious student of garden science the library of **The Royal Horticultural Society** – the Lindley Library – is of the utmost value. Botanists and naturalists in general will find much important material here, some of it unobtainable elsewhere in London, and, in some instances, in the whole country. The horticultural aspect, as one might expect, is stressed, but there is much on systematic botany with a close connection with horticulture. The Lindley Library contains floras and monographs of plant genera which have a horticultural interest. The collection is well indexed and easily consulted. The Cory Bequest (1936) added a number of rare and important items to this fine library. A feature of this valuable bequest was the books with illustrations of plants, particularly the coloured illustrations of the late eighteenth and early nineteenth centuries. Among the important acquisitions received since 1949 may be mentioned three folio volumes of paintings of Chinese plants, made under the direction of John Reeves, a merchant who was in China from 1812 to 1831,[12] and a large, unpublished collection of beautifully executed coloured drawings of British plants by the late Miss Dorothy Martin (1882–1949). The Lindley Library is estimated to consist at present of about 33,000 volumes and pamphlets. The library is an 'outlier' of the National Central Library. The importance of this fact to students can perhaps be realised when one remembers that the Lindley Library is probably the most complete horticultural library in the world. The library catalogue published in 1927 has 488 pages.

To round off this account of natural history libraries in London, the attention of the student should perhaps be drawn to the libraries of certain other institutions to which the advanced student may seek access, should the more obvious and better-known repositories of books on his subject fail him. This may happen in difficult 'border-line' subjects, where natural history shades, for example, into anatomy, physiology, or into clinical or veterinary medicine. For instance, though hardly any mention has been made of the Science Library in the present account, it should be unnecessary to emphasise the paramount importance of this great general library of science for natural

---

[12] For a description of these drawings, see *J. Roy. Hort. Soc.* 78 1953, 209–213. It may be noted that the large collections of drawings made by John Reeves and his son, J. R. Reeves, are in the library of the British Museum (Natural History).

history as well as for the many other scientific disciplines which are its province. However, the student of natural history should also bear in mind the libraries of the Royal Society, the Patent Office, the Royal Society of Medicine, the Royal College of Surgeons, the London School of Hygiene and Tropical Medicine, the Royal Veterinary College, to name just some of the further sources of information.

The biologist is indeed confronted in London with an overpowering wealth of material, but although biologists, and taxonomists in particular are, or should be, bibliographically conscious, there remains a good deal to be done in the matter of indexing and making generally known the contents of such libraries as I have mentioned above. Such works as the *World list of scientific periodicals* are available, but the issue of more accession lists, bibliographies of special subjects, hand-lists of current periodicals, lists of early books, of drawings, and manuscripts, and the like would help students greatly.

CHAPTER III

THE SCIENCE LIBRARY

By the late H. T. Pledge
Keeper

IF this essay has any interest, it will be that of an account, by the only person concerned throughout, of a curious episode in the history of British librarianship, an episode of some moment to librarians, though not, perhaps, to present-day users. For during most of the life of the present edition of this book the postal loan service of the Science Library – the episode in question – will be a thing of the past.

That this episode is the only thing of wide interest in the history of the library does not enable us wholly to by-pass what went before, for this proved potent in the fate of the experiment. The Science and Art Libraries of the old South Kensington Museum were conceived quite naturally as part of that Museum and, like it, as learned bodies, though extremely useful ones. When, early in this century, the Museum split into the Victoria and Albert and the Science Museums, and the libraries went with their respective halves, they continued to be viewed as learned bodies. All the Victorian dignity of science as an Activity of the Spirit, almost as the successor of religion, doubtless informed the sedate life of the place. There was plenty of time to carry out all the checks and longhand fair-copying of the old-style librarianship. At least, so we may suppose.

The first war proved to be a harsh commentary on this. War, and industry after the war, needed science. Research stations sprang up, official and industrial. Few of them started with any libraries to speak of. But the Victorian inheritance of enlightened philanthropy was still strong in the library world. The Central Library for Students was founded to bring to scattered hungry minds the library resources of the whole country. Librarians with a new impulse began to sally forth from their still rooms shouting their wares in comparatively brazen voices. Such were the inspirations which fermented in Dr. S. C. Bradford's mind during the first half of the 'twenties. When he succeeded to the Keepership of the Science Library in 1925, they found

48

scope in the opening of the resources of the library to research institutions throughout the country by means of postal loans.

The writer has only verbal tradition of the part played by Dr. Bradford in bringing this result about. The atmosphere was not encouraging. Local interests felt themselves threatened. On the other hand he also enjoyed a good deal of informal support of a type which is harder to come by in these departmentalised days.

The opening of the loan service was not by any means Dr. Bradford's only step. The Wembley Exhibition is said to have shown with what curious ease one could obtain the gift of enormous numbers of publications from all over the world merely by asking for them. Nor were most of these publications the second-rate ones. This discovery was followed up by Dr. Bradford and by his successors. The *World list of scientific periodicals* was combed. An elderly member of staff, who already displayed some of the eccentricity of the old-time antiquary, lost the rest of his wits in scanning the 25,000 entries. The collection of periodicals grew mightily. Under 4,000 in 1925, it reached 11,000 before the end of the postal loan service. Of course, many of these presentations failed to sustain themselves. Stoppages and re-starts were frequent, adding to the general chaos of births, deaths, fusions and fissions of the journals themselves, which reflected the tumult of the scientific movement. Like a millionaire, the library could never tell exactly how rich it was at any given moment, to the furious exasperation of users who expected the virtues of the old stately ways without their narrowness. Complaints were incessant but, from the first, the loan system was an almost embarrassing success.

In fact, the automatic nature of its success lost it the interest of its initiator, who became far more interested in information work, and in particular in the Universal Decimal Classification as a tool for the inquirer. It was here that he was well served by the old tradition of graduate librarianship, natural where libraries had always been regarded as parts of learned institutions. In those days of a shortage of jobs in science, it was easy to form a graduate cataloguing staff. At its highest point, just before the war, the library had nine scientists on its staff. Thus the subject-classification of the collections, and their use through this in answering inquiries, became a feature of the service. All in all a certain leadership may be claimed for the library in the 'thirties.

A monstrous card-index, amounting to three to four million cards, all classified by the system, grew and grew in the limited space available. Some cards were printed, some typed, all too many were in archaic handwriting. They were in all languages. Not without, at times, a hint of the ludicrous, the U.D.C. was shouted from the house-tops. H. G. Wells came to the library, seeking his fantasy of a World Brain. He did not return.

In fact, despite the qualified workers and the monstrous index, the first condition for successful inquiry work was lacking, as indeed it still often is in inquiry work everywhere, namely a sufficient volume and closeness of use. Incessant touch between staff and user was best achieved in the countless specialised research and information centres then springing up; and their competition was fatal to this vast central scheme. All Dr. Bradford's efforts to 'prime the pump', to get an amount of business which would have justified the staff needed constantly to edit and re-edit the card-index, failed. He was indeed himself far too little aware of how elaborate was the servicing needed by the index. It was little used, and there came a time, after his death, when it was quietly parcelled up and the costly cabinets dispersed among other libraries. Its passing made little difference to the amount of inquiry work accomplished. Many inquiries are still dealt with, many more could be. Historical and humane aspects of science are naturally a speciality.

The keepership of E. Lancaster Jones, who succeeded Dr. Bradford, was one of much-needed consolidation, but it was, in fact, mainly a war-time one, with half the staff, and half the books, away. The decree that the valuable parts of the collections were to be evacuated to safety was fortunately interpreted to mean those of value in the antiquarian book market. Some of these were consequently chivvied from place to place as many as four times before they slowly returned home in the late 'forties. The library was thus able to give its indispensable services to the war-effort without the complaints and competition of local users, many of whom had indeed thoughtfully vanished for the duration. The loan-service, already a triumphant success, now acquired practically a monopoly in the preoccupations of the staff.

After the war, the demands upon it at once became tremendous. Science was the order of the day. Every up-to-date firm aspired to set up a research department. Enrolments on the loan-list were for some years incessant, and if the number of loans did not rise proportionately this must have been partly due to the mutual interference of users. They were competing for the same small section of the huge accessions which continued to roll in. This continuity was due to presentations: purchase grants then bore no relation to need, except to the national need for rigorous economy. Awkward features of traditional accessions policy began to come to light and could not be readily altered. To acquire, if possible, all of what Americans excellently call archive-material, at all costs to derivative work, was not, before the war, in such visible conflict with the demands of industry as it became after-wards when funds were so short. Not only funds; space was never, after 1939, found in the Museum site for nearly the whole collection. A succession of distant stores for almost a third of the books imposed dismal burdens on staff and users.

And not only space: before the war, staff kept broadly in proportion to the demands on the library. After the war, this was not so. After the war, too, the original vintage of scientific staff was in all-too-acute demand elsewhere, in units new and old. Harwell, the British Council, the Patent Office, the Science Museum itself, the new Lending Unit precursor of the National Lending Library, all received key personalities from the Science Library.

It was after the war that the seasoned wisdom of Lancaster Jones, who had died prematurely just after weathering the troubles of the conflict itself, was most seriously missed. It is very doubtful if he would have ventured on the uncharted seas of photocopy services and of inter-library loan-organisation, even in order to give an appearance of taking urgent action in an almost desperate emergency. What users wanted was simply loans, loans and yet more loans; and he might well have seen that these other schemes could come to seem a mere screen to cover the failure to provide books, storage space and staff – the things, and the only things, really needed to give a vastly improved service. The stores need not have been in London, for only a small and known fraction of the collections was in heavy and post-haste demand.

As a fact, however, the extreme shortage of books after the war led to the organisation by the library of a private interlending scheme among its registered borrowers, a scheme which became difficult to stop and most expensive in staff time, partly because it could be used by participants as much to free themselves from the tedium of con-sulting a catalogue as for any other purpose.

As a fact, too, a photocopy service was forced upon the users, taking a leaf out of the book of the U.S. Department of Agriculture where such a scheme had been a great success. Certain periodicals, for which there were almost incredibly long waiting lists, were withdrawn from loan altogether. Photocopies were offered instead, at a sufficiently cheap flat rate, and on a sufficiently simple system, to come to be used for many journals other than these particular ones. The cheapness sprang from the simple observation that clerical work, arising out of preliminary estimates of price and the like, accounted for a large fraction of the cost of the older type of photocopy system. Copies sold had, in 1958, reached the respectable figure of 30 per cent of the whole external issues of the library.

Though the resulting entanglements in copyright law and in other directions led to much waste of staff time, the Photocopy Service was in the spirit of the age and showed the library still in some sense in the forefront of events. To it there still came learners from all parts of the world. Many of these must have been impressed by what they saw, for many temporary members of staff come from the antipodes and elsewhere in the Commonwealth.

There came a time when committees at a comparatively high level scrutinised the library services at the disposal of industry, and the Patent Office and Science Libraries came in for some rearrangement of function. It is not within the scope of this chapter to comment on their findings. But the evident lack of space in South Kensington, the theoretical possibility of carrying on postal loans from anywhere in England even when half are to users in Greater London, and the local needs of the expanding Imperial College, have led to the initiation of a new loan library, with the ultimate resumption by the Science Library of its pre-Bradfordian function. The new loan library has as a nucleus a large fraction of the more industrial elements in the old collections, and with these go a non-academic element in the Science Library activities which, perhaps, its museum atmosphere was never wholly fitted to serve. In its new work the library reading room not only serves the outside visitor as before, but it is dovetailing with scientific and humanistic libraries in the College and in the Victoria and Albert Museum. The Ancestral Voices in the very title of the old Science and Art Department find themselves curiously restored to authority in what is, presumably, the oldest science centre in the world; though the phrase, Science Centre, was not in use when the old Queen dedicated these institutions to her Albert's holy shade.

A short account of the Science Library. Aslib *Report of Proc. of 1st Conference, 1924,* 27–29.
BRADFORD, S. C. Why the Science Museum Library changed to the U.D.C. *Lib. J.* 55 (12) 1930, 1000–1005.

HOLMSTROM, J. E. Records and research in engineering and industrial science. 2nd edition. Chapman & Hall, 1947, pp. 238–240.

LYONS, Sir H. Recent developments in connection with the Science Library. Aslib *Report of Proc. of 4th Conference, 1927,* 49–52.

PARKER, H. J. Science Museum Library. *Libri* 3 1954, 326–336.

SCIENCE MUSEUM, LONDON. Report(s) of the Advisory Council. (Annual.)

SPRATT, H. P. Libraries for scientific research in Europe and America. Grafton, 1936, Chapter I.

—— Technical science libraries. *Year's work in Librarianship,* 6 1933, 114–134.

THOMPSON, A., and EDWARDS, P. I. The Science Museum Library Supplementary Loan Service. *Lib. Assn. Rec.* 58 (8) 1956, 293–298.

URQUHART, D. J. The Science Museum Library, in IRWIN, R., editor. The libraries of London. The Library Association, 1949, Chapter 3.

CHAPTER IV

THE LIBRARY OF THE VICTORIA AND ALBERT MUSEUM[1]

By A. W. Wheen
Keeper

THE library of the Victoria and Albert Museum, South Kensington, S.W.7, is a reference library for the study of the history, philosophy, technique and appreciation of the arts. It is open to the public free on weekdays, 10 a.m. to 6 p.m., holidays excepted. Admission generally is by reader's ticket, for which application is to be made to the Director and Secretary of the Museum; holders of British Museum reader's tickets, or cards of membership of the National Art Collections Fund and certain other institutions are also admitted.

The library, now the largest specialised collection of art literature in the world (it comprises some 500,000 volumes and 300,000 photographs), had its modest beginning as the working library of the first School of Design in Ornamental Art established at Somerset House in 1837, the outcome of a Select Committee on Arts and Manufactures appointed by Parliament in 1835 to "inquire into the best means of extending a knowledge of the arts and the principles of design among the people (especially the manufacturing population) of the country".

The machinery of the Industrial Revolution had been running for more than two generations, and, under the powerful momentum of accelerating technical invention, it ploughed on through depression after depression, until in certain fields, particularly textiles, pottery, Birmingham ware and fancy goods, the production of luxury for the middle class was an accomplished fact. Yet all was not felt to be well. In the field of industrial art the traditional crafts had been dislocated, the apprenticeship system had been disrupted, the craftsman was sinking into proletarian misery and competent designers for the new

[1] Much of the historical information in this account is from an article by A. Van de Put, F.S.A., formerly Keeper of the Library, in *Aslib Information*, No. 26, December 1935.

processes in the new materials were not forthcoming. Among men of taste the achievement produced only despondency. "I believe", protested one, "that the attempt to supersede the work of the mind and hand by mechanical process for the sake of economy, will always have the effect of degrading and ultimately ruining art." In the more sensitive manufacturer, made conscious of the sales value of art by the competition of superior French wares, it produced puzzled irritation. "People of taste are fond of complaining", it was asserted in apology, "of the many ugly patterns which our manufacturers are continually sending forth, when with the same trouble and expense, so much finer patterns may be produced; but they would not do so, if they only considered how many ugly tastes our manufacturers have to cater for." And to the new enthusiasm of the educationist it offered opportunity. "In former times", said one, "artists were workmen and workmen were artists, . . . it is very desirable to restore this happy connection." The Select Committee accordingly recommended the establishment throughout the country of Schools of Design, charged with instruction of the artisan population in the direct application of the arts to manufacture; and, aimed at the consumer, the simultaneous foundation of libraries, public galleries and museums for the improvement of the public tastes – "in all of which the practical application of the arts to manufacture should be deemed an essential element." But the time to implement these recommendations unfortunately fell on an hour of trade depression; the first Normal School of Design was set up under the Board of Trade in rooms on the top floor of Somerset House and the spacious programme of libraries, museums and galleries dwindled to a mixed assortment of 'casts, examples and books', the instructional equipment of the School of Design.

The results did not answer to the expectation. The fundamental principle of industrial design, that "scientific improvements in machinery, and economy in construction of it, are intimately connected with perfection of form", though clearly stated at the time, was imperfectly understood; the notion of design was restricted to that of ornament, and it was found impossible to bend the academic system of art education to the humbler requirements of industry. After repeated inquiries and reforms it was eventually declared in 1849 that "to the classes for whose benefit it was established, the School appears to be nearly useless".

Following the Great Exhibition of 1851, which so painfully exposed to the contemplation of men of taste the anarchy and decay into which the industrial arts had fallen, the original proposals of the Select Committee for improving public taste by the foundation of galleries, museums and libraries were revived. In February 1852 the Department of Practical Art was established, temporarily housed at Marlborough House, and there in September a Museum of Manufactures was opened, containing the casts and objects belonging to the School together with a collection of ancient and modern industrial art which had been shown at the Great Exhibition and purchased for £5,000 at the instance of the Prince Consort, who had perhaps been prompted by a private memorandum submitted by Gottfried Semper, the great German architect. These objects together formed the nucleus of the present Museum collection. The School library, consisting of a lending library of 1,000 smaller works on the theory and history of art, and a reference section of 500 large illustrated volumes on architecture and decoration, many cut up to furnish the classes as examples, became the Museum library, open to the public from 10 a.m. to 9 p.m. daily, Saturdays excepted, at a fee of 6d. a week or 10s. a year. In 1855 the Museum and the library, with the newly constituted Department of Science and Art, passed under Order of Council to the Lord President of the Committee of Council in Education, and in 1857–58, to make room at Marlborough House for the Prince of Wales, the collections were transferred to South Kensington.

The first classified, printed catalogue had been issued in 1855, followed by an alphabetical supplement in 1857, when the library contained some 6,000 volumes, 2,200 prints and drawings and upwards of of 1,000 photographs. In 1860 readers totalled 4,560.

Once established at South Kensington, the expansion of the Museum collections was astonishingly rapid. After 1860 similar museums sprang up throughout Europe. By 1880 an unprecedented and incomparable body of material was available for comparative historical study. Despite its avowed and reiterated orientation toward aesthetic and technical education, it was inevitable that the Museum should, in its development, fall into line with the historicism that was so marked a feature of nineteenth-century thought. From the first it was maintained that "a collection of works of art is best arranged on an historical basis to combine taste and instruction". The classification by techniques and materials, e.g., ceramics, metalwork, textile, woodwork, etc., devised primarily to aid the technical student, favoured in the event the connoisseur, the antiquarian and, most important, the historian of the arts. On the evidence made available in these great collections, the history of the arts has since been written.

The development and organisation of the library, in so far as it is a reference department of the Museum, has been parallel to that of the Museum, following generally a technical and ethnographical classification. But the scope of the library always greatly exceeded that of the Museum, in that it covered not only the industrial, but also the fine arts, music only excepted. In 1868, when a great expansion of the book collection was initiated, the library was newly styled the 'National Art Library', a title which lapsed, however, in 1900 in favour of the 'Art Library', when the Board of Education absorbed the former Departments of Science and Art and of Education. This rapid expansion of the library was concurrent with the compilation of the most comprehensive bibliography of the earlier literature of art ever to be published. The project originated in a suggestion made by Charles Dilke in the *Athenaeum* prior to 1851 and subsequently developed by Henry Cole, Director of the Museum, in which he recommended "the preparation of a general bibliography of art instead of a catalogue dependent on the accidental collection of works". Book titles obtained from British and foreign sources were assembled and edited at the Museum over a period of many years, the first sheets being printed in the advertisement columns of *The Times,* and thereafter, during 1868–69, in *Notes and Queries*. In 1870 was published *The first proofs of the universal catalogue of books on art, compiled for the use of the National Art Library and the Schools of Art in the United Kingdom,* two volumes of 2,188 pages followed in 1875 by a supplement. Though far from scientific by modern standards, this bibliography served the library at once as a catalogue and list of *libri desiderati*. In 1890 an author card-catalogue superseded the occasional, printed but unpublished, lists of new books supplementary to the *Universal catalogue*. Between the years 1881 and 1901 was issued the well-known series of Class Lists of books on the various arts; supplementary material for the revision of these lists, though accumulated until 1904, when a subject index was started, has never been published. The library has now three separate series of subject-indexes: the first in manuscript volumes covering the acquisitions in 1890; the second, acquisitions from 1904–32; the third, in which it is hoped eventually to incorporate the second, acquisitions from 1933. Together these indexes, though always under revision, constitute the largest classified bibliography of the literature of art in existence. During the recent war the library remained open; but as a measure of safety these index volumes were microfilmed, and one copy is now in the Library of Congress, U.S.A. Index material for the years

1891–1903, in so far as it was not incorporated in the published Class Lists, unfortunately remains unavailable to students.

In 1884 the library moved into the galleries designed by Captain Francis Fowke, which it still occupies on the south side of the Museum courtyard. During the year 1899, while the Cromwell and Exhibition Road fronts were under construction from designs of Sir Aston Webb, the character of the Museum, which had long endured great confusion from insufficient space, was clarified and simplified. The various scientific and technological collections were moved elsewhere, the old name 'South Kensington Museum' was changed to 'Victoria and Albert Museum', and the collections formed into a specialised museum of the fine and applied arts. The library also was reorganised at the same time; its very large collection of prints and drawings were formed into a new department of 'Engraving, Illustration and Design' now styled 'Prints and Drawings', and the book collections were assigned the status of a museum department, styled the 'Library and Book Production Department', with an exhibition gallery.

The library is intended for the use, on the one hand, of all practitioners of art, for architectural and art students, industrial and commercial designers, theatrical and graphic artists, typographers and artistic craftsmen of every sort; and on the other, of art historians, aestheticians, art critics, connoisseurs and collectors. Though it has been the practice to avoid as far as possible duplication of archaeological literature represented in the British Museum Library, the special purposes of the art library make it inevitable that a large amount of such literature should be included – material which is now doubly valuable in view of the heavy losses suffered by the British Museum in this branch during World War II. In addition to this public use, the collection serves as a central reference library for the other Museum departments. The contents include much manuscript material relative to the arts; ancient and modern printed books, both British and foreign; catalogues of collections, public and private; sale catalogues; sets of periodicals and transactions of learned institutions, covering the history of art of all countries, styles and periods.

The range of subjects includes architecture, sculpture, painting, the graphic arts, ornament, the art of the theatre, textiles, costume, ceramics, glass, woodwork, furniture, interior decoration, metalwork, jewellery, enamels, coins, medals and seals, arms and armour, clocks and watches, illuminated manuscripts, calligraphy, book illustration, printing, bookbinding, topography, biography, heraldry.

In normal times in the Book Production Gallery is displayed a collection drawn from the library and from the Department of Prints and Drawings, arranged to illustrate the history and technique of the arts of the book. The exhibition comprises illuminated and calligraphic manuscripts; printed books showing the evolution of printing, type design and book illustration; a representative selection of European and Near Eastern fine bindings; and an exhibit illustrating the several techniques of book production.

During the latter part of the nineteenth century, before the character of the Museum had been so strictly defined and narrowly specialised, the Museum was bequeathed two famous private collections of general and historical literature, the Dyce and Forster Libraries. The former, bequeathed by the Rev. Alexander Dyce, critic and editor of Elizabethan dramatic literature, contains a number of manuscript copies and many first and rare editions of the works of almost all the outstanding English dramatists, scholars and critics of the sixteenth and seventeenth centuries, as well as of Italian poetry, plays and romances, and editions of the Greek and Latin classics. The Forster Library, bequeathed in 1879 by John Forster, for many years editor of the *Examiner*, historian, biographer, and friend of Charles Dickens, is remarkable for its collection of English nineteenth-century literature, a very extensive group of seventeenth-century broadsides and pamphlets, a valuable collection of rare Swiftiana, together with numerous manuscripts and letters of literary, historical and artistic interest, among them three notebooks of Leonardo da Vinci, illustrated with drawings; above forty volumes of correspondence of David Garrick; and original manuscripts, proofs and editions of many of the novels of Charles Dickens.

In 1940 the late Mr. H. J. B. Clements bequeathed to the Museum his collection of more than 1,150 bindings decorated with British armorial book stamps, which, in conjunction with the catalogue prepared by himself, illustrate the whole history of English book-collecting from the sixteenth to the twentieth century.

In other departments of the Museum are a number of beautiful bindings in the making of which craftsmen other than the binder played the chief part, books in wooden boards covered with ivory or metal, enamelled or set with precious stones. In the Department of Prints and Drawings are numerous pages and cuttings from illuminated manuscripts, of which an illustrated catalogue has been issued.

CHAPTER V

THE PATENT OFFICE LIBRARY

By F. W. Gravell
Formerly Librarian, The Patent Office

FUNCTION AND HISTORY

THE Patent Office Library is a State public reference library, presenting
a world-wide coverage of the industrial arts and of the sciences from
which these arts derive. The Patent Office, more correctly called the
Patent Office and Industrial Property Department of the Board of
Trade, is administered by a Comptroller-General, who is responsible
for the granting and registration of patents for invention, designs and
trade marks. The library was established in the Patent Office to promote invention by the stimulus of free and easy access to scientific and
technical information. The venture was so successful that when the
Government, in 1950, was considering the establishment of a Science
Centre on the South Bank of the Thames, in London, the Patent Office
Library was selected as the best library of its kind available to form the
basis of a National Scientific Reference Library in that Centre. The
plan for this Centre has since been abandoned, for the present at any
rate, but a scheme is now going forward to move the Patent Office and
its library to the South Bank site, adjacent to Waterloo Bridge, and to
develop the library as a national collection under the name of 'The
National Reference Library of Science and Invention'.

The library was opened to the public on 5th March, 1855, as 'The
Library of the Great Seal Patent Office', following the establishment of
the Office under Patent Commissioners three years earlier by the
Patent Law Amendment Act of 1852. This Act gave to the Commissioners power to grant patents for invention, as distinct from the
grant of letters patent for other royal privileges. An invention is defined
in the Act as a "manner of new manufacture". This definition has,
broadly speaking, governed the scope of the collection of books and
periodicals forming the library. In medicine, for example, the collection
is limited to drugs and appliances and in agriculture to fertilisers,

insecticides and the tools and mechanics of cultivation. Agricultural products are, of course, covered in so far as handling, preserving and processing are concerned. Similarly, in forestry, the emphasis is on forest products.

The provision of a public reference library by the Patent Office can best be understood by an appreciation of the underlying purpose of a patent system. This is to stimulate the productivity of a country by inducing inventors to allow their ideas to be published, in return for the privilege of using a new process, or manufacturing and selling a new article, for a limited term of years, under government protection. The publishing of its series of specifications containing original ideas of manufacture is a vital part of the work of the Patent Office. Experience shows that one invention, or improvement, provokes another and so the industry of the country is advanced. The Patent Commissioners saw, in undertaking their work of disseminating technical information, that information of all kinds on the industrial arts and the sciences could serve as a stimulus to invention, and so they established the library as a centralised effort to collect such information from every country and make it publicly and freely available.

The library owes its existence to the Clerk to the Commissioners and Superintendent of Publications, Bennet Woodcroft. He appears to have been the moving spirit behind the activity of the Office in the early years. His own personal library of science and industrial art was first lent, and subsequently purchased, to form the nucleus of the book collection. As Superintendent of Publications, Bennet Woodcroft was also responsible for the publishing of patent specifications which were granted under the earlier laws and, together with other letters patent, were in manuscript form on parchment rolls, in the custody of the Master of the Rolls. Mr. Woodcroft also inaugurated the various series of Abridgments of Specifications of Patents, a pioneer effort in abstracting technical literature. These publications all took their place as important reference works in the library collection.

The library began its existence in a long narrow passage under the Patent Office and was popularly known as 'The Drain Pipe'. In response to the numerous complaints of users and the recommendations of a 'Select Committee on the Patent Office Library and Museum', new rooms for the library were opened in 1867 on the second floor of the Office, occupying a space 60 ft. by 49 ft. The present building, occupying its own site in the centre of the Office buildings, was opened in 1902. This building covers an area of 140 ft. by 60 ft. and is

50 ft. high, with two galleries 19 ft. wide running the length of the building on either side. It was erected at a cost of £166,000 and designed by Sir John Taylor. The public access area was extended by the opening of a lower ground floor in 1954. This area had, until then, been used as a reserve stack. The expansion of the library beyond the capacity of the public building has been met by the installation of reserve book stacks in a number of separate locations.

THE PATENT MUSEUM AND THE LIBRARY

A Patent Museum was formed and opened in 1857 at South Kensington in proximity to other exhibition collections. Some years later an agitation arose to secure the removal of the library to a site adjacent to the Museum. A Select Committee of the House of Commons was appointed "to inquire as to the most suitable arrangements to be made respecting the Patent Office Library and Museum". A most exhaustive inquiry was conducted and the report issued in 1864 stated that the library was most useful in connection with the work of the Office. This decision strongly emphasised the primary function of the library as part of the machinery necessary to the effective working of the Patents Act. The value of the library as an educational institution is considerable, and the collection presents unique opportunities for historical studies, but its real function is that of a bibliographical workshop for the manufacturing industries. The Patent Museum was transferred to the Science and Art Department on 1st January, 1884, in accordance with the provisions of the Patents Act of 1883.

GROWTH AND USE OF THE COLLECTION

According to the estimate of Mr. Woodcroft in his evidence before the Select Committee of 1864, the library had then grown to a collection of 30,000 volumes, the specifications being "a very small part". By 1902, when the new building was occupied, this total had trebled. The present-day collection is estimated at 380,000 volumes and occupies roughly nine miles of shelves. The patent literature forms about a quarter of this last total; the United Kingdom specifications total approximately two million and the series for the United States of America is approaching three million. More than half the total collection consists of periodical sets, of which about a half of the titles held, approximately 7,000, are current titles. The remaining quarter, or less, of the library collection is composed of textbooks, pamphlets and manufacturers' catalogues. The number of separate accessions, including periodical titles and pamphlets, but excluding manufacturers' catalogues, is now over 103,000.

The value of the library lies not only in its world-wide collection of published technical and scientific information, but equally in the freedom of access given to all who wish to use it. Admission formalities have been reduced to a minimum – the signing of a visitors' book each day and the depositing of bags and umbrellas in the cloakroom. A system of open access to the shelves has been in operation from the beginning and has contributed greatly to the increasing use made of the library by the public. Upwards of 2,000 readers sign the visitors' book each week and the grand total of signatures during more than one hundred years is nearly eight and a half million. The open access facilities are supplemented by numerous catalogues and indexes and by the provision of staff information desks at appropriate points. A service from the reserve stacks is also maintained. In general the literature of the last thirty to forty years is in open access and all earlier material must be applied for from the reserve stacks. The collection is open to the public from 10 a.m. until 9 p.m. from Monday to Friday and from 10 a.m. to 1 p.m. on Saturday.

COLLECTIONS OF BRITISH PATENT PUBLICATIONS IN OTHER PUBLIC INSTITUTIONS

The Patent Law Amendment Act of 1852 empowered the Commissioners of Patents to present copies of all published specifications and other publications to public libraries and museums. The Commissioners interpreted this provision very liberally and in 1884 complete sets of Patent Office publications were being sent to 47 towns in the United Kingdom and 70 public offices, seats of learning, societies, etc. in the Empire and foreign countries. In addition, complete sets of abridgments of patent specifications were placed with 367 mechanics', literary and scientific institutions, whilst 75 other libraries at home and abroad were receiving minor grants. Each complete collection at this time comprised 3,960 volumes and cost the Office £4,150 to produce. This widespread distribution of patent information can be taken as the original intention behind the amending Act. The enforcement of economy in government expenditure, the growth of collections to unwieldly proportions and the demise of many local institutions have reduced this distribution to a small fraction of the earlier liberality. Today only 21 public libraries in the United Kingdom receive and make available complete sets of Patent Office publications. The distribution to other bodies has been similarly curtailed, except that a free exchange of publications has been maintained between the Patent Offices of the countries of the world.

This dissemination of patent literature has naturally resulted in the receipt by the library of a considerable amount of literature sent in exchange. Foreign patent specifications and proceedings of learned institutions have been received in this way. In addition, many institutions, private and governmental, donate their publications.

Acquisition by purchase is, however, the chief source of the supply of books and periodicals. Since the Second World War, the purchasing power of the library has steadily increased. This increase is partly accounted for by the need to keep step with rising prices, but the chief reason is the decision of the Government to permit the library to intensify its stock in readiness for its role as a national scientific reference library. This intensification is still within the limits of its present coverage, the field of invention, and it is envisaged that a wider coverage will be undertaken when the library assumes its wider responsibility, covering the field of science and technology generally. The present allocation for all publications purchased is £12,800 p.a.

Very precise arrangements are made for binding in order to keep all the literature in a suitable condition for open access consultation. The present grant for this purpose is £11,000 p.a.

DISPOSAL OF OLDER MATERIAL

In 1951 the Technical and Scientific Libraries Committee of the Advisory Council for Scientific Research recommended that the proposed National Scientific Reference Library be developed from the Patent Office Library. In this report the principle of limited conservation of material was put forward for the library, in place of the policy of unlimited preservation which had prevailed up to that time. A period of fifty years was suggested as an economic limit for the preservation of technical and scientific literature, except for patent specifications and the more important periodicals in the field. In 1956 a small subcommittee representing librarians and users endorsed this principle and set out the categories of literature which could be dispensed with. It also outlined procedures for the method of disposal in order to ensure that copies were preserved as far as necessary in other libraries in this country. This disposal procedure has now been established and it is hoped to regulate the size of the library to a very large extent by balancing the intake against the disposals. The increasing output of literature in scientific and technical fields will tend to make this a losing battle, but it will, at any rate, postpone the advent of saturation point in a new building very considerably. The proceedings of important learned and professional societies and outstanding periodicals on a subject will still be kept indefinitely, together with all the home and overseas patent records, but, subject to journals discarded being available elsewhere in the country, an endeavour will be made to limit the Patent Office Library collection to the 500,000 volumes recommended by the 1951 Committee.

The microfilming of early patent specifications and records has been considered, but so far no economic method of doing this has been found.

THE ARRANGEMENT OF THE LIBRARY COLLECTIONS

The general and detailed arrangements of the library are set out in a leaflet, *Guide to the use of the library*, distributed by the Patent Office. This arrangement is in four main sections: (1) United Kingdom patent publications and official records; (2) Overseas patent publications; (3) Technical and scientific periodicals; (4) Books, pamphlets and trade catalogues.

UNITED KINGDOM PATENT SECTION

A search in this section can be made by the patent number, the name of the patentee or the subject of the patent. Published specifications, name indexes and classified subject abridgments of specifications are available for each kind of search. The life of a patent from the day of application until its expiry can be traced in copies of official registers which are maintained in the library.

OVERSEAS PATENT SECTION

Except for the smaller countries, this section contains numbered series of patent specifications, annual indexes and patent and trade mark journals from foreign countries and from the Commonwealth. In most cases it is possible to search by number, name, or subject, but the provision is more restricted than in the United Kingdom Section, except in the single instance of Germany. The German specifications are available in classified subject order as well as in numerical order.

This classification is, however, an arrangement of one specification in one place and does not provide cross references.

TECHNICAL AND SCIENTIFIC PERIODICALS SECTION

This is the largest section of the library and contains a very wide range of periodicals, all of which can be said to have some connection with the field of invention. Many sets of learned societies, professional institutions and trade periodicals go back to the date of their first appearance. Only a few scientific subjects can be regarded as outside the range of invention, and the exceptions become fewer with the passage of time and the progress of science.

The emphasis is placed on periodicals for two reasons: (1) the periodical is generally the earliest form of publication of a new development (apart from a patent specification), and (2) the periodical article usually contains the detail of a study or development and is consequently most frequently referred to in the literature of the subject. Textbooks, with the exception of a few original monographs, are summaries of development, and act as a means of consolidating information on a subject that has already been written up in articles scattered in periodicals.

The Patent Office Library made several attempts to index the articles contained in its large collection of periodicals, but these have all been abandoned in favour of the collecting of indexing and abstracting journals to form a comprehensive key to this literature. There is now, within the Periodical Section, a section devoted to periodical bibliographies of all kinds which serves as a general index to the whole periodical collection.

Various lists of periodicals held by the library have been published through the years. The last complete list was published as an alphabetical subject list in 1924. In recent years it has only been possible to issue an alphabetical list of titles of current periodicals. The second edition of this list appeared in 1958 under the title *Periodical publications in the Patent Office Library. List of current titles.* The *World list of scientific periodicals* includes the Patent Office Library collection.

TEXTBOOKS, PAMPHLETS AND TRADE CATALOGUES SECTION

The textbook collection is intended to cover only scientific and technical books at research level and books covering the technical processes and productions of industry. Works at a student or introductory level are not normally included, but are acquired in some subjects when more advanced books are not available. Pamphlets and manufacturers' catalogues are applied for and included when they are of sufficient size and interest. It has not yet been possible to make these collections comprehensive, or even representative of the whole of industrial activity. In recent years the purchase of textbooks has been made on a much wider scale than formerly and can now be regarded as fairly representative of the output of most of the European countries and North America in scientific and technical books.

CATALOGUES

The catalogues now in use in the library provide, in general, for search under authors, subjects and titles of periodicals. The author catalogue up to 1930 is in the form of a loose-leaf scrapbook, consolidating the author entries of all books received up to that date. From 1931 onwards, this catalogue is on cards filed as a consolidated supplement.

The author entry is the basic entry of a unit card cataloguing system, introduced in recent years. The subject catalogue is in classified order with an alphabetical index of subjects. There are two separate title indexes of periodicals: one is an index of all titles held of both closed and current sets, the other is a visible strip index of current titles only. The visible strip index is available as a printed publication and is referred to in the earlier section on periodicals. An alphabetical subject list of periodicals in the library is also available in the reading room; this is a revision of an earlier printed publication, kept up to date with sheaf supplements. Various minor but useful indexes are available in the reading room for the assistance of the reader in consulting trade catalogues, dictionaries and bibliographies. The catalogues above mentioned are guides to the use of the textbook and periodical sections. The patent sections are served by their own separate indexes and arrangements. A series of separate subject guides to the collection was issued in the early part of the century, but it was abandoned on account of expense and insufficient demand.

The author catalogue arrangement is mainly that laid down by the Joint Anglo-American Library Associations Code. Periodicals are entered under earliest titles in the author catalogue, with references from later titles. In the periodical lists the current title has preference. The practice followed by the *British union-catalogue of periodicals* and the American *Union list of serials* of listing periodicals of corporate bodies under the names of those bodies, except when the title is distinctive, is followed in the Patent Office Library. The *World list of scientific periodicals*, with its arrangement under first word, has not been followed.

CLASSIFICATION

The classification of textbooks and periodicals is distinct from the classification of patent literature. Patent classification schedules are designed to facilitate the work of a patent examiner in his official search for novelty and are built upon elements of construction and processes of manufacture, employing characteristics of arrangement peculiar to this purpose. Most countries have their own separate classifications, but the German classification is followed by several neighbouring countries. The Council of Europe is sponsoring an international patent classification and all the countries within the Council are now printing international class marks on their patent specifications, in addition to their own class mark. Searching by subject in the patent literature must still follow the scheme of each country and classification schedules for a number of countries are available in the library. Separate arrangements of the specifications themselves are only provided in the library for the United Kingdom and for Germany. The United Kingdom provision is that of the *Abridgments of patent specifications* by subject groups, supplemented by classified arrangement of current full specifications. For Germany there is a one place arrangement of full specifications.

The scheme in use for the arrangement of textbooks and periodicals was devised by a former librarian, Mr. E. Wyndham Hulme; it is essentially an arrangement of the books themselves, and not a scientific or logical scheme into which books are fitted. The scheme was called "a 'relative' system of shelf classification" and, in the words of Mr. Hulme, was "designed to meet the peculiar requirements of inventors, searchers, and others who, as a rule, are more deeply versed in the practice than the literature of their respective sciences". The notation is 'mixed' and employs a combination of one or two letters, followed by figures read as decimals. The distribution of the letters and figures is, in general, an arbitrary one. Subjects are frequently distinguished by a change of the first or second letter, but no attempt has been made to show the arrangement or subordination of topics by the notation as a whole. The U.S. Library of Congress Classification Schedules were made use of freely in the drawing up of the original scheme. The classification, as it is today, may not be quite what Mr. Hulme intended, but the principles of his 'relative' system foreshadowed the trend of modern book classification.

PHOTOCOPYING SERVICES

The Patent Office has pioneered in the photocopying of documents. The service was begun in 1918, when an early Photostat camera was presented by Sir Robert Hadfield. In 1929 the service supplied 154,979 half-sheets and had increased to 637,900 half-sheets by 1947. At the present time the output is at least 1,500,000 half-sheets, and these are produced mainly by means of microfilming and Xerography. Photo-copying by Xerography, using microfilm beforehand, is being developed as the standard means of photo-reproduction in the library. The aim is to operate the microfilm cameras in the library as a service to readers on the spot and to supply the enlarged photoprint by Xerographic process very quickly. Any patent specification, and any single article of a periodical required for purposes of private research and study, can now be supplied at a reasonable cost.

CLIENTELE

A considerable amount of reading in the library is of a quick reference type, resulting in an atmosphere of movement and activity not usually associated with libraries. A high proportion of the readers are regular users, employed by industrial firms and scientific and technical institutions as literature searchers and information officers. In many cases this work involves spending much, if not all, of the working day in the library. The estimated use of the library provided by a count of signatures in the visitors' book must take this long use into con-sideration, since a reader is only required to sign once each day. Early reports on the library described the clientele as being drawn from the ranks of "professional men, agents of foreign and provincial inventors and practical mechanics and operatives". Patent agents and their employees still make extensive use of the facilities, but the individual inventor and technician has very largely disappeared and his place has been taken by people employed to locate and supply scientific and technical information. This means that, whilst the total number of readers does not change much from year to year and is even less than it was in earlier years, when use in the evening was greater, the library is actually serving a much wider public through the bibliographical representatives of industrial and technical bodies, who now form such a large part of those making use of its facilities.

A recent census of readers has produced the following summary of their interests and activities:

Average number of persons using the library on any week-day   430

Categories of users:

Firms, including Patent and Trade Mark Agents   74%
Government departments, Research associations, Universities, Hospitals, Publishers, etc.   12%
Private individuals   14%

Percentage of readers using four main sections of the library:

| British patents | 69% | Periodicals | 78% |
| Foreign patents | 58% | Textbooks | 63% |

Frequency of visits by readers:

Every day	6%
Most days	24%
Occasionally	70%

Length of time spent on each visit:

A full working day	10%
Long periods	33%
Short periods	57%

BRIEF ANALYSIS OF THE BOOK AND PERIODICAL COLLECTIONS
BY SUBJECT AND BY LANGUAGE

The following breakdown of language of books and periodicals received in 1958 is given as an indication of the current efforts of the library to provide a collection in line with the aims of its founders, who, in 1855, described it as "a public library of research within the Patent Office, to consist of the scientific and mechanical works of all nations".

Books, including pamphlets and trade catalogues:

English language	73%
German language	$16\frac{1}{2}$%
French language	5%
Other languages	$5\frac{1}{2}$%

The following table gives the approximate number of volumes by main subject group in open access only; i.e., 1921 to date, but not including patent specifications and patent journals.

Subject Groups	No. of volumes		
	Books	Periodicals	
		Current boxes	Bound volumes
General reference	1,920	15	760
Scientific research; industrial property	780	50	1,600
Printing; photography; textiles; dyeing; ceramics; glass	1,230	206	2,440
Applied mathematics; physics; optics	930	184	2,880
Publications of scientific and technical societies	—	203	3,220
Magnetism; electricity; electronics	1,260	243	5,840
Atomic physics	300	42	220
Mechanical, structural and civil engineering; transportation	2,370	578	19,980
Architecture and building	360	114	1,300
Military, naval and marine engineering	810	59	1,420
Sanitary and municipal engineering	1,080	146	1,980
Medical sciences; dentistry; pharmacology	1,170	76	1,740
Food technology; brewing; agricultural and horticultural sciences; timber technology	2,190	335	5,900
Geographical and geological sciences; mineralogy	750	116	3,300
Mining; metallurgy; fuels	2,280	234	5,240
Chemistry; chemical industries	3,840	413	8,220

Periodicals, acquired by purchase only:

English language	43%
German language	$24\frac{1}{2}$%
French language	12%
Russian language	$6\frac{3}{4}$%
Italian language	4%
Dutch language	$2\frac{1}{2}$%
Other languages	$7\frac{1}{4}$%

Representatives of many nations are to be found using the library every day. They are attracted by the books and periodicals in their own language and covering their special technical interests. The concern with international patent protection is also an important factor in the attraction of foreigners with industrial connections to the Patent Office and its library.

THE LIBRARY AND PATENT LITIGATION

The primary concern of the Patent Office is with novelty and the date of making such novelty public. The library is therefore very much concerned with the establishment of a date of publication for everything which it offers to its reading public. Whilst it may be easy to prove the date of publication of an English publication from a number of sources, or from the publication itself, it may often be difficult, if not impossible, to prove a date of availability to the British public in the case of a publication which has come from overseas. To meet this need, the library dates every publication coming from overseas with the date of shelving. This date is regarded in law as the "effective publication date in this country" and the library is recognised in law as a place of effective publication. Library material may be cited in opposition to the grant of a patent applied for on a date subsequent to the library date stamp carried by the cited material. The provisions of opposition to patent grants by interested parties increase the validity and, consequently, the value of patents eventually sealed and the library, with its wealth of material, makes an indispensable contribution to the extended search. The official search for novelty in the Patent Office is limited by the Patents Acts to the last fifty years of patents granted in the United Kingdom, but there is no time limit in a backward direction to the citation of other publications.

WAR AND PEACE

The library functioned almost without interruption through the two world wars, but with some curtailment of its services. During the second war the position was frequently very precarious, but, apart from blast damage, the building and its contents survived. The Patent Office maintained a very efficient A.R.P. Squad throughout this second war and a number of fire bombs were extinguished and the buildings saved from the destruction by fire that overcame many city buildings not so well guarded. The library was only closed to the public on four days on account of enemy action during the whole war period.

Scientific and technical literature is acquiring a place of increasing importance in our modern world of rockets and atoms and in all our strivings for the peaceful uses of man's inventions. Bibliographical research has become the acknowledged preliminary to laboratory and workshop experiment and the Patent Office Library occupies a unique position as a universal provider of the information necessary to this unceasing quest.

CHAPTER VI

THE NATIONAL CENTRAL LIBRARY

By S. P. L. Filon
Librarian and Secretary to the Trustees

and I. P. Gibb
Deputy Librarian

IN his book on *Library co-operation in Europe* (1935), Mr. J. H. P. Pafford
pointed out that Great Britain is the only country which, while
possessing a considerable library service, has no state-supported lending
service. This state of affairs, however, has not prevented us from
developing, in the course of the last thirty years, one of the most highly
organised national lending services in existence.

The need for a national lending service, as apart from local services,
was felt for some considerable time before the existence of the National
Central Library, or even of its forerunner, the Central Library for
Students. For instance, one of the earliest of the numerous suggestions
foreshadowing the creation of the Central Library for Students was
made at the L.A. Conference of 1906 by J. McKillop who suggested
that the L.C.C. Education Committee should establish a central library
for the provision of expensive books for students. The idea of 'store' or
'central' libraries to supplement the public library service by providing
the more expensive and out-of-the-way books was put forward by
S. Kirby in the same year. A. J. Philip of Gravesend, who was responsible for inaugurating the first interlending system in London, proposed
the establishment of a Central Reference Library and Clearing House
for London and in 1913 the suggestion made by a group of librarians
that a central loan library should be created was warmly supported by
Dr. A. W. Pollard, the future Hon. Librarian of the Central Library
for Students. Dr. Pollard further advocated a petition for a grant from
the Board of Education.[1]

[1] For fuller summaries of these papers and bibliographical references see
Chapter 2 of NEWCOMBE, L. Library co-operation in the British Isles. Allen
& U., 1937.

War, however, came in 1914 and prevented any of these suggestions being put into practice. It is indeed a curious fact, commented upon by Mr. Pafford, that the seed from which was to spring the National Central Library and our present national interlending system was sown not by librarians but by those concerned with popular education. The Central Library for Students was founded in 1916 by Dr. Albert Mansbridge and a group of persons interested in adult education. The Carnegie United Kingdom Trust agreed to make a grant for the purpose of establishing the new library and of covering expenses during an initial experimental period of five years.

The purpose of the Central Library, as defined in its first annual report, was "to ensure that all *bona fide* students coming under its notice shall be helped in their studies, if they are unable to obtain the use of the necessary books elsewhere". The report further states that the "development of the library will depend largely upon its relationship with existing libraries . . . it will need to be complementary and supplementary to such institutions. . . . It will supplement the book supplies of libraries which are unable, for various reasons, to store a number of duplicates of books for which, owing to the development of local studies, there is a temporary demand." It is clear from this that the library was not originally intended to serve the general public, as it does now, but only adult classes or private students who found it difficult to obtain books. The future connection with the public library system is already implicit, however.

The Central Library for Students began in a small way in a house in Tavistock Square with a staff of two and a stock of 1,392 books, which was inherited from its rather obscure predecessor, a library for Workers' Educational Association and University Tutorial Classes at Toynbee Hall. During the following years the stock and the issues rose steadily. The connection with the public libraries became closer and closer, active collaboration beginning in 1917, when the first book was borrowed by a public library (Westhoughton P.L.). The first public library to subscribe to the Central Library was Kendal Public Library (1918). In 1920 the Carnegie United Kingdom Trust made a special grant of £1,000 to the Central Library for six years on the understanding that the library would make every effort to aid 'rural libraries' (as County Libraries were then called), by acting as a reservoir of expensive books and duplicate copies.

The beginnings of the present organised system of interlibrary lending really go back to the year 1923–24 when, to quote the eighth annual report, "the Carnegie United Kingdom Trust have made grants to three special libraries in London (the College of Nursing, King's College for Women and the Royal Aeronautical Society) on condition that the works in the possession of these libraries are available for the clientele of the Central Library for Students". These are described in the report as 'Outlying Libraries'.

Already in 1919 the national importance of the Central Library for Students was being recognised. The Adult Education Committee of the Ministry of Reconstruction in their Third Interim Report on Libraries and Museums expressed the need for a state-aided circulating library and recommended that the Central Library for Students should be regarded as the nucleus of such a library, the three main functions of which would be: (1) to act as a reservoir from which to supplement the book collections of local libraries by supplying on loan local demands for larger and more expensive works than public libraries can provide; (2) to supply bibliographical information; (3) to act as a clearing house and enlist the co-operation of public, central, technical and other libraries. In the same year (1919) the Library Association, at their Annual Conference, passed a resolution agreeing with this and suggesting to public libraries the desirability of making an annual subscription to the Central Library. The resolution also strongly recommended that the library should receive a government grant.

In the meantime the Central Library continued to receive financial support from the Carnegie Trust, after the expiration of the five-year experimental period. Colonel J. M. Mitchell, the Secretary to the Trustees, was an enthusiast in the cause of library co-operation and in his *Report on public libraries* (1924), he suggested that "the Central Library in Dunfermline should have in its possession the catalogues of all public libraries in Scotland (the principle would apply in England but it would mean a number of central libraries each with its own district) and should be able to borrow books from any public library for the use of another". This clearly points to the later Regional System and to the principle of a central clearing house.

Full official recognition of the necessity for a national system of inter-library lending came in 1927 with the publication of the Report of the Departmental Committee on Public Libraries. This proposed a voluntary system of co-operation, the chief recommendations being: the establishment of a system of regional libraries, the expansion of the Central Library for Students into a national centre linking up the regional libraries and the creation of a central cataloguing agency.

The report recommended further that the Central Library for Students should receive an interim government grant of £5,000 per annum and that a committee should be set up to work out details of the transfer of the library to the control of the Trustees of the British Museum.

However, when the payment of this interim grant came up for discussion by the House of Commons, the question was referred to the Royal Commission on National Museums and Art Galleries, whose Final Report (Part I), published in 1929, only recommended a grant of £3,000 to the Central Library towards the cost of: (1) supply of bibliographical information; (2) the promotion of the Outlier System of libraries; (3) the preparation of a union catalogue.

In accordance with the wishes of the Treasury, the Trustees of the Central Library for Students adopted in 1930 a new constitution, which brought into being the National Central Library. The main differences between the new and the old constitutions lay in the composition of the governing body and to some extent in the object for which the library was being re-created. The National Central Library would no longer be controlled by private trustees but by a Board of Trustees at least half of whom were to be *ex-officio* members, appointed by such bodies as the Trustees of the British Museum, the Library Association and the Carnegie Trustees. Certain of the powers of the Trustees were to be delegated to an Executive Committee, appointed mainly by official bodies. Under the new constitution the chief objects of the Library were to be:

1. To supply on loan to libraries, or in exceptional cases to individuals, books for study.

2. To supply such books on loan to groups of adult students.

3. To act as a clearing house for mutual loans of such books between other libraries.

4. To act as a centre of bibliographical information both for national and international purposes.

It is worth comparing these objects with those for which the Central Library for Students was founded: for, whereas in 1916 the emphasis was on loans to individuals, these are now to be the exception, and in fact, from 1930 onwards, the individual students who had formerly been served by the Central Library for Students were normally supplied with books by the National Central Library only through the intermediary of the Public Libraries or University and Special Libraries, thus making full use of the resources of local libraries before tapping those of the N.C.L.

In the following year the Library was granted a Royal Charter of Incorporation. This confirmed the new constitution already adopted by the Trustees of the Central Library. Two years later (1933) the Library found a more suitable home in its present premises, situated between University College and the headquarters of the University of London, still within the 'sphere of influence' of the British Museum and most appropriately next door to Chaucer House. The opening of this new building by His Majesty Majesty King George V brought the Library for a brief moment into the limelight and to the notice of the general public.

With the establishment of the Library in its new building, the period of rapid growth and change was succeeded by one of consolidation and of the steady realisation of existing plans. It seems fitting at this point, therefore, that some description should be given of the manner in which the Library is organised and of the way in which it carries out the functions already outlined. Before doing this, however, a word must be said about the relationship of the Library to the Regional Systems, to the Universities and to the Outlier Libraries.

Concrete proposals for the establishment of regional systems originated, as has been said, with the report of the Departmental Committee on Public Libraries in 1927, but, although a small regional system covering the County of Cornwall came into existence in 1928, this was hardly more than a 'pilot' scheme and it was not until 1931 that the first full-scale systems were established: those for the Northern and the West Midlands areas. To each of the new regional systems the Carnegie Trustees made a grant for the purpose of building up a union catalogue of the works in the libraries co-operating, in order to facilitate inter-lending and make the fullest use of the library resources of each region. These union catalogues were to be duplicated and combined at the National Central Library to produce a National Union Catalogue. In the years following, the Welsh, the South Eastern, the East Midlands, the Yorkshire, the North Western and the South Western systems were created, the Yorkshire system dispensing, however, with a union catalogue. At the National Central Library itself were housed the South Eastern Regional Bureau and the 'London Union Catalogue' or headquarters of the London interlending system, covering most of the Borough Libraries in London. The National Central Library acted as the clearing house to which were sent requests for loans which could not be satisfied within the regions. Using as its chief tool the National Union Catalogue, the library then tapped the resources of the other Bureaux.

Interlending between the universities dates from the year 1925, when the Joint Standing Committee on Library Co-operation was created by the Association of University Teachers. The Committee established an Inquiry Office at Birmingham University for the purpose of arranging loans between the university libraries and also some special and foreign libraries. In October 1931 this Office was transferred to the National Central Library and the work of acting as clearing house for inter-university loans was taken on by its Information Department.

Something has already been said regarding the origin of the Outlier Libraries. These agree to lend their books to other libraries through the agency of the N.C.L., in return for which they are entitled to borrow books from the N.C.L. itself, or, through it, from its other outlier libraries or from the co-operating university libraries or the libraries in regional systems. Originally the Carnegie Trustees made special grants to the majority of new outlier libraries so that by the year 1931 a total of £84,425 had been granted by the Trust to this group of libraries. After this year these grants were terminated as the funds set aside were exhausted. Many of the Outlier Libraries contributed cards to the special Outlier Union Catalogue which the N.C.L. was in the process of building up. The majority of the outliers are special libraries, but originally this group contained a considerable number of municipal and county libraries, which have since become absorbed in the regional systems (such, for example, as Croydon Public Library and Derbyshire County Library), so that at the present time, with the exception of a very small number of public library outliers in London, the outliers are all special libraries. They cover a wide field of knowledge and include in their numbers such very different libraries as Dr. Williams's Library (theology), the London School of Economics and the Science Library. Those London borough libraries which contribute to the London Union Catalogue are each of them outliers of the N.C.L. and form collectively what amounts to a separate regional system. Applications to the N.C.L. can be forwarded by the L.U.C., while requests for loans by the N.C.L. are sent direct to individual libraries.

The organisation of the work of the Library is as follows. There are now, in addition to a Headquarters Department which includes a Finance Section, three main departments which, in order of seniority, are: the Adult Class and Accessions Department, the Interlending

Department, and the British National Book Centre. These departments carry out different functions of the Library and reflect different stages in its growth.

The Adult Class Department, recently amalgamated with the Accessions Department, fulfils one of the original objects of the Central Library for Students, that is, lending books to organised classes of students. Its bookstock, before being in great part destroyed in 1941, was based on the original stock of the Central Library. It now contains copies of books for class use, many of them duplicated because they are needed by several different classes at the same time. The tendency in recent years has been to purchase the type of work which adult classes cannot conveniently obtain from local libraries or other sources, which involves the purchase of more expensive and specialised works. Applications for loans are made by classes either through a public library in the case of classes organised by the Workers' Educational Association, which also sends requests direct, or through the extra-mural departments of universities in the case of university tutorial classes. Classes send in their requirements in the shape of lists of books, these being required usually for several months. The majority of classes begin in the autumn, the books being returned some six months later in the spring; some classes, however, meet during the summer. The books are sent to the classes, addressed to the tutors, in wooden boxes.

A separate Accessions Department was established in 1950 to build up the main lending bookstock of the Library. Previous to this a 'Library Department' had been responsible both for purchasing and accessioning books and for checking requests for loan in the catalogue, which meant that the work of building up the bookstock was made subsidiary to the daily routine of checking requests. It was therefore found advantageous to separate the two functions. Now, the part of building up the main lending stock, consisting of some 160,000 volumes, is combined with that of purchasing and making available the books for Adult Classes, which now total 50,000. The two collections of books, built up it is true on very different principles, can now nevertheless be used to some extent in conjunction.

The books purchased for the Library's main lending stock are now selected on the following principles: (1) that at least one request to borrow the work has been received; (2) that if still in print they should not cost less than 25s.; (3) that a loanable copy of the book has not been traced in any co-operating library. Relatively few recent British books are now purchased, as the coverage of these by Regional Systems has become more and more complete in recent years. Since January 1959 no currently published British books are normally purchased in view of the scheme for complete coverage of British books listed in the *British National Bibliography* which has been undertaken on a co-operative basis by the Regional Library Systems. Most of the Library's purchases consist at present of American books, of monographs published by learned societies (such as the publications of the Camden Society and Roxburghe Club), and of foreign books. A stock of highly specialised material not available for loan from other libraries is therefore being built up. Not all books are obtained by purchase; a considerable number of gifts of books both by libraries and by private individuals are received by the Library, some of considerable value, such as certain privately printed works and the collection of books on the Napoleonic period presented by the late Professor Holland Rose. The bookstock suffered a very great loss when the Library's premises in Malet Place were almost entirely gutted by fire during an air raid in April 1941, about 105,000 volumes out of a total of nearly 180,000 being destroyed.

The bookstock of the Library has been gradually built up again since the war but is still little bigger than its pre-war size, owing to the relatively small amount of money available for the purchase of books. For the year 1959–60 the book fund, out of which binding and the purchase of books for adult classes (as well as of bibliographies and reference books for the Interlending Department) had to be paid for, only amounted to about £6,000. When compared with the book funds of the larger and even of the average public library, this amount is plainly inadequate, even if the Library's bookstock is regarded as only filling in gaps in the general interlending stock available over the country as a whole. Indeed, in order to fulfil properly the Library's duty to provide bibliographical information, it would be easy to spend most of the present book fund on bibliographies and reference books.

The Library possesses an author catalogue on cards for its own stock and also a classified catalogue, now discontinued. Since 1960 in order to save space books are arranged on the shelves in accessions order; previously they were classified on the Dewey System.

The Interlending Department was inaugurated in 1931, when it was termed Information Department. Its functions were originally: (1) to build up the National and other Union Catalogues needed to locate books in co-operating libraries; (2) to give bibliographical information about books; (3) to trace in other libraries and arrange for the loan of books not in the Library's own stock, loans from which were formerly the responsibility of the Library Department (the old name for the Accessions Department before it became responsible solely for the building up of the library's stock). From 1951 the Information Department was enlarged with the addition of some of the Library Department's staff and given the task of dealing with all applications for loan, whether or not the books sought were in stock. At the same time a special sub-section of the department was established to deal with the union catalogue work which previously had been done in a haphazard way in the intervals of dealing with loan requests.

The old name Information Department was to some extent a misnomer as the supply of factual information was not required of it as in most special libraries. Even the supply of bibliographical information has been circumscribed by lack of staff though, of course, bibliographical research is done in connection with many of the requests received for specific works. The provision of special *ad hoc* bibliographies on restricted subjects is, however, undertaken within the limits imposed by the staff available. It would be desirable to implement fully the clause in the Charter referring to this type of work but more cannot be done without additional funds.

A very extensive library of bibliographies and reference books has been built up and is used mainly to check the requests sent in by libraries. Many libraries still have very poor bibliographical resources and much unnecessary work has to be done at the N.C.L. and the Regional Bureaux to verify titles which libraries should be in a position to check themselves. There are a good many requests, however, the verification of which is beyond the resources of most libraries, such as foreign titles or papers in journals and periodicals.

The necessity of verifying the authors and titles of books, and the titles of periodicals asked for, is largely a result of the inadequate bibliographical apparatus at the disposal of most local libraries and regional bureaux. It is a task which takes up a large proportion of the time of the library-trained staff of this department, who make use for this purpose of a fairly comprehensive collection of general and current bibliographies (e.g., the *United States catalog*, the *Cumulative Book Index*, the *British National Bibliography*, the catalogues of the British Museum and the Bibliothèque Nationale, the *Deutsches Bücherverzeichnis*, *British union-catalogue of periodicals*, *World list of scientific periodicals*, Library of Congress *Russian accessions*). The British Museum is visited to check details of books there, both by consulting the catalogues (which will not be so necessary when the new published catalogue is completed) and by seeing the books themselves. By the generosity of the Rockefeller Foundation, a Bureau of American Bibliography was set up before the war and among other bibliographical tools provided was the Library of Congress Catalogue, which is of course of great value to the Library. The work of this bureau is now integrated into the general bibliographical work of the Library.

For tracing a loanable copy of the work requested, the chief instruments are the Union Catalogues. The National Union Catalogue or combined catalogue of the Regional Systems has already been mentioned. It takes the form of a sheaf catalogue arranged alphabetically by authors, each entry being of the briefest kind and containing only such details as are necessary for the identification of an edition. It is no more than a finding list and has no pretension whatever to bibliographical completeness, as have some American Union Catalogues. The different Regional Systems are indicated by the colour of their slips, the library which actually possesses the book not being shown, as application for the loan of a book located in the catalogue is made to the appropriate Regional Bureau and not to the local library. The book is then located by the Regional Bureau in the Regional Union Catalogue. A considerable amount of space in the National Union Catalogue is saved by combining on one slip all the locations for a book which is in several Regions. The catalogue is estimated to contain approximately one million entries; about one in three of the titles checked in it is located.

The second main source of locations is the Outlier Union Catalogue. This has been built up partly from contributions from outlier libraries (including some of those now absorbed in the regions) and partly from the results of searches made for books not already noted in the Union Catalogues. Both positive and negative results of searches are recorded, as it is always useful in the case of further applications for the same book to know what work was previously done and when, as it is obviously not desirable or practicable to repeat a search too frequently. It is on cards and arranged by authors, periodicals being kept in a separate sequence, and it contains approximately half a million entries. Its efficiency is high, the search results, of course, increasing the proportion of applications for which entries can be found; this proportion is about 50 per cent.

By 1960 considerable arrears of union cataloguing had accumulated in respect of both catalogues. It was decided that the two catalogues ought to be combined in card form. As a first stage therefore the arrears of entries for the National Union Catalogue were copied by Xerography on to cards and are being filed into the Outlier Union Catalogue. Later stages of the project will, it is hoped, comprise the insertion of additional entries for books in special libraries and the conversion of the present National Union Catalogue on to cards to produce one unified catalogue.

Other sources which are used to obtain locations are the London Union Catalogue and the South Eastern Regional Catalogue, both housed at the Malet Place premises. The L.U.C. is checked for material especially likely to be found there, and the staff of the S.E.R.L.B. check the 'wants' list sent out regularly to Regional Bureaux.

A fairly high proportion (one-half to one-third) of works dealt with by this department are either not located in any union catalogue or printed catalogue of a library from which they can be borrowed, or it turns out that the works located are not actually available for loan when application is made for them. This means that search lists have to be drawn up, duplicated and sent to various groups of libraries. This involves a good deal of clerical work as, at the present time, two lists per week, each of two or three hundred titles, are sent to the Regional Bureaux and two to the universities, while a number of shorter special lists are sent to groups of outliers such as medical or agricultural libraries. This somewhat cumbersome method of locating books takes a good deal of time, especially as most libraries take a considerable time to check them, owing to lack of staff, but it is doubtful whether this procedure can ever be wholly dispensed with, even when the union catalogues approach completion, especially in cases where a rigorous search has to be made.

More clerical work is involved in the process of arranging the actual loan. On each application form are marked, in serial order, all the procedures that may have to be applied in order to obtain the required book. The locations found in the union catalogues are first used, but if the book proves to be unobtainable from these libraries, one or more special outliers may be tried according to the nature of the book, and the inquiry may have to be included on a bureau or university list. When all the sources tried have failed, the final process consists, normally, in informing the borrowing library that the book is unobtainable.

A word should be said here about foreign loans. These were originated by the Birmingham Office of the Joint Standing Committee on Library Co-operation of the A.U.T. and they became the responsibility of the N.C.L. in 1931. The system adopted by most countries is briefly as follows. An application from a local library in any country is forwarded to the recognised national centre in that country (generally the national library), which transmits it to the national centre in the foreign country considered most likely to possess a copy of the work required. The book, assuming that it exists in that foreign country, is then either lent by the national centre of that country, or is located elsewhere by that centre, by means of a union catalogue or by some other method. If it is available, it is then transmitted through the national centre to the borrowing library. The object of this procedure is to make sure firstly, that a book which is asked for on loan does not exist in the country of origin of the application and, secondly, that the book is searched for in a systematic manner in the country to which the request is sent. The machinery for lending between one country and another is slow and inclined to be expensive and hence should not be used except in cases of real need and where a book is not obtainable in the borrower's own country. Before and immediately after the last war, the demands on this service were quite small; in 1938–39 this country lent 508 books to different foreign countries and borrowed 283. By 1959–60 this had increased to 3,494 books and periodicals lent abroad through N.C.L. and 1,871 books and periodicals borrowed from other countries; in addition 398 and 478 photographic copies respectively were arranged through these channels. There are now sixty-two overseas countries with which the N.C.L. has interlending arrangements; in addition requests are accepted from all recognised Commonwealth libraries. The countries with which most interlending is arranged are Germany (West and East), France, U.S.S.R., U.S.A., Italy, Czechoslovakia, Hungary, Yugoslavia and Spain.

Mention might be made here of the two foreign language union catalogues which the N.C.L. has compiled: The Russian Union Catalogue and the German Union Catalogue (1939–49). The Russian Union Catalogue contains entries for approximately 80,000 books and 4,000 periodical titles, comprising 115,000 issues, in libraries in this country; additions are regularly made but owing to the greatly increased demand for Russian books and periodicals (applications for which are dealt with by the editor of this catalogue) less progress in cataloguing other libraries' holdings can now be made. It is to be hoped that financial resources will in future permit an expansion of this most important work. In 1959–60 2,463 applications for Russian books and periodicals were received; of these 62 per cent were supplied either from resources in this country, or by international loan. The German Union Catalogue (1939–49) is now virtually complete and contains approximately 11,400 entries for books and 3,600 for periodicals. The editor of this catalogue deals with all applications in German, Dutch and the Scandinavian languages. This language specialisation in Russian and Germanic is a major factor in the high percentage of successes achieved, and it is a principle which might well be extended.

The British National Book Centre was the successor to the wartime Inter-Allied Book Centre, the administration of which was taken over by Unesco and handed over to the N.C.L. in 1947. Its functions are to act as a clearing house for the re-allocation of unwanted books and periodicals in this country and throughout the Commonwealth. This is done by means of monthly lists of books and periodicals, based on cards submitted by donor libraries; these lists are circulated to some 500 libraries and in 1959–60 over 100,000 books and periodicals were re-distributed in this way. These functions are really a continuation of those already undertaken by the Library on a small scale in pre-war days, when the N.C.L. acted as the distributing centre through which books and periodicals, discarded by libraries or presented by individual donors, could be passed on to other libraries where they were most needed. In the year 1938–39, 7,977 books and periodicals were distributed to 117 libraries. It has now been possible to extend the work of redistribution to a selected number of foreign libraries.

We have now surveyed briefly the early history and development of the Library and its organisation and routine functioning have been outlined.

As regards the all-important financial aspects of the Library's development, one cannot do better than quote the following words written by the former librarian, Mr. R. H. Hill:[2] "The development and potentialities of the library have always outstripped the available financial provision. From the outset to 1929 it was financed almost entirely by voluntary contributions from Trusts, libraries, and private subscribers. In 1930 its growing importance as a national asset secured some recognition by an annual grant from state funds of £3,000. In the second year of the grant, however, grounds of urgent national retrenchment reduced this sum to £2,850 and in the next three years to £2,700. This was restored for 1935–6 to £3,000. For the next five

[2] *Library World*, May, 1946, p. 156.

years the grant was increased to £5,000 conditional on continued support from the Carnegie Trustees and a considerable increase of contributions from libraries. Although the latter condition was not fully implemented, the grant was continued for 1938-9. Imperative need for economy in Government expenditure reduced the annual sum to £4,800 in the first year of the war, to £3,500 in the second, and to £4,500 in the remaining years. It is true to say that the development of the library, and even its continued existence on any scale, have only been made possible by the continued generosity of the Carnegie Trust, and during the last war by the timely aid of the Rockefeller Foundation." Since these words were written, costs have risen steeply and it is gratifying that the Treasury has continued to play a major part in the maintenance of the Library; the grant of £7,500 for 1946-47 has become £52,000 for 1959-60. The Report of the Minister of Education's Committee on Public Libraries (Roberts Committee), published early in 1959, makes the recommendation that a much greater financial contribution towards the Library's costs should be provided by local authorities.

At the outbreak of the war, the stock of the Library had reached approximately 170,000 volumes. The total issues, including those made as a result of the Library's 'clearing house' activities, but excluding those of the Adult Class Department, rose to a peak, 53,091 in 1933-34, then fell during 1934-36 to 36,142, after which they rose again steadily to 46,715 in the last pre-war year, 1938-39. The cause of the fall in issues was undoubtedly the fact that many libraries which had been applying direct to the N.C.L. were now sending their requests to their Regional Bureaux and that a good proportion of these requests was being satisfied from within the regions.

During the war the Library, like so many others, suffered severe handicaps. Many members of the staff left in order to undertake war service and they had to be replaced, as far as possible, by temporary staff who, though inexperienced in this type of work, performed wonders. Owing to the foresight of the librarian, Dr. L. Newcombe, the Information Department, together with its irreplaceable union catalogues, was evacuated to Hertfordshire in the autumn of 1939 and was thus spared the fate of the Library and Adult Class Departments which suffered such heavy damage by enemy action in April 1941. The Adult Class Department lost the whole of its own stock, with the exception of some 5,000 books out on loan at the time, while the main stock of the library was reduced to 72,612 books.

The issues naturally declined during the early years of the war, the total (including Adult Classes) having decreased from 58,683 in 1938–39 to 39,420 in 1940–41. If the following year, 1941–42, saw an increase to 43,410 in the total issues, in spite of the disastrous loss of stock with which it began, the explanation lies in the greatly increased number of applications received and in the consequent expansion of the Library's 'clearing house' functions. The increase of that year was continued and by 1945–46 the total issues were 59,671, thus exceeding the figure for the last pre-war year, while in 1946–47 the total reached 66,000. The rebuilding of the stock was proceeding steadily at the same time, the total number of volumes in the Library being 105,974 at the end of February 1947. By 1960 the total had reached approximately 210,000 volumes.

At the end of 1944 the librarian, Dr. L. Newcombe, retired and was succeeded by Mr. R. H. Hill, who came to the N.C.L. from the Bodleian Library, of which he was Secretary. Dr. Newcombe's period of office which began in 1926 thus corresponded with the most critical years of the Library's development: it saw the change from the Central Library for Students to the National Central Library, the creation of the regional systems and their union catalogues, and the growth of the outlier system of libraries, both of which developments owe so much to him. Mr. Hill retired in March 1958, Mr. S. P. L. Filon being appointed librarian in his place. Mr. Hill was faced with the task of consolidating the work of Dr. Newcombe and of re-establishing the smooth working of the interlending system after the stress and strain of the war period. He was successful in persuading the Treasury to increase their recognition of the national importance of the Library's work by steeply rising increments in the annual grant-in-aid. He widened the scope of the system of specialised co-operating libraries. His reign saw internal reorganisations of the administration of the Library which facilitated the building up of its stock and the compilation of the essential union catalogues. The placing of the interlending system on a national basis and its adequate financing remained, however, an unsolved problem. It is hoped that the Roberts Report will usher in a new era.

In the spring of 1945 the Information Department returned to London but, as it could no longer be housed in the blitzed premises at Malet Place, had to be accommodated in a house in Woburn Square, some five minutes' walk from the main building. The main premises were fully restored to use in 1951. The Library must now look forward to the time when it moves to a new building in Store Street, provided as a replacement by the University of London who wish to take over the present premises.

The Library Co-operation scene is changing rapidly and will probably continue to do so; the development of Regional and Inter-Regional subject specialisation schemes, the recommendations of the Roberts Report and the foundation of the National Lending Library for Science and Technology are all bound to have a marked effect on the work of the N.C.L. So, too, are the technical developments which it is hoped the library will be able to utilise; for example, TELEX was installed for speeding-up the communications between the N.C.L. and co-operating libraries at home and abroad, and photocopying and Xerography which are already playing an increasing role in inter-lending and which would be much assisted by the Library possessing its own photographic unit. Moreover, the large numbers of books collected under subject specialisation schemes may possibly lead to some system of national or local depositories, similar perhaps to that of the Mid-West Inter-Library Center in the U.S.A. or the projected University of London depository in this country; this would also have a marked effect on inter-library loans. The next decade is one of great potentialities for which the Library must be a flexible unit ready to adapt itself to changing circumstances.

CHAPTER VII

PARLIAMENTARY LIBRARIES

THE LIBRARY OF THE HOUSE OF LORDS

By Christopher Dobson
Librarian

IT was not until the year 1826 that any active steps were taken to supply a library for the House of Lords. In that year a librarian was appointed, and Sir John Soane was instructed to fit up a room for the accommodation of a library. At first the books consisted of little more than a collection of Reports and Parliamentary Papers, most of which were transferred from the Parliament Office. In 1827, however, the librarian obtained authority to spend over £900 on the purchase of books and binding. This collection, of which a printed list is in existence, was chiefly of a legal character. In the same year the Earl of Rosslyn became the library's first benefactor by presenting a collection of printed House of Lords Appeal Cases and Writs of Error from 1702 which had belonged to his father and to his great-uncle, Lord Chancellor Loughborough.

In 1834, when the Houses of Parliament were destroyed by fire, the House of Lords Library was thus only eight years old, and was of comparatively small extent. It is recorded that, while the fire was raging, the books were passed along a file of soldiers to St. Margaret's Church, and that all were saved.

In the same year the French Chamber of Peers made an important gift of nearly 2,000 volumes in the French language, mainly of a parliamentary character, but including a number of historical works such as Anselme's *Histoire généalogique . . . de la maison royale de France* (1726–33), and a complete set of *Almanachs royaux*, mostly bound in contemporary morocco. Their arrival was delayed for two years while Sir Robert Smirke was erecting suitable temporary accommodation for the library out of the ruins left by the fire. The sudden acquisition of so many volumes in difficult circumstances may partly account for the fact that few volumes were added during the following decade. In

1848, however, the books were moved from the cramped quarters into Sir Charles Barry's four beautiful rooms overlooking the river, which now form the main library, and from that date the importance of the library was more fully recognised. Gradually the policy was adopted, which has been continued to the present day, of building up a good general library round a more specialised nucleus of legal and parliamentary books. On the general side preference has been given to such sections as English literature and history in its widest sense, but the classics and books on theology and art have not been overlooked. Fiction, in the accepted use of the term, has never taken any prominent part.

In 1856 Lady Truro, whose husband had been Lord Chancellor from 1850 to 1852, presented his law library. This collection, most of which is preserved as a separate entity in what is known as the Truro Room, consists of about 3,000 volumes. It includes not only the law reports and legal textbooks ordinarily used by a lawyer of the first half of the nineteenth century, but also considerable sections on the history of law and of parliamentary institutions. The gem of the collection is a fine copy of Statham's Abridgment which was printed for Richard Pynson by Guillaume le Talleur at Rouen about 1490; and a large number of volumes and several pamphlets are of sixteenth- and seventeenth-century dates.

Among the many other gifts which have been received, one in particular should be recorded. This is Sir William Frazer's bequest, made effective in 1899, of eleven folio volumes of Gillray's political caricatures which contain several items of special rarity.

The library possesses complete sets of the *Journals* of both Houses; sets of the Sessional Papers of both Houses from 1801; two complete sets of *Hansard* and a collection of debates published prior to 1800; the *London Gazette* from the beginning in 1665; *The Times* newspaper from 1794; and a collection of printed Private Acts from the year 1719.

An important section consists of books on the specialised subject of Peerage Law, including the proceedings in Peerage Cases, both printed and in manuscript. The printed cases date from the early part of the eighteenth century; and among the manuscript material are four bound volumes of reports prepared by the late J. H. Round, of which a detailed calendar is given in his *Family origins* (1930). The legal section of the library now includes five sets of the Law Reports from 1865, three sets of the English Reports, five sets of Sessions Cases, three sets of

All England Law Reports, a set of Lloyd's List Reports, and other reports. Complete runs of legal periodicals include the *Law Quarterly Review*, the *Harvard Law Review* and the *Toronto Law Journal*.

Among a large number of sets of publications issued by historical and other societies are those of the Pipe Roll, Canterbury and York, Navy Records, Champlain, Harleian, Surtees, Walpole, Wren, Selden and Stair societies. In some instances a subscription has followed a gift of sets of earlier volumes. The library also possesses a practically complete set of the publications issued by the Commissioners on the Public Records and by the Public Record Office. Several series of pamphlets include the collection of tracts, mainly relating to Ireland, which belonged to the third Sir Robert Peel and was purchased for the library in 1897. It consists of 287 bound volumes and the contents are for the most part of eighteenth-century date. They were catalogued in detail for one of the printed appendices to the general catalogue compiled by Sir Edmund Gosse, Librarian from 1904 to 1914.

This catalogue, which is exclusive of the legal section, was printed in 1908, and slips have been inserted giving the additions to 1913. For subsequent additions the card-index system has been used. There is a separate card-index catalogue for the legal section, both on an author and subject basis. The total number of volumes in the library is about 70,000.

From time to time there have been disposals of duplicate books and others that have been found to have little practical value for this library. Since 1945 several thousand volumes, including Colonial Papers, Australian and Canadian Sessional Papers and duplicate law books, have been given to other libraries, such as Rhodes House Library at Oxford, the Institute of Commonwealth Studies and the libraries of the Inns of Court. But selection of books for disposal has to be made with care. Even apparent duplicates cannot be discarded with impunity. It was found recently in examining copies of the second edition of Stair's *Institutions of the law of Scotland* (1693) that there were at least three separate issues of that edition, a fact which appears to be unrecorded.

Today the library performs several related functions. It is used for the legislative work of a Second Chamber, and for the varied needs of members of the House of Lords. It supplies the books, sometimes in great numbers, for the judicial work of the House as the supreme Court of Appeal in Great Britain and Northern Ireland; and especially of late years it has acted practically though not perhaps nominally, as a departmental library for the Lord Chancellor. In certain instances facilities are provided for those engaged in special lines of research who wish to consult books which are not available in the British Museum or elsewhere.

When the House of Lords is not sitting for public business, visitors are shown a selection of manuscripts displayed in the Queen's Room. Most of these form part of the large accumulation of House of Lords manuscripts which are stored in the Victoria Tower in the custody of the Clerk of the Parliaments. One case contains the original letter of Charles I to the House of Lords in 1641, pleading for Strafford after his attainder; the warrant for the execution of the King, signed by Oliver Cromwell and other members of the Court set up for his trial, which was produced at the trial of the regicides in 1660 by Colonel Hacker, the first of the three officers to whom it was directed; and the declaration from Breda signed by Charles II on the eve of the Restoration. A second case includes a commission for the prorogation of Parliament signed by Elizabeth I, with the Great Seal attached, and the original Act embodying the Petition of Right of 1628 showing the cut which removed the King's conditional approval. In a third case is one of the original manuscripts of the Articles of Union between England and Scotland signed in 1706 by the Commissioners of both countries, headed respectively by the Archbishop of Canterbury and the Lord Chancellor of Scotland. A fourth case contains the manuscript Prayer Book formerly attached to the Act of Uniformity of 1662, which is known as the 'Annexed Book' and is the authority for our present Prayer Book; together with the Prayer Book of 1636 with the alterations and additions made in the handwriting of William Sancroft, afterwards Archbishop of Canterbury, who acted as secretary to the Committee of Revision in 1661. A fifth case contains a holograph letter of James I to Cecil; a letter to the Speaker of the House of Peers written by Prince Rupert in 1646 and signed by him and Prince Maurice; and, of special interest, two of the letters written to each other by the King and the Queen which were captured by Fairfax in the King's cabinet at the battle of Naseby in 1645. In a sixth case, the display of other manuscripts is changed periodically.

It is fitting to record with feelings of thankfulness that during the war of 1939–45, although the library was in the immediate zone of damage, no harm was caused to any of its books.

(These notes are largely based on a lecture delivered at the University of London School of Librarianship in April 1948 by Sir Charles Clay,

C.B., Librarian to the House of Lords 1922–56, and subsequently printed in the last edition of this book in 1949.)

THE LIBRARY OF THE HOUSE OF COMMONS

By Strathearn Gordon
Librarian

THE germ of the House of Commons Library can be traced back to a dumpy little manuscript volume bound in leather and known as 'Seymour'. It is the diary of a Clerk of the House of that name who in 1547 kept a diary showing the Bills dealt with by the Commons. His successors developed the idea into a more detailed record of proceedings, the value of which was soon apparent to the House, and to this day one of the main duties of the Clerk is to supervise the production of an accurate *Journal*. For generations the library of the Commons remained a rudimentary and peripatetic organ, for the manuscript *Journals*, and doubtless the few books of procedural precedents then existing, travelled round in the Clerk's luggage as his private property.

In the middle of the eighteenth century the Commons started to interest themselves in their records. They ordered the *Journals* to be printed and Addressed the King for a building in which to keep them and their Papers. But it was not until Mr. Charles Abbot was elected Speaker in 1802 that the true foundations of the library were laid. Fortunately for posterity he had a mania for preserving the national archives and as Speaker he concentrated upon the masses of neglected records under his hand. The well-known 'Abbot Collection' was classified and bound, and the system of dealing with the great annual accretion of Papers was laid down and continues in force to this day.

These records were dispersed all over the Palace and across the road in Abingdon Street until the inconvenience resulted in the foundation of the first library at the request of Mr. Speaker Manners-Sutton in 1818. It was a single room 17 ft. square called 'The Ancient Committee Room' or 'Speaker's Chamber', situated over the outer Lobby of the old Chamber in St. Stephen's Chapel. Mr. Benjamin Spiller was appointed the first librarian and such were his labours that by 1832 a committee reported that he had died of overwork.

Almost from the start books overflowed into 'closets and presses' in the corridor outside. A new library was build in 1827, overlooking Cotton Garden to the river, and it was from here that Macaulay dated some of his pleasant letters, filled with political gossip. The positions of both libraries are shown in *The Topography of the Old House of Commons* by Dr. O. C. Williams. The almost total destruction caused by the Great Fire of 1834 enabled Sir Charles Barry to build the fine existing suite of rooms, which came into use shortly before 1852. It consists of four large apartments, each 60 ft. long, called rather unimaginatively A, B, C, and D Rooms, and a smaller entrance hall called from its window the Oriel Room. Adjoining the latter is the galleried Reference Room, for long known as the Map Room. D Room, which is known as the Speaker's Library, serves him as an official conference room, and to receive distinguished visitors; while C Room is the only remaining non-smoking and silence room. The suite is on the Principal Floor and overlooks the Terrace beside the Thames. The rooms are very high so that the upper shelves are 16 ft. above the ground and have to be reached with long ladders. Galleries have often been recommended and would certainly ease the use of the library, but the expense of re-channelling the ducts and wiring which pierce the old building would be very great and the aesthetic results of building galleries might divide the opinions of Members acutely.

At any rate, whatever the defects of Barry's library, it has served its purpose tolerably well. He evidently intended it as the principal amenity for Members outside the Chamber for both work and recreation. There is already an historic quality about it. Ministers have their rooms, but much of the work of the Opposition and of backbenchers is done in the library. Many famous speeches have been written at the long tables and many political jests whispered among the green armchairs. Members take their ease there, too, while silent annunciators warn them of the business proceeding in the Chamber. Sometimes, in clear sunlight, the river scene through the tall windows has the detailed brilliance of a painting by Canaletto; and often the green velvet curtains are comfortably drawn against winter fogs. But the view which many Members prefer is of the moonlight and yellow lamps glittering on the river on a fine night.

The library has always been the special care of the Speaker. From its earliest days the House decided that he should be assisted in his responsibilities by a committee, but that he should always appoint all the staff. During the formative years the Library Committee included outstanding Members such as Gladstone, Disraeli and Lord John Russell, but by 1861 interest seems to have waned and it was not re-appointed. Since 1922 the Speaker has appointed (usually sessionally) an unofficial, all-party, advisory committee of Members to keep him in touch with the wishes of their colleagues and to advise him on all matters concerning the library. With a body of over 600 busy people such as form the House of Commons, possessing widely different backgrounds, needs and working habits, opinions as to the most suitable library are bound to vary. Hence, since its foundation in 1818, it has been thought best by the House of Commons to confide the control of the library to the impartial authority of the Speaker, who, with the advice of his committee, acting also in a non-party spirit, endeavours to please all Members by adopting a middle course.

The policy of the library regarding its holdings has changed since 1818. The core has always been, and must remain, official publications. These include one of the finest collections of nineteenth-century government records which exist in any country. To these must now be added the endless stream of documents produced by international bodies. The original aim was to provide a good 'Library of historical and constitutional information'. The fire of 1834 was a turning point. Almost the whole of a priceless collection of parliamentary manuscripts and archives was lost, with about half the holdings of books, many of which were thrown out of the windows or damaged by water. But the new premises provided space for the leisurely acquisition of a fine 'country gentleman's library' rich in travel, topography and French works, which stood in fixed locations on the somewhat gloomy shelves, graduated from the elephant folios below up through the quartos and octavos to the little duodecimos near the ceiling. Fiction, except for the classics, and scientific works were excluded. But most Members possessed their own books. They were accustomed to their library and lodged few complaints.

The inevitable renovation started in 1945 and is still in progress. Faced with the needs of the post-war House of Commons, a Select Committee under the chairmanship of Sir George Benson, who remains the Chairman of the Speaker's Advisory Committee, made sweeping recommendations for an expansion of the staff to provide extended services for Members. Much has been accomplished. Every book has been cleaned and appraised for disposal or retention. All books and pamphlets are being re-catalogued. Comprehensive card author and subject catalogues and a strip index of holdings have replaced the old author catalogue contained in a single volume. Expert advice has been enlisted to make good the manifest deficiencies, and holdings have been graded according to demand. The problem of space will be partially solved by 1962, when the great Victoria Tower at West-minster will be made available for the purpose for which it was originally intended – the storage of documents of both Houses of Parliament. The total holdings are at present estimated at 100,000 volumes. Since not everything can be kept, apart from official publications, which should be available to Members, emphasis is directed upon their specialised work and interests – law, constitutional and general history, and works bearing upon every aspect of Parliament, in particular biography and memoirs. Gaps have to be filled from as good a collection of reference works as can be got together. For the declared object of the Select Committee of 1945–46 is being strenuously pursued: "a Reference Library to provide Members with the maximum assistance in their multifarious duties".

Modern equipment has been installed in the library, new armchairs designed and the lighting and heating improved. An up-to-date Reference Room has been formed to provide Members with a wide range of newspapers and periodicals and to give quick answers to queries on any subject. Research and statistical sections answer the specific questions of Members of a more complicated nature and provide bibliographies and statistical memoranda in time for debates in the Chamber. These services are only limited by the stipulations that the queries must be directly concerned with the parliamentary duties of Members and that the latter must always expect factual replies of a non-partisan nature.

To perform this work candidates for the senior staff grade are now required to possess a good honours degree of a British university and if possible some exceptional knowledge of languages. These are the qualifications demanded of Assistant Keepers at the British Museum, to whom Library Clerks are equated as regards status and conditions.

Much of the groundwork of this reconstruction has been simple. What is more difficult is the attempt to perfect the existing services. Members of Parliament work, or wish to work, at great speed. Their requirements are extraordinarily diverse. Often, through no fault of their own, their references may be somewhat vague. No doubt, given time, their queries could be unravelled reasonably easily in any large library. But speed is the essence of House of Commons service. The solution which is being attempted is by a wide system of specialised indexes, mostly of the visible strip type, which are kept constantly up to date. These include a comprehensive Index of Parliamentary and other Papers, Debates and Motions; Indexes of Questions; of past

Business; of future Business; of Chairmen of Committees and Commissions; of Colloquial names of Reports; of International Affairs; of Home Affairs; and many others.

The House of Commons Library is not very large. Nor is it stuffed with treasures, though it possesses some. The unique interest of working therein lies in the opportunity it affords of devising means to help an interesting community who are engaged in duties of very great responsibility.

The library is only open to visitors by means of Members' conducted tours on days when the House is not sitting. Students who wish to consult documents which are not available elsewhere (of which there are very few) may sometimes secure the Speaker's special permission to work in the library on non-sitting days.

CHAPTER VIII

GOVERNMENT DEPARTMENTAL LIBRARIES

By D. W. King, O.B.E.
Librarian, The War Office

and R. G. C. Desmond
Deputy Librarian, Ministry of Agriculture and Fisheries

THERE are some forty libraries attached to government departments in London, and it will obviously not be possible to give a detailed account of every one in this brief survey. Nor for that matter will it be necessary, for while some possess imposing collections running to many thousands of volumes, others contain little else than sets of departmental manuals and similar publications. But whatever the character of the libraries under review, no effective survey can be made without giving some general indication of the functions they perform and the type of material they contain. It must be appreciated that they are 'special organisation' rather than 'special subject' libraries. As Linda Morley explains: "The special organisation library in corporations, government agencies [departments], etc. . . . has peculiar administrative problems flowing out of this affiliation. The ultimate objectives of such libraries are those of the parent organisation by which they were established and financed. . . . The subject librarian has a predetermined subject for which he seeks individual clients . . . the organisation librarian . . . has a predetermined clientele for whom he seeks subjects and specific information."[1] In brief, the object of a departmental library is to serve the staff of the department of which it forms part. Given this objective it necessarily follows that the library's acquisitions are based on the requirements of this staff. The fact that this staff includes in many departments officers actively engaged in historical and other forms of research does, however, make their collections of special value to the student. In the three service departments the historical sections are linked with the departmental libraries. In the Foreign

[1] *J. of Doc.* 3 (1) 1947, 24-25.

99

Office the departmental library proper forms part of the Research Department. In the case of the Colonial Office and Customs and Excise the library is intimately associated with the administration of the departmental record sections.

The first task of a departmental library is to provide a well-balanced collection of literature on all subjects relating to the department's immediate field. This will, of course, include all the publications issued by the department itself. In the case of certain offices these number thousands. It will include, too, the publications of administrative departments performing similar functions in the dominions, colonies, and frequently foreign countries, together with a good selection of non-official literature. But no departmental library functions efficiently if it confines its acquisitions solely to the department's immediate field. There is a general basic stock every library must possess – sets of Public General Acts, Statutory Instruments, Parliamentary Debates and Sessional Papers, etc. In addition, the needs of each of the department's special branches must be met. The War Office Library, for instance, provides Clergy Lists for the army chaplains branch, the Ministry of Works Library books on heraldry for the branch concerned with the decoration of streets and public buildings on ceremonial occasions. Lastly, the departmental library has educational work to perform. The Assheton Committee on the Training of Civil Servants, which reported in 1944, drew attention to the part the library could play in staff training by the provision of suitable reading material. Most departmental libraries now have stocks of introductory books on the machinery of government, public finance, and other aspects of national administration, for the use of new entrants to the service.

Nearly all the libraries under review issue bulletins and circulars to publicise their contents. These appear at fortnightly, monthly or quarterly intervals and are an essential means of keeping the staff of a department, often stationed in the provinces many miles from their library, informed of the latest additions to the stock. Since these lists cover a limited subject field, they become quite useful specialised bibliographies of current literature, and often include departmental publications not sold by H.M. Stationery Office and consequently not listed in the *Daily List*. For example, the monthly *Accessions to the War Office Library* records numerous regimentally produced historical pamphlets which are difficult to trace through any other bibliographical source; likewise the *Monthly List of official Colonial Publications*, prepared by the Colonial Office Library, is the only comprehensive checklist of current literature published in the colonies. The Ministry of Works Library produces a six-monthly consolidation of its fortnightly accessions lists and provides an annual index to periodical articles. In the past certain of the older libraries such as the Foreign Office and the War Office issued printed catalogues and a few are still being published: further volumes are being added to some forty catalogues of manuscripts and Oriental books in the India Office Library; and another supplement is being prepared to the catalogue of the Library of the Royal Botanic Gardens, Kew, originally published in 1899 with a supplement in 1919.

Though departmental libraries exist primarily to serve the staff of the offices of which they form part, most are prepared on occasion to make their resources available for reference by outside inquirers. A few, such as the Ministry of Education and the Ministry of Agriculture, Fisheries and Food, admit members of the public as a normal practice, but the majority prefer to deal only with bona fide inquirers seeking specific information within the department's field and not readily obtainable elsewhere. Even among the libraries which do not normally admit outside inquirers few, if any, would refuse applications from suitably sponsored research workers. Borrowing facilities are available to other government departments and frequently to other libraries. Several government libraries are prepared to loan books through the National Central Library, and quite a number now participate in the Science Library supplementary loan scheme.

In dealing with the individual libraries, pride of place must be given to those of the older departments (the Treasury, the Home Office, the Foreign Office, the Colonial Office, the Board of Trade, the War Office, the Admiralty, Customs and Excise, etc.). These libraries date back at least to the early part of the nineteenth century, and in the course of years valuable collections numbering many thousands of volumes have been built up.

The Combined Library of the **Treasury and Cabinet Offices** at Great George Street contains some 60,000 books and pamphlets. A large proportion of the stock is made up of official publications – this is one of the few libraries which possess a complete set of Sessional Papers. The non-official literature deals mainly with finance, economics and the various aspects of public administration. Worthy of special note is the Lister collection of prints, etc. illustrating the history of Whitehall. Sub-libraries exist in the Cabinet Central Statistical Office and the Treasury Organisation and Methods Division with material strictly relating to the sections they serve. A printed catalogue in two volumes (one author, the other subject) was published in 1910. There is an independent library containing literature on staff training and related subjects attached to the Treasury Training and Education Division. The office of the **Treasury Solicitor** has a law library at its headquarters at Storey's Gate.

The library of the **Home Office** in Whitehall consists of some 45,000 volumes and pamphlets. Among the subjects covered are law and legal administration, criminology and law enforcement, child welfare, etc. The stock includes complete sets of Public General and Local Acts, Sessional Papers and reports, etc., as well as a number of sixteenth- and seventeenth-century books – the latter an indication of the distant origin of the department. Non-official visitors are only admitted to the library when sponsored by a senior officer of the department.

The Library of the **Foreign Office** is linked with the Research Department under one director. The Library of Printed Books, so called to distinguish it from the manuscript and other collections, is housed in Cornwall House, Stamford Street, with about 100,000 books and some 6,000 pamphlets on all aspects of international law and relations, and a comprehensive map collection. A dictionary catalogue was published in 1926.

The libraries of the **Colonial and Commonwealth Relations Offices** are jointly administered, and their combined stock of over 114,000 books and pamphlets constitutes one of the best collections of literature on the colonies and dominions in existence. The legal section with complete sets of Colonial Acts and ordinances is used extensively by other departments. Although the Colonial Office Library was founded in 1854, much of the stock is considerably earlier and boasts many rare items. A printed catalogue was issued in 1896, and a supplement in 1907. The Commonwealth Relations Office Library is in Downing Street not far from the India Office Library in King Charles Street, which since 1947 has formed part of the Commonwealth Relations Office.

The **India Office** Library was founded in 1802 by the East India Company whose archives are preserved here, and the holdings amount to some 223,000 books and 25,000 pamphlets, including a large number of works in Sanskrit, Arabic, Persian and modern Indian languages. Until 1948 the library was legally entitled to requisition on publication a copy of every printed work published in British India, including

Burma. Every aspect of Indian life – cultural, historical, religious, sociological and administrative – is covered by the library. One important special collection is the Johnson collection of Indian and Persian miniature paintings. With this wealth of material, particularly priceless manuscripts, this library constitutes a unique collection serving the needs of Indologists throughout the world.

In 1949 the Library of the Imperial Institute was taken over by the Colonial Office when that department assumed responsibility for the scientific and technical activities of the Institute. The scientific work was performed by two sections: the Colonial Products Laboratory and the Minerals Resources Division of the Colonial Geological Surveys. In 1957 the greater part of the library stock – about 90,000 volumes – was transferred to Gray's Inn Road with the Colonial Products Laboratory which was renamed the **Tropical Products Institute.** Two years later it became a research establishment of the Department of Scientific and Industrial Research. After the material relating to overseas agriculture and forestry had been allocated to the Tropical Products Institute, some 50,000 geological items remained to form the Library of the **Mineral Resources Division of the Overseas Geological Surveys.**

The **Board of Trade** Library in Horse Guards Avenue possesses some 150,000 volumes. As is the case with most of the older departmental libraries, the stock includes complete sets of Sessional Papers and similar material. The general literature covers all aspects of economics, trade and industry, and there is an extensive collection of trade exhibition catalogues. A statistics library providing an international coverage on trade and production is open for reference in Lacon House, Theobalds Road.

The Library of the **War Office** in Whitehall, with its origins in the seventeenth century, contains about 340,000 books and pamphlets. Besides an exhaustive collection of British and foreign works on military subjects, it has a wide selection of books on history, topography and technology. The military collection includes a large number of sixteenth- and seventeenth-century books, and an almost complete set of United Kingdom, Indian and other Commonwealth regimental histories. A printed catalogue in four volumes was published during the years 1906 to 1916 and annual supplements were issued up to 1940. A branch library at Chessington covers technical subjects.

The **Admiralty** Library, at Admiralty Arch, has a large collection of 140,000 items mainly concerned with the historical and adminis-

trative aspects of naval affairs. A printed catalogue was published in
1911. Scientific and technical literature is dealt with in the Admiralty
by the Centre for Scientific Information and Liaison at Queen Anne's
Mansions, St. James's Park.

The **Customs and Excise** Library at King's Beam House, Mark
Lane, contains two distinct types of material – modern technical
works on articles and trades subject to indirect taxation and valuable
record material of interest to the student of social history and the local
antiquarian. It contains about 26,000 books.

Though the **General Post Office** is one of the oldest departments, its library, housed at Headquarters Buildings, St. Martin's-le-
Grand, is of comparatively recent date. The bookstock, which amounts
to some 3,500 items, includes material on all subjects of concern to the
staff of the department; the library's holdings also include the department's records. There is also a technical library on all subjects relating
to telecommunication engineering at the Post Office Research Station,
Dollis Hill, which is not open to the public.

We next come to the libraries of the departments formed during the
course of the nineteenth century (Education, Agriculture, Health,
Scottish Office, Inland Revenue and General Register Office).

The Library of the **Ministry of Education,** Curzon Street, dates
from the special collection of books assembled for the Educational
Exhibition of 1854, since when the stock has grown to more than
150,000 books and pamphlets – the most comprehensive collection of
literature in its special field in the country. Of particular importance to
students are the many reports of commissions, statistical returns,
diverse material on institutions and societies, and a unique collection of
the official papers of other countries. Early children's books and old
works on teaching methodology are some of the bibliographical
treasures of this library.

The Main Library of the **Ministry of Agriculture, Fisheries and
Food,** Whitehall Place, includes in its collection of 120,000 volumes the
major works in agriculture published since the early nineteenth century.
A considerable number of foreign agricultural serial publications are
obtained through international exchange arrangements. The Cowan
and Cotton collections on bee-keeping, particularly strong in eighteenth
and nineteenth-century works, are rich in a number of rare items. Some
of them are recorded in a chronological list of early books in the library
published in 1930. A useful bibliographical tool, now in its fourth
edition (1958), is a classified list of standard and recent works on

agriculture, horticulture and food which are in the library. The Library of the Ministry of Food was absorbed when that department was merged with the Ministry of Agriculture and Fisheries in 1955. Located in Great Westminster House, Horseferry Road, it houses about 10,000 volumes on food technology and nutrition. The Royal Botanic Gardens, Kew, also form part of this department, and a brief description of its library will be found in Chapter II.

The Library of the **Ministry of Health,** in Savile Row, traces its beginnings back to the early days of the Poor Law Commission, but it did not grow appreciably until the establishment of the Local Government Board in 1871. Its stock of about 80,000 items includes a valuable collection of pamphlets on the poor laws and the care of the poor published between approximately 1670 and 1850, and the only complete set in the country of the annual reports of medical officers of health of local authorities in England and Wales. The principal interests of the library are public health and medical services, and although it has a good historical collection on infectious diseases, in particular cholera and smallpox, it does not attempt to acquire a wide range of purely medical literature. It is of interest to note that it is one of the few libraries in this country where the Bliss classification scheme is used. *Hospital abstracts* is now one of the library's functions.

The libraries of the Scottish Home, Agriculture, Health and Education Departments are in Edinburgh but a small collection of books is maintained at the Scottish Office in Whitehall.

The Library of the **Board of Inland Revenue,** at Somerset House, comprises about 20,000 items dealing with public finance and taxation. Also at Somerset House is the Library of the **General Register Office,** with a stock amounting to some 17,000 volumes. Its collection of British and foreign census returns and reports on vital statistics is probably unique.

The remaining libraries in this brief survey belong to departments which have come into existence during this century.

The **Air Ministry** Library has approximately 59,000 books and pamphlets, housed partly in Whitehall Gardens and partly at Adastral House. The stock is representative of all types of material of concern to the Royal Air Force. The **Meteorological Office,** which is attached to the Air Ministry, has its own library, a collection of some 80,000 items on meteorology and geophysics, housed at Bracknell, Berks.

The **Ministry of Labour and National Service** Library in

Almack House, King Street, contains some 35,000 volumes covering the whole field of labour conditions and industrial relationships.

The Library of the **Ministry of Pensions and National Insurance,** John Adam Street, since its foundation in 1916, has acquired publications concerning pensions, grants and allowances awarded as the result of service in the Armed Forces. In 1953 the Ministry of National Insurance, established nine years earlier, was merged with the Ministry of Pensions and its library of books on social welfare was combined with the Pensions Library. The present library numbers about 25,000 volumes but part of the stock is located at the two central offices at Blackpool and Newcastle upon Tyne.

The Library of the **Ministry of Transport,** Southwark Bridge Road, established in 1920, has fluctuated in size as the result of a number of departmental amalgamations: the mergings of the Ministry of Shipping in 1941 and the Ministry of Civil Aviation in 1953, the loss of its civil aviation functions to the present Ministry of Aviation in 1959, and the consolidation of its shipping functions consequent on the transfer of the Admiralty's duties in relation to merchant shipping to it. With the exception of aviation, its stock ranges over all transport: railways, roads, motor transport, shipping, docks, harbours and canals. An important feature of this library is the collection of Local Acts and Orders relating to transport undertakings; also meriting special note is a set of local Turnpike Acts, 1801 to 1867.

The **National Assistance Board** Library, Old Burlington Street, has a small but representative collection of material on social welfare and related topics.

The **Department of Scientific and Industrial Research** (which is not an administrative department and therefore, strictly speaking, falls outside the province of this chapter), maintains a small central library at Charles House, Regent Street, together with a central catalogue of the holdings of most of the D.S.I.R. research station libraries. The Tropical Products Institute, the Government Chemist's Department, and the Geological Survey, each with its own library.

The Reference Library of the **Central Office of Information** in Hercules Road, Westminster Bridge Road, was founded at the outbreak of the last war as a part of the Ministry of Information. When the Central Office of Information replaced the Ministry in 1946, the library began to specialise mainly in literature reflecting British life and customs, and now has a stock of approx. 30,000 volumes. The Central Office of Information also has a small Social Survey Library on the methodology of social research and sample surveys, and a Photographs Library at its Hercules Road address. The stock of 500,000 photographs on the topography, economic and social life of the country, the Commonwealth and the colonies can be examined by the public and photocopies can be purchased.

The **Ministry of Aviation** represents a revival of the old Ministry of Aircraft Production which the Ministry of Supply absorbed in 1946. In 1959 the Ministry of Supply was re-organised as the Ministry of Aviation and took over the civil aviation functions of the Ministry of Transport. The Central Library is housed in St. Giles Court, St. Giles High Street, and its stock of 47,000 books and pamphlets relates to various branches of technology and civil aviation. There are also technical libraries at many of the Ministry's research establishments outside London.

The **Ministry of Housing and Local Government** in Whitehall came into being in 1951 as the successor to the Ministry of Town and Country Planning, and at the same time assumed those functions of the Ministry of Health relating to housing, local government, drainage and water supply. This involved the transfer of about a quarter of the Ministry of Health's Library to the new department whose library now has a stock of about 70,000 items.

The Ministry of Fuel and Power, now the **Ministry of Power** at Thames House South, Millbank, was established in 1942 and the nucleus of the present stock of its library came from the Department of Mines' collection at the Board of Trade. It has a comprehensive collection of 80,000 books and pamphlets on mines and quarries, minerals, coal, gas, electricity, petroleum and hydraulic power undertakings. The Library of the Safety in Mines Research Establishment is at Sheffield.

The Library of the **Ministry of Works** at Lambeth Bridge House, Albert Embankment, contains about 50,000 books and pamphlets. The greater part of the stock is naturally devoted to building technology and includes a large collection of photographs of ancient monuments and historic buildings; there is also a special collection on Londiniana.

There remains a number of other government libraries in London such as that belonging to the Agricultural Research Council and that of the Nature Conservancy which is described in Chapter II. They are not departmental libraries but, like the national museums and galleries, possess substantial libraries on their particular interests, and sometimes special collections of exceptional value, and should therefore be briefly mentioned. The London Museum Library, for instance, has important collections on the Suffragette Movement and the Fire and Great Plague of London, and the National Maritime Museum houses the Phillip Gosse collection of books on piracy. The National Gallery, the National Portrait Gallery and the Tate Gallery maintain comprehensive collections on the history of painting which are occasionally made available for consultation by serious inquirers. The Imperial War Museum, on the other hand, has a reading room where facilities are freely available to members of the public to consult the stock of some 80,000 items on the two world wars.

DEPARTMENTAL LIBRARIES

DOWNIE, P. M. The library of the Ministry of Education. Education, Libraries Bulletin, No. 8 1960, 6-10.

FOUNTAIN, A. E. The library services of the British Ministry of Health. *Libri*, 3 1954, 32-38.

FOUNTAIN, A. E., and KING, D. W. Government libraries in Britain, in SEWELL, P. H. ed., Five years' work in librarianship, 1951-1955. The Library Association, 1958, 87-93.

HIRST, F. C. The Ministry of Agriculture, in Library resources in the Greater London Area. No. 5: agricultural libraries. The Library Association, Reference and Special Libraries Section (South Eastern Group), 1956, 11-15.

KING, D. W. The War Office library. *Lib. World*, 61 (720) 1960, 254-255.

MALLABER, K. A. Books in the Board of Trade. *O & M Bulletin*, 7 (4) 1952, 40-47.

PARROTT, C. The Foreign Office library. *Lib. World*, 61 (720) 1960, 251-253.

STAVELEY, R., ed. Government information and the research worker. The Library Association, 1952.

SUTTON, S. C. A guide to the India Office Library. H.M.S.O., 1952.

TREASURY. Guide to government libraries. 2nd edition. H.M.S.O., 1958.

WALFORD, A. J. Assistance in government libraries, in HEPWORTH, P. Primer of assistance to readers. 2nd edition. Association of Assistant Librarians, 1956, 40-43.

WALFORD, A. J. Government libraries. *Lib. Assn. Rec.* 52 (11) 1950, 410-415.

CHAPTER IX

THE LONDON BOROUGH LIBRARIES

By James D. Stewart

Formerly Borough Librarian of Bermondsey

To get a clear idea of the municipal public libraries of Metropolitan London, it is advisable to take a brief glance at their origin and history.

In the middle of the last century when the first Public Libraries Act was in operation, Metropolitan London was divided up into sixty-seven parishes, each one of which could become a separate Library Authority. The honour of being the first London area to adopt the Act is held by the Parish of St. Margaret and St. John, Westminster, which took this then momentous step in 1856. Just over a quarter of a century – twenty-seven years to be exact – elapsed before Wandsworth followed this example, with Fulham three years later in 1886.

This long interval was not actually barren, because a great deal of unobtrusive work was done in the education of opinion regarding the need for the public provision of books. That this spade work had its effect is shown by the fact that in 1887, when the first edition of Greenwood's *Public libraries* appeared, eight areas had adopted the Act. These areas were Battersea, Bermondsey, Chelsea, Finsbury, Hammersmith, Kensington, Lambeth and the remainder of Westminster.

In 1890 an Amending Act came into force and gave further stimulus, resulting in nine areas adopting the Acts between 1890 and 1895. At the end of the century, twenty-two of the Metropolitan areas had library services.

In 1900 a London Government Act had the important and far-reaching effect of amalgamating the sixty-seven parishes into the present system of twenty-nine areas comprising the Cities of London and Westminster, and the Metropolitan Boroughs. This not only brought together the appropriate adjoining local parishes into more convenient units, but also had the effect of promoting the adoption, between 1901 and 1920, of the Public Libraries Acts for the remaining London Boroughs. Their adoption by Paddington and St. Marylebone in 1920 completed the process for the whole of the Metropolitan area.

The administrative framework for the Metropolitan municipal public library service is now as follows. There are twenty-nine independent library authorities, each providing a more or less complete service within their areas. Each of these systems consists of a central library surrounded by satellite branch libraries. The only variation from this is in the case of the City of London which, so far, has confined its provision to the large reference library at Guildhall and has left the setting up of local lending libraries to the semi-private City Institutes, such as those at Bishopsgate and St. Bride's.

A great deal of argument, during which a great deal of uninformed nonsense has been talked, has gone on for many years regarding whether or not this is the right administrative framework for the library service of the Metropolis. At first sight this assemblage of twenty-nine independent library authorities would appear to be a cumbersome method of providing a service that should be more or less uniform over the entire area, and this gives a deceptive plausibility to the suggestion that there should be one central authority for library purposes. This question of centralised versus local administration has been so much to the fore in recent years that it may be as well to devote a few minutes to its practical effects so far as library services are concerned.

It must be remembered that London presents a library problem quite distinct from that of any other part of the United Kingdom. This distinction arises largely from the fact that London, as the capital, contains in addition to its municipal libraries, the immense national library resources of the British Museum, the Science Library, the Library of the Patent Office, etc., and the vast semi-private, but usually available, resources of numerous specialised organisations having their headquarters in London. So far as reference library provision is concerned, therefore, it is probable that nowhere else in the world is the advanced student and research worker so well provided for as he is in the London area. In most other large cities, for example, in Birmingham, Manchester and New York, the municipal public library has to take the place, so far as it can, of the great national reference libraries; but in London the situation is obviously quite different. This, while it eases the situation, does not absolve the London Boroughs from providing good reference libraries, and later on I will outline briefly their present state and the plans for the future.

The circumstance that there are few comparable library areas anywhere else in the world makes a contrasting examination of the results of centralised and local control very difficult; but in those areas where a single authority controls a very large system, the following divergencies from the London situation exist. There is usually a large 'central' library which is much more complete and extensive than any municipal library existing in London today. Within its limits, which are chiefly those imposed by accessibility and transport, this kind of central library provides, for the centre of its area, a service far beyond that provided by any municipal library in London. The remainder of the area is covered by branch libraries of varying sizes. These branch libraries cannot, as a general rule, bear comparison with the local central libraries of the London Boroughs, and do not provide anything so good as the service given in the boroughs all around and outside the central area.

The position, therefore, is that while London lacks the superlative *central* municipal library service given in the few comparable areas, the level of the service given over the whole area, and especially in those parts at a distance from the centre, is very much higher in London than it is anywhere else. In other words, the library 'coverage' given throughout all parts of the Metropolitan area is undoubtedly better as it stands than anything that would have resulted from a centralised control.

As a former London Borough librarian I may possibly be accused of prejudice, but I have been sufficiently long in the service to take a detached view of this problem. I have seen large library systems in operation in this and in other countries, and I am convinced that the ordinary resident in Metropolitan London, including the man living on the outskirts as well as the man living at the centre, has at his immediate disposal a far better library service, for ordinary purposes, than exists anywhere else. Further, my experience in other capacities of large centralised organisations has convinced me that local control results in greater attention being given to special local needs, and provides much greater opportunities for personal initiative and experiment.

And lastly, it must be realised that the average Metropolitan Borough has resources which enable it to provide a library service at least comparable with that of most of the large provincial towns. It may surprise most people to know that for years two adjoining London Boroughs between them have provided more money for the purchase of books than is provided by the largest provincial city in the country.

I make no apology for introducing these theoretical considerations into what is intended mainly as a statement of facts, because they have a considerable bearing on the more recent developments of London's public library service with which I am mainly concerned. And I may even hope to persuade you that local control combined with a larger-area co-operation is an excellent method of making the best of both worlds.

A brief summary of the present condition and work of the London Borough libraries is advisable at this point. The present estimated population of Metropolitan London is about 3,260,000. To serve this there are 156 public library buildings containing a stock of about 5,550,000 volumes. The administrative and clerical staff (excluding manual workers) numbers 1,395. The total number of books issued from the lending libraries during last year was over 33,300,000 (excluding school libraries); and in addition large numbers were used for reference purposes. The total expenditure was over £2,300,000. If you care to compare these figures with those of any other library area in the world, you will realise that London's library organisation, though it may not be ideal, more than stands up to any comparative analysis.

My real purpose, however, is not to hold London up either as a good or a bad example of administrative control, but to describe some of the influences and processes that have been at work in recent years to turn this assemblage of independent libraries into one closely knit system by means of mutual understanding and co-operative effort. First, however, let me admit that Metropolitan London is most favourably placed for the kind of inter-library co-operation I am going to describe. Its units (i.e. the London Boroughs) are all within reasonable distance of one another and are more or less comparable in size and resources. This means that each borough can be expected to take an equal share in any enterprise. This is an important factor, because the situation in most areas of the country is that one or more very large libraries are surrounded by numbers of very small libraries, which naturally makes inter-library co-operation and the financing of special schemes difficult to adjust, and throws most of the burden on a few of the participating libraries.

Another special feature in which Metropolitan London differs, I believe, from every other part of the country, is that it has an active Metropolitan Boroughs' Standing Joint Committee, which exists for the purpose of advising the Metropolitan Boroughs on any matters that concern London as a whole. This Metropolitan Boroughs' Standing Joint Committee, consisting of representatives from each authority, has within its organisation an Advisory Body of Librarians, to which it refers for consideration any matters affecting the Metropolitan public libraries. There is also in London an Association of Metropolitan Chief Librarians, which meets monthly for the practical discussion of library affairs; and any matter for which such a course seems appropriate can be referred by this Association to the Metropolitan Boroughs' Standing Joint Committee. The unusual advantages of such an arrangement are clear; any development of library practice which secures the approval of the Metropolitan Chief Librarians can be taken direct to the Standing Joint Committee representing all the library authorities in the area; and, if it appears to be desirable, is then recommended to the individual library authorities. I should say that the Standing Joint Committee has no power to enforce any course of action upon any of its constituent authorities, but if a majority of the latter approve any particular scheme, it is usually only a matter of time before all fall into line.

The circumstance that has brought about this change in the relations between the library authorities of London was the formation in 1929 of the London Union Catalogue. This is, in effect, the Regional Library Bureau for the Metropolitan area, and it was financed during its first few years by the Carnegie United Kingdom Trust. In 1934, when it became necessary to transfer the financial responsibility for the London Union Catalogue from the Carnegie United Kingdom Trust to the constituent libraries, the obvious body to take control was the Metropolitan Boroughs' Standing Joint Committee; and that body has controlled the organisation, through its Advisory Body of Librarians (first elected for this special purpose) since that date. The London regional system is the only one in the country which is controlled by such a semi-statutory body.

Incidentally, the creation of the London Union Catalogue organisation, with its extensive inter-library lending scheme, was also the first real step forward towards the linking up of the independent library systems in the area. As is now the case in all regional systems, it then first became possible for a reader at any one of the 156 library buildings in the Metropolitan area to have at his command the total non-fiction stock of all the Metropolitan libraries. How important a step forward this was is not always fully realised today; but it is only necessary to think back to the 1920s when the reader was, in most cases, limited to the few thousand books that happened to be in the library building he visited, and to compare this with his present more fortunate state in having over 5,500,000 books available immediately and about

20,000,000 further books available through the National Central Library, to realise that it was indeed a very long step.

This went some distance towards removing the old and well-founded complaint that public library service in London was very largely decided by place of residence, and that the man on one side of the street might have at his disposal a much better service than the man who happened to live on the other side of the street.

During the early days of the war, the opportunity was taken to bring about another reform through the medium of the Metropolitan Boroughs' Standing Joint Committee with the agreement of the boroughs. This was a scheme for the inter-availability of readers' tickets, whereby a reader registered at any of the Metropolitan Boroughs can use his ticket anywhere in the Metropolitan area, with the sole remaining exception of Chelsea. This scheme, originally intended to overcome the difficulties experienced by readers during the London blitz, when large movements of population took place and large numbers of workers were diverted to unaccustomed districts, has proved so useful and well-appreciated that it has now become an ordinary feature of London's library work. How much it is appreciated is shown by the great numbers of books (over a million) borrowed by readers using their tickets outside their home areas. Is it too much to hope that one day this principle will be extended to cover the whole country?

A development such as this brings many minor problems in its train, and one of these was the appearance in the library issue-trays of readers' tickets of various shapes and sizes. This prompted the Association of Metropolitan Chief Librarians to consider the standardisation of such forms as readers' tickets, bookcards, etc.; and, at a later date, various other forms in common use in libraries, particularly those used for inter-library communications of one kind or another. The emergence of such devices as photo-charging has both simplified and complicated progress along these lines.

It is worth noting, at this point, that so far as details of library administration are concerned, decisions taken by the Association of Metropolitan Chief Librarians become effective without reference to any other body.

Experience gained from the use of the London Union Catalogue and its inter-library loans has more recently concentrated attention on library bookstocks, and two main developments that have taken place are of considerable interest. For a long time the London Union Catalogue office has been useful, not only in providing more copies of certain books, but also in preventing the complete disappearance from the London area of many of the older books. While this kind of advice, based on current usage, was and is valuable, it was felt to be insufficient as regards library stocks in general, and the first organised attempt to solve this problem on a larger scale was the creation of a Metropolitan Joint Fiction Reserve. It had been found, especially since the war years, when so many books were destroyed, that many works of fiction (including books for children) had become difficult to obtain, if they were not in danger of total disappearance. The Joint Fiction Reserve was established for the purpose of ensuring that somewhere in the London area copies of all works of fiction likely to be required by the student of literature, or by the reader having some definite purpose, would be available. The method adopted has been to allocate a small part of the alphabet to each of the London Boroughs, and to make them responsible for the books written by authors whose names come within these alphabetical limits. Thus Battersea is responsible for all fictional authors from A to BAI, Hammersmith for all between FR and GN, and so forth. Each library is expected to make a deliberate effort to collect books within these limits, and is assisted in this by all the other libraries contributing appropriate books as they are withdrawn from current circulation.

This scheme came into operation on 1st May, 1946, and considerable stocks of standard and older works of fiction have been built up; and it is satisfactory to note that an active use has been made of them. Those who are familiar with union catalogues will know that works of fiction are not usually represented in such compilations. This is the case in London, so that the method of working the scheme has been simplified by supplying each library with an alphabetical and borough key to the collections (*see Appendix B*), and all requests are made direct to the holding libraries, either by post or telephone.

The second plan, instituted in 1948, for improving the stocks of books available in the London area, is much wider and more far-reaching, and consists of a scheme whereby each library in the area specialises in certain subjects. Wherever there are a number of independent libraries in an area, it is obvious that each of these must be a 'general' library attempting to represent all subjects and all kinds of books. The result of this is that each library naturally limits its purchases to the best and most commonly needed books in each field of literature and makes no attempt, apart from certain local interests, to represent particular subjects with completeness and adequacy. From this it follows that while each borough in London might have a reasonable selection of books on a special subject, duplicating neighbouring selections to a considerable extent, London as a whole would be without any really specialised collection such as would be needed by the advanced student and research worker.

In order to overcome this defect the whole field of knowledge was divided into appropriate sections and allocated by agreement to the boroughs (*see Appendix A*). Each authority agreed to make additional financial provision for this scheme, and valuable special collections on all subjects are being built up over the area.

It is important to realise that the creation of these specialised collections is *in addition* to the book provision which has existed heretofore; and also that the scheme is a long-term one, enabling each library to build up these specialised collections as circumstances, including accommodation, will allow. It is expected that in this way each borough library will come to possess a departmental library in its own special subject, with all the resources of a similar department in a well-equipped university library; and it is obvious that even in the meantime this additional provision will bring about a gradual but most valuable expansion of the resources available. These specialised collections include both reference and lending and essential periodical material, and are available, partly through the inter-library lending scheme, to all readers in the London area.

Another more recent co-operative scheme, brought about by post-war changes of population, is concerned with foreign fiction. In arranging this scheme it has been assumed that all Metropolitan libraries maintain adequate stocks of fiction in French, German, Italian and Spanish. Other languages have been distributed amongst the London Boroughs in accordance with the details set out in *Appendix C* to this chapter.

A minor development in mutual stock-building has been the provision of over a thousand sets of plays (each set comprising one copy per character) for the convenience of play-reading groups, etc.

A great many other matters concerning London library administration and methods might receive attention, but only a few can be indicated here. The question of reference library provision is one of these. As already indicated, the great national reference libraries in London make an incomparable provision for the advanced student and research worker, although difficulties arising from lack of accommodation and time spent on travelling limit the general usefulness of these institutions. At the other end of the scale, the reference libraries contained at present in the borough libraries are mainly equipped, and fairly well equipped, for the less advanced and elementary student; but they cannot be considered adequate. There is an obvious need therefore for for one or two much larger reference libraries to be provided by the municipalities, and various proposals to effect this are under consideration. The City of Westminster has done much in recent years in creating an extended reference library of this nature, and this, together with the Guildhall Library, serves the central area well. For the outlying areas, agreements have been reached for extended reference libraries to be provided at Battersea, Deptford, Hammersmith, Islington, Lambeth and Woolwich.

The scheme of specialisation already outlined gives increasingly valuable help in this development.

A good deal of work has also been done on such details as bringing about uniformity in the hours during which library services are available, and in the standardisation of other rules and regulations affecting the public use of the libraries.

A number of other co-operative developments of the work of the London libraries have been the subject of reports and detailed consideration, but have been delayed by the political considerations and uncertainties regarding the possible new administrative areas into which the Metropolis may or may not be divided. These must remain in the background for the present, but the foregoing gives sufficient details for a picture, even if only an outline one, of the Metropolitan public library service as it exists at the present moment. It should also be clear that it is possible for a number of quite independent authorities and administrators to work together for area as well as local purposes, and to become a co-ordinated body for the service of the public.

The methods and ideas described might with great advantage be considered in other areas of our country where any convenient geographical assemblage of libraries – even if only a few – makes them possible and useful. Even in these days of increasing compulsion and regimentation, there are still great opportunities for the friendly voluntary co-operation that results in mutual helpfulness and the improvement of the public service.

METROPOLITAN SPECIAL COLLECTIONS

Under the terms of this scheme (instituted in 1948), each library in the Metropolitan area undertakes to maintain a special collection dealing with certain specified subjects. This is achieved by (*a*) the purchase of all books dealing with the subjects published in this country, as well as the principal foreign publications; and (*b*) the permanent preservation of their books, as well as other books transferred to the special collection from other libraries. Periodical literature on the subjects is included in the scheme, but on a less comprehensive scale, depending chiefly on demand.

METROPOLITAN SPECIAL COLLECTIONS

SUBJECT ALLOCATIONS

Dewey Classification	*Library*
000–099 (excl. periodicals at 050, 071–079 and special Bibliography)	Bermondsey
100–199 (excl. 133–135)	Hampstead
133–135	Battersea
200–219	Hammersmith
220–259	Deptford
260–289	Fulham
290–299	Westminster (St. Martins Branch)
300–329	Hammersmith
330–339	Poplar
340–354	Hammersmith
355–379	Paddington
380–389	Holborn
390	Kensington
391	Chelsea
392–399	Kensington
400–499	Kensington
500–509	Camberwell
510–529	Camberwell
530–549	Islington
550–559	Camberwell
560–569	Chelsea

Dewey Classification					Library
570–579	.	.	.	.	Deptford
580–589	.	.	.	.	Chelsea
590–599	.	.	.	.	Southwark
600–609	.	.	.	.	Woolwich
610–618	.	.	.	.	St. Marylebone
619	.	.	.	.	St. Pancras
620	.	.	.	.	Woolwich (Plumstead Branch)
621–621.2	.	.	.	.	Woolwich (Plumstead Branch)
621.3	.	.	.	.	Woolwich Central
621.4–621.6	.	.	.	.	Woolwich (Plumstead Branch)
621.7–628	.	.	.	.	Woolwich (Eltham Branch)
629	.	.	.	.	Hackney
630–649	.	.	.	.	St. Pancras
650–659	.	.	.	.	Holborn
660–679 (excl. 675)	.	.	.		Lambeth
675	.	.	.	.	Bermondsey
680–689	.	.	.	.	Shoreditch
690–699	.	.	.	.	Battersea
700–709	.	.	.	.	Westminster (St. Martins Branch)
710–729 (excl. 712	.	.	.		Battersea
712	.	.	.	.	St. Pancras
730–769	.	.	.	.	Westminster (St. Martins Branch)
770–779	.	.	.	.	Finsbury
780–789	.	.	.	.	Westminster (Central Music Library)
790	.	.	.	.	Greenwich
791–792	.	.	.	.	Westminster (St. Martins Branch)
793–799	.	.	.	.	Greenwich
800–819	.	.	.	.	Stepney
820–829	.	.	.	.	Westminster (South Audley Street)
830–849 (excl. the subdivision listed below)	.	.	.	.	Bethnal Green
839.2	.	.	.	.	Westminster

Dewey
Classification   *Library*

839.3	Westminster
839.31	Westminster (St. Martins Branch)
839.32	Westminster
839.5	Wandsworth
839.6	Wandsworth
839.7	Wandsworth
839.81	Chelsea
839.82	Southwark
849.9	Westminster
850–858	Westminster (St. Martins Branch)
859	Hackney
860–868	Westminster (St. Martins Branch)
869	Poplar
870–888	Southwark
889	St. Pancras
890–895 (excl. the subdivisions listed below)	Fulham
891.85	Kensington
891.86	Hampstead
892.49	Stepney
894.511	Hammersmith
896–899	Kensington
900–913 (excl. 913.3) . . .	Wandsworth
913.3	Southwark
914–919 (see 940–999)	
920–929	Kensington
(individual Biography A–G)	Kensington (Brompton Branch)
(remainder) . . .	Kensington Central
930–939	Southwark

940	⎫	Wandsworth
941–942	⎪	Lewisham
942.1	With corresponding	Guildhall
943–949	classes of 914–919	Wandsworth
950–969	⎪	Stoke Newington
970–999	⎭	Hackney

APPENDIX B

METROPOLITAN JOINT FICTION RESERVE

The following libraries have agreed to collect out-of-print and older work of fiction, mostly now otherwise unobtainable, by authors as follows:

A–BAI	Battersea	HOZ–KEL	Kensington
BAJ–BEL	Bermondsey	KEM–L	Lambeth
BEM–BOR	Bethnal Green	MA–MAY	Lewisham
BOS–CAP	Camberwell	MAZ–MOO	St. Marylebone
CAQ–CHD	Chelsea	MOP–OO	Paddington
CHE–COL	Deptford	OP–PIC	Poplar
COM–CRH	Finsbury	PID–RNZ	St. Pancras
CRI–DEL	Fulham	ROA–SHA	Southwark
DEM–DRY	Greenwich	SHE–SN	Shoreditch
DRZ–FOZ	Hackney	SO–THI	Stepney
FR–GN	Hammersmith	THL–TRD	Stoke Newington
GO–GRD	Hampstead	TRE–WEB	Wandsworth
GRE	Holborn	WEC–WI	Westminster
GRI–HOY	Islington	WJ–Z	Woolwich

APPENDIX C

FICTION IN FOREIGN LANGUAGES

NOTE: It is assumed that *all* Metropolitan libraries maintain adequate stocks of fiction in French, German, Italian and Spanish.

Afrikaans	Westminster
Czech	Hampstead
Danish	Chelsea
Dutch	Camberwell, Deptford, Islington, Westminster
Greek (modern)	St. Pancras
Hungarian	Hammersmith
Norwegian	Holborn, Paddington, Southwark, Woolwich
Polish	Kensington, Lambeth, Lewisham, Stoke Newington
Portuguese	Poplar
Rumanian	Hackney
Russian	Battersea, Finsbury, Fulham
Serbian	Hammersmith
Swedish	Bermondsey, St. Marylebone, Shoreditch, Wandsworth
Yiddish	Stepney

CHAPTER X

THE GUILDHALL LIBRARY

By Raymond Smith
late Librarian

and A. H. Hall
Librarian

THE Guildhall Library has a definite and unique, if rather circumscribed, contribution to make to librarianship in general, and to the
Metropolitan area in particular; and we hope it will be of some use to
students and others to know what it is and what it does.

Guildhall Library has developed along quite peculiar lines, and its
structure and growth are due to the changing society in which it has
been set. Even today it takes as its inspiration the ideas and ideals of the
people who founded it in the fifteenth century, and fostered its growth
thereafter. Even today it claims that it is striving to carry out policies
and purposes which derive from a remote past: the leaves of the tree
are green, the trunk is knotted and gnarled, and the roots very far down.

The origins of the library cannot in truth be referred to in the
singular, since it has had two, and an interval of nearly 400 years
separates them in time. How the two growths stemming from these
roots have coalesced and grown together will be the first part of the
story.

In 1423 that rich and pious merchant Richard Whittington died. In
his will he left money for charitable purposes; and his executors, with
the executors of one William Bury, set up the first Guildhall Library.
Contemporary records tell us very little about the collection thus
inaugurated; but it is known that the main purpose of it was for the
use of students, and those engaged in instructing the people; and we
also know, what is of equal importance, that it was described by contemporaries as Libraria communis, the common library, at Guildhall.
That it was mainly theological in character is a fair guess. Indeed the
only surviving relic of it – acquired some years ago from an antiquarian
book-dealer – is a metrical version of the Bible by Peter de Riga.

This library endured for some 125 years; and then, probably in 1549, the whole collection was 'borrowed' in its entirety by the Duke of Somerset, possibly for the purpose of furnishing his new palace, Somerset House in the Strand. It is believed that the Corporation was not the only owner whose treasures were confiscated in this arbitrary way for the same purpose.

It may be assumed that the Corporation were dismayed by this calamity; it does not appear that they made any effort to recover their lost treasure, and certainly they made no effort to establish another library at Guildhall for nearly 300 years. Not until the early nineteenth century was any attempt made to get together another library – the early nineteenth century which saw the inception of the modern spirit of historical inquiry, and the beginning of the publications of the Record Commission.

In 1824 the Corporation appointed a committee to "inquire into the best method of arranging and carrying into effect in the Guildhall, a library of all matters relating to this City, the Borough of Southwark, and the County of Middlesex".

We would emphasise the exact terms of reference. The library was to be highly specialised, devoted to "all matters relating to" a given geographical area. The precise implication of this will be more fully realised when the history and pre-history of the City is considered: the Celtic settlement; the Roman occupation and desertion; the medieval city, rich in political and economic power; the guilds; the struggle for independence and self-government; the arrest of the five members; the Plague, the Fire; the growth of a greater London; the struggle between Court and City in the eighteenth century; the dominance of the City in the economic life of the country in the nineteenth century; all these are "matters relating to this City".

The point must be made that this library was founded and maintained by the Corporation out of its Privy Purse, and not by the ratepayers. And although it was for many years a private library open only to members of the Corporation and accredited students, in 1873, when the present building was completed, it was opened to the public. Thus it became – and still is today – the only public library solely for reference maintained by a local authority. To this point we will return later; but first we want to deal with the growth of the library and the gradual development of its policy.

In 1850 the first Library Act was passed. It is difficult for us today, surrounded as we are by public and private libraries of every description, to realise the position of the poor student in London in that year. Then, apart from the British Museum, there were no public libraries in the metropolis. A hundred years earlier a plea had been issued for a "publick mercantile library" in the City. Gibbon, half a century earlier, had deplored that "the greatest city in the world is destitute of a public library". But in 1850 Charles Knight could say, "I, who carry on my vocation in London, who have been in London five-and-twenty years, I say with shame . . . that there is not a single library, from Whitechapel to Hyde Park Corner . . . from Lambeth or Southwark to Marylebone, or in any other part, where a poor man can walk into a public library and obtain without purchase, or without hire, a single volume for his consolation."

In 1857 the City of Westminster adopted the Library Acts, but thirty to forty years passed before London possessed, generally speaking, the provision that had been made years before by Manchester, Liverpool and Birmingham. It is true that in 1853 the Library Committee of the Corporation reported in favour of establishing a free library and free circulating library, but a public meeting called in 1855 by the Lord Mayor rejected the suggestion. Ratepayers would have none of it.

Meanwhile the small library formed by the Corporation in 1824–28 was growing in size and in importance, and while the chief emphasis was still on London books, many works were added illustrative of London's growth or necessary to a library of any size. Reports made in 1832 and 1835 show that works on English history and topography had been acquired on a large scale, "together with lectures on the Constitution, parliamentary works, and a collection of dictionaries, glossaries, etc., so important in every public library".

During the next thirty-five years the collection had expanded steadily. In 1868–72 the present library was built, and the Common Council resolved that its books and library treasures "should henceforth be devoted to the free use of the public".

The next important step in library development in this country was the passing of the Public Libraries Act of 1892. We would stress the point that until the passing of this act Guildhall was, with the exception of Westminster, the only municipal reference library of any size in London. This factor, and the other factor that Guildhall was solely and wholly a reference library, gave it a unique position. It is obvious that by sheer force of circumstances the scope of its intake had to be widened; and Guildhall by reason of the number and variety of the calls made on it, became not merely a local collection with a general background, but – what was in those days – a large library of general reference.

From the 1890s onwards, however, the public library position in London began to change; slowly at first, but with increasing acceleration. The poverty-stricken Carnegie and Borough Libraries of the early days developed prodigiously; the Library Association was formed and instituted professional examinations, and the passing of the Public Libraries Act of 1919 removed the penny rate limitation which had been such a terrible handicap to library development. This meant that some of the work formerly done by Guildhall was being done – on a smaller scale perhaps, but nevertheless being done – in twenty-eight other Metropolitan centres. Guildhall no longer stood alone: it was one of a number; though even today we venture to think it is in some respects *primus inter pares*.

Events in the greater world outside were not without repercussions even in the small sphere of the City's library. The war of 1914–18 affected very badly the City's private purse, and in 1922 the City, which had for nearly a hundred years maintained a quasi-public and public service at no public cost, adopted the Libraries Act with effect from 1921, and the library became rate-supported. World War II was, for us, a major tragedy. On the night of 29th–30th December, 1940, Guildhall was set on fire from sparks which spread from a neighbouring church, and part of the library was burned out; while many thousands of volumes were damaged by fire, water and subsequently, ice. If we could have had a select fire, we would have welcomed it; we lost much valuable material but much lumber too. The Library Committee determined to turn the tragedy into victory, by seizing the opportunity for overhauling the remaining stocks, and by re-constituting from the grounds upwards on the lines of a declared policy. This briefly was, and still is, to maintain: (*a*) the London collection, (*b*) a general reference library, (*c*) the special collections which the library has acquired during its long existence, (*d*) a commercial reference collection.

The contents of the library may best be considered under these heads of policy.

LONDON COLLECTION

The collection covers the City, the County and, to a lesser extent, Greater London. The City section, which is the most comprehensive collection on that area to be found anywhere, includes printed, graphic and manuscript material. The manuscripts form a particularly strong feature of the collection. The Corporation was one of the first, if not the first, local authority to collect local records, and today three large rooms are required to house them. The records of most of the City livery companies and those of the majority of the City parishes are in the custody of the library, and recently the probate records, including the original wills, of the Archdeaconry Court and Commissary Court of London have been passed over to the library by the authorities at Somerset House. For many years the library has been recognised by the Master of the Rolls as a depository for manorial records, and within the last few years it has been designated by the Bishop of London as the diocesan record office for the City. Under this latter authority, the library has recently had transferred to it the episcopal registers, visitation books and other records of the London diocese which range in date from 1306 to 1927, and also other diocesan records previously housed at St. Paul's. Apart from the records already mentioned, and records of business houses, insurance companies and other City institutions, there is also a large number of deeds relating to City property. These include the library's greatest treasure – the purchase deed of Shakespeare's house in Blackfriars with his signature attached.

It should be pointed out that there are at Guildhall two separate but complementary collections of manuscripts: one in the Guildhall Records Office consisting solely of records originating in the business of the Corporation, and going back in almost unbroken sequence to medieval times; and those in the library, which, from the description above, will be seen to cover activities in the City outside those of the Corporation. For the benefit of students and others, the Library Committee published in 1951 a guide to both collections of records. It is hoped to publish a second edition of this guide in a few years' time. In the meantime, however, the Committee has started a series of small handlists giving details of the holdings of various classes of records in the library. So far there has been issued in this series a list of the Vestry minutes of parishes in the City. Other lists in preparation will include Churchwardens' accounts and Parish registers. The Library Committee also publishes, normally once a year, a journal entitled *Guildhall Miscellany*. This journal contains articles of a historical, antiquarian or literary interest based wholly or in part on material to be found in the library or Guildhall Records Office. By this means the Committee hopes to make more widely known contributions to knowledge within these special fields which would otherwise find little opportunity of publication.

The printed material in the library's London collection includes practically all the more important works of all periods written on the area. It is particularly strong in the ephemeral political and social pamphlets of the seventeenth, eighteenth and early nineteenth centuries. A notable feature of the collection is an almost complete set of London directories from the mid-eighteenth century to date. Colour-plate books also figure largely and include a rare issue of Shotter Boys' *London as it is*, 1842.

The London collection of prints and drawings is the richest in the country. Fine prints and drawings are well represented, including the collection made by the late Viscount Wakefield of Hythe and presented by him to the library. The main purpose of the collection, however, is topographical record, and there is a wealth of material, which, although of negligible artistic merit, is invaluable from this point of view.

There is an extensive range of maps of London dating from the sixteenth century to the present day. The rarest item amongst them is the Agas plan of London, *c.* 1570, of which only two other copies are known.

GENERAL REFERENCE

This section contains the more important works, useful for reference, on all subjects with the exception of technology and science. These two subjects are not represented except by works of an encyclopaedic nature, and inquirers in these fields are directed to nearby libraries specialising in these subjects. The library does contain, however, works on the historical side of these subjects.

SPECIAL COLLECTIONS

These collections, in the main, support, or are complementary to, the London collection and the general reference section. The most notable are: *English history.* – The library contains all the major printed source material such as the Calendars of State Papers published by the Public Record Office and publications of English local record societies. *English local history and topography.* – All the standard county histories and most local histories are available. A special feature is the series of local directories and poll books dating from the eighteenth century, which are probably the most extensive in the country. *English genealogy and heraldry.* – This collection was developed as source material of the lives of the many prominent London citizens whose family roots are to be found throughout England. It contains a large number of printed and typescript parish registers for all parts of the country and long runs of peerages and similar publications. The literature of heraldry is well represented and includes many of the earlier heraldic writers from the sixteenth century onwards. *Official and legal publications.* – These include a complete set of House of Commons papers and reports from 1835 with many of an earlier date, together with complete sets of Commons and Lords debates and journals. The file of the *London Gazette*, complete to date from its commencement in 1665, is one of the few in existence. Of particular value is the long file of public and local Acts of Parliament, which extends (with some minor gaps) from the earliest Statutes. Another important holding in this section is the file of law reports, particularly those of the late eighteenth and early nineteenth centuries.

There are also a number of special collections bequeathed or deposited which fall outside the general scope of the library. These include the library of the Gardeners' Company on practical horticulture, the library of the Clockmakers' Company on horology, the Cock collection on Sir Thomas More, the Willshire collection of prints illustrating the early development of engraving, and an extensive collection of playing cards belonging to the Company of Makers of Playing Cards.

COMMERCIAL REFERENCE COLLECTION

This important section of the library provides for the needs of business men working in the City. The separate Commercial Reference Room contains British and overseas directories, trade and professional periodicals, the principal London, provincial and many foreign newspapers, time-tables, general and statistical handbooks, etc. An outstanding feature of the room is the extensive range of foreign directories which covers all parts of the world and is the most comprehensive collection readily available to the public in London. Another much used item is Moody's British Company Service, which gives, on cards, up-to-date information on all British public companies. The Guildhall is the only public library in London which has this service. The Library Committee issues from time to time a publication entitled the *C.R.R. Courier* showing the additions which have been made to the room and other information concerning its contents.

In addition to the Commercial Reference Room, much material useful to the business man, such as statistical publications and manuals of commercial practice, is kept in the main library. Also obtainable in the main library are long files of periodicals, notably *The Times* (from 1806), *Stock Exchange Daily List, Financial Times,* etc.

The library is a modern, up-to-date and live public reference library. It is equipped with those mechanical aids which are now common in the larger libraries of the country, such as photo-reproducing apparatus, microfilm reader and duplicating machine.

The procedure for obtaining books is extremely simple and rapid. No reader has to wait more than a few minutes for the material he wants, whether it be printed, manuscript or graphic.

All types of readers use the library – some quarter of a million a year – but they can be divided into three main classes, namely the workers in the fields of London history and topography, the ordinary reader who requires a particular piece of information in any field, and the business man who wants directories or statistical or other information in commercial fields.

The library forms an integral part of the public library system of London and indeed of the whole country. Owing to its long existence and its policy, the library contains much material not otherwise readily available to the public. It therefore ranks as one of the most important national reference libraries, and inquiries are received from every part of this country and from abroad.

The library plays its part in the various library co-operative schemes, both local and national. Its stock is recorded in the London Union Catalogue, and through that body and the National Central Library it will lend to other libraries works not available elsewhere. It keeps in touch with library affairs through the Library Association, and particularly, in its own field, through the Reference, Special and Information Section of that Association.

Although the library is for reference only, a special duplicate collection of London books has been formed from which students can borrow. In the Commercial Reference Room a collection of recent, but not current, foreign directories is available for loan by business men in the City. Furthermore, since 1957 the Corporation has made considerable annual financial grants from rates funds to the three institutes (St. Bride's, Bishopsgate and Cripplegate) in support of the lending libraries maintained by them out of their charitable funds. The main purpose of these grants is to provide lending library facilities for the resident population and those working in the City without adequate lending library facilities in their dormitory areas.

From what has been said, it will be appreciated that Guildhall is unique; it fits into no category; it is a public municipal library with no general loan facilities to its residents or to people who work in its area except as mentioned above. It is a special library with a background of general reference works or, conversely, a general reference library built round a highly important nucleus of local and specialised material. It is part privately and part publicly owned; its building and private collections are leased to the library authority; and it serves an area with a day population estimated at 400,000 and a night population of just over 5,000.

CHAPTER XI

THE LIBRARIES OF THE LONDON COUNTY COUNCIL

By Miss I. Darlington
Archivist and Librarian, The Members' Library

and H. R. Mainwood
Organiser of Education Library Services

THE libraries administered by the London County Council, known respectively as the Council's Library and the Education Library, are not public libraries within the meaning of the Acts but they both give service in their own fields to the people of London and to students in general. They are entirely different in scope and purpose and they are therefore treated separately here. The libraries in Council training colleges, technical colleges and schools are described with the Education Library since they all come under the supervision of the Organiser of Education Library Services.

The Council's Library. This library, sometimes known as the Members' Library to distinguish it from the Education Library, is intended primarily to serve members of the Council and its staff in carrying out their multifarious duties. It performs in fact the same kind of function for the Council that the library of the House of Commons fulfils for the Council's august neighbour across the river. Its coverage comprises on the one hand, local government and local government services of all kinds, and on the other, London in all its aspects. It started from humble beginnings with the collection of blue books and technical literature taken over from the Metropolitan Board of Works in 1889 but it has grown into a special library of considerable size and value in its own field and it is now used for reference by many people outside the Council's service.

On the local government side beside general works on local government in the British Isles and abroad, the library carries a stock of books on social welfare in all its branches, education, public health, town planning, architecture and housing, road and bridge construction, main drainage, etc. It also contains the raw material for a study of that

very complicated subject the development of London local government, in the minutes and reports of all local authorities, public boards
and public utility undertakings in the County of London, and of many
in the Home Counties, as well as in those of superseded authorities such
as the Metropolitan Board of Works, the School Board for London
and the London Boards of Guardians and the reports of the London
vestries back to 1855. These are, of course, all printed and are additional
to the archives of London authorities whose functions have been taken
over by the Council, in the Council's Record Office.

More general works of reference include *Hansard* back to 1803, a set
of local Acts relating to London which has been calendared and
indexed, and many parliamentary papers and reports.

Some books on the history and topography of London are a *sine
qua non* for those whose duty it is to administer its social services and
plan its future, but this side of the library received a big impetus when
the Council in 1900 agreed to co-operate with a voluntary society, the
London Survey Committee, in the production of an annotated list of
buildings of architectural and historical interest in the London area.
From the beginning a large proportion of the necessary historical
research devolved upon the Council's officers and, under the scholarly
guidance of Mr. W. Braines, the scope of the library was enlarged to
include all obtainable books and pamphlets on London, and also maps,
prints and drawings of London. Though in books on the City of
London it cannot approach the riches in the Guildhall Library, it has
now a very comprehensive collection on the Metropolitan and Greater
London areas.

Many eighteenth- and nineteenth-century maps and plans of London
were inherited by the Council from its predecessors the Commissioners
of Sewers, the Metropolitan Buildings Office and the Metropolitan
Board of Works. The collection has grown during the years by purchase and gift and now comprises some 4,000 items. The print and
drawing collection (over 18,000 items) has been largely acquired by
gift but individual items and bulk collections are purchased when
opportunity offers. The biggest accession was the purchase in 1923–24
of a large part of the Gardner collection, though the Council's representative at the auction sales was careful not to bid against the libraries of
Metropolitan Boroughs who wished to buy for their local collections.
The London books of John Burns, given to the Council by Lord
Southwood in 1943, include many extra illustrated volumes of standard
works on London including three sets of Pennant. Recently some

thousands of postcard views have been presented to the library. These are often of value in filling gaps in the topographical record of vanished streets and buildings.

The photograph library illustrates both London and Londoners. It is growing at the rate of about 5,000 items a year as copies of most of the photographs taken currently of the Council's activities are added to it. It will in time include a full photographic survey of buildings of architectural and historical interest in London.

All the visual material is now available in one large room which can be used by members of the public as well as by the Council's staff.

In 1938 a series of catalogues of the library's stocks was projected but, owing to the outbreak of the 1939–45 war, only one of these was finished and printed. This was the *Catalogue of books on London history and topography* which forms a good bibliography of books published in that field before 1939. The author and classified catalogues of the library are on cards. The classification scheme, though it owes much to Dewey and U.D.C., has been devised to fit the peculiar coverage of subjects in the bookstock, and it is also used, with some necessary adaptations, for the photograph library. The collection of prints and drawings is arranged and catalogued topographically, and a subject index is being built up. A quarterly list of new accessions is circulated in the Council's service and to other libraries in the London area. From time to time bibliographies on particular local government services are compiled and similarly circulated.

About 120 periodicals are taken regularly; many of these are kept for two years only, but sets of some such as *The Times, The Municipal Journal, The Builder, The Illustrated London News, The Annual Register*, etc., are kept permanently.

In 1912 Henry Harben, a former member of the Council, bequeathed to the library the material he had accumulated during the compilation of his *Dictionary of London*. The bequest included not only all types of printed and graphic material but also a collection of original records, mainly leases and indentures of sale of London properties dating from the thirteenth century onwards. From this time the Council accepted gifts of records but did not actively seek them. The first occasion on which it was found necessary to intervene in order to preserve an important record series was in 1931, when the Council took over the eighteenth-century copy memorials from the Middlesex Deeds Registry in order to save them from the waste-paper merchant. Over a period of years a complete set of volumes of copy memorials and memorials from 1709 to 1946 (over 11,000 volumes in all) was transferred to the Council, while the original rolls from 1709 to 1837 were sent to Middlesex Guildhall.

The Council agreed from the outset to support the work of the British Records Association and in the early 1930s helped the Association by giving temporary accommodation to some of the accumulations of records from solicitors' offices pending their sorting and dispatch to different parts of the country. In the 1930s some interesting London records were obtained from this source but latterly the flow has been reduced to a trickle since the Association now sends most of the London records it receives to the appropriate Metropolitan Borough Council reference library. Lists of these records are, however, deposited with the Council for the use of students.

The Council's Record Office was recognised as a Manorial Repository by the Master of the Rolls in 1943 when a long series of court books for the Manor of Stepney were transferred from the Public Record Office. Other manorial records have been acquired from time to time.

When work was resumed on the *Survey of London* in 1946 the research worker ran into difficulties because of the heavy war damage which had been inflicted on so many of the buildings – churches, institutions, solicitors' offices, etc., which had housed records which were essential raw material for the historical side of the survey. Many of these records were in a sorry state from fire, water, or exposure to the elements, while others were in peril from the continued drive for paper salvage. It became obvious that in many cases the only way of preserving them was to take them over and from 1948 onward a policy of collecting records of London interest was actively pursued. Additional trained staff were recruited as assistant archivists and in 1956 a repair shop was installed with a full-time repairer.

The office was recognised as a diocesan repository by the Bishop of Southwark in 1952 and by the Bishop of London in 1955. A complete parish by parish survey of the church records of South London has been carried out, and a similar survey of those of London north of the Thames is in progress. The records of 144 parishes have now been deposited. Many estate, institutional and business records have also been acquired either by gift or on deposit. The records of the Council and its predecessors, though physically separated from non-official records, are administered within the same office, the whole serving the purposes of a normal county record office for the County of London except that it contains no sessions records. The latter are kept by the Clerk of the Peace at Newington Sessions House since, under the provisions of the Local Government Act, 1888, the Clerk of the Peace for the County of London and the Clerk of the London County Council are separate officials.

The library and record office each have a microfilm reader and microfilm copies are acquired from time to time of material which will supplement the stock. Recently a set of microfilm copies of the index to *The Times* has been purchased and the experiment is being tried of buying microfilm copies of *The Times* itself and of some other frequently used periodicals to save storing the originals. Limited use can be made of the photographic unit in the department of the Architect to the Council for supplying photographic copies of material to readers. The library is not, however, yet fully equipped for the increasing part which photographic techniques will undoubtedly play in library provision in the future. There is on the premises a bindery where confidential papers and rare books are bound or repaired but other binding is done commercially. For most of the repair work on documents, prints and maps, traditional methods are used, but with the help and advice of the Council's Scientific Adviser, experiments with new materials and techniques are being successfully carried out.

Both the library and its ancillary collections and the record office can be used for reference by students and other interested members of the public. They are open Monday to Friday 9.30 a.m. to 5 p.m., Saturday 9.30 a.m. to 12.15 p.m. Documents can be seen on Saturday in the library only if advance notice has been given of requirements.

The Council's Education Library Service forms part of the London Education Service. In addition to the Education Library at County Hall, there are libraries staffed by full-time and part-time professional librarians in the Council's teacher training colleges, technical colleges, colleges of commerce, schools of art, day colleges, and the larger secondary schools.

The Education Library itself is maintained in Room 453 on the fourth floor at County Hall. It contains some 170,000 volumes, and includes books of all types other than class textbooks. Books on the history, theory and method of education and on psychology and child study are important sections, and periodicals, over 100 in number, concerned with these and other subjects are available. The library is open from 9.0 a.m. to 6.0 p.m. on Mondays to Fridays during school terms, and from 9.0 a.m. to 4.30 p.m. during school holidays. On Saturdays, it is open throughout the year from 9.0 a.m. to 12.0 noon. All teachers, lecturers and staff employed by the L.C.C. may borrow directly from the library, and others may use it for reference. The library is an outlier library of the National Central Library, and books are lent to and borrowed from other libraries. Books for use in school and college libraries may be borrowed for periods of up to three terms. Normally, single copies only of individual titles are lent, but the particular needs of individual schools are met as far as possible. One school may choose a general collection, another may need books on a particular topic, another may require more advanced books for individual pupils. A display collection of books suitable for primary and secondary school libraries is maintained at the library.

Each of the teacher training colleges administered by the Council – Avery Hill, Battersea, Furzedown, Garnett, Philippa Fawcett and Shoreditch – has a library built up to meet the special needs of students and staffs, the largest having bookstocks of well over 20,000 volumes.

Colleges of Further Education aided by the Council consist of three Colleges of Advanced Technology (Battersea College of Technology, Chelsea College of Science and Technology and Northampton College of Advanced Technology): The Polytechnic (Regent Street), Borough Polytechnic, Northern Polytechnic, North-Western Polytechnic, Woolwich Polytechnic, City of London College, Cordwainers Technical College, Sir John Cass College, together with Morley College. All of these colleges receive substantial financial assistance from the Council, and their library provision is described in Chapter XVIII.

The technical colleges, schools of art and colleges of commerce maintained wholly by the Council are each concerned with a range of related subjects. While their libraries naturally specialise in these subjects, they also contain books of more general interest for use in connection with the liberal studies which form a normal part of the curriculum of many courses both for full-time and part-time students. The following list indicates the specialist interests of the colleges, and the approximate size of their bookstocks and holdings of periodicals at the end of 1960.

		Books	Periodicals
Technical Colleges:			
Barrett Street Technical College, Barrett Street, W.1.	Dressmaking, design, embroidery, hairdressing, tailoring, furriery.	3,500	66

		Books	Periodi-cals
Technical Colleges—continued.			
Brixton School of Building, Ferndale Road, S. W.4.	Architecture, building, engineering, science and mathematics, decoration and fine arts.	9,000+ 2,500 pamphlets, reports, etc.	175
College for the Distributive Trades, Charing Cross Road, W.C.2.	Advertising, display, management and merchandising, textiles and general commodities, food commodities.	5,000	125
Hackney Technical College, Dalston Lane, E.8.	Mechanical engineering, instrument engineering, horology, electrical engineering, chemistry, building subjects.	5,000	75
London School of Printing and Graphic Arts, Back Hill, Clerkenwell Road, E.C.1.	Printing, bookbinding, design, graphic reproduction, administrative studies.	13,500	300
Norwood Technical College, Knight's Hill, West Norwood, S.E.27.	Chemistry and biology, commercial and liberal studies, physics and mathematics, telecommunications and electronics.	11,250	170
Paddington Technical College, Saltram Crescent, W.9.	Electrical and mechanical engineering, motor vehicle engineering, science, science laboratory and medical laboratory technology, chiropody, physiotherapy, glassworking.	4,500	100
Poplar Technical College, Poplar High Street, E.14.	Mechanical engineering and naval architecture, electrical engineering and physics, marine engineering, flour milling.	4,000	140
Shoreditch College for the Clothing Industry, Curtain Road, E.C.2.	Dressmaking, tailoring, clothing technology, machine embroidery, management and work study, sewing machine repair and maintenance.	4,000	72

		Books	Periodi-cals
Technical Colleges—continued.			
South East London Technical College, Lewisham Way, S.E.4.	Building and structural engineering, mechanical engineering, electrical engineering and applied physics, catering and needlecrafts.	7,250	200
Technical College for the Furnishing Trades, Pitfield Street, Shoreditch, N.1.	Furniture, upholstery and soft furnishing, musical instrument technology.	3,500	50
Wandsworth Technical College, Wandsworth High Street, S.W.18.	Mechanical, production and electrical engineering, audio-visual aids, building, nursery nurses.	6,500	100
Westminster Technical College, Vincent Square, S.W.1.	Civil engineering, mechanical and gas engineering, cookery and hotel operation.	10,000 (incl. 3,500 pamphlets)	160
Schools of Art:			
Camberwell School of Arts and Crafts, Peckham Road, S.E.5.	Painting, sculpture, design and crafts, printing.	5,000	60
Central School of Arts and Crafts, Southampton Row, W.C.1.	Book production, interior design, furniture and pottery, theatrical design, printed textiles and weaving, industrial design for light engineering industries, silversmiths' work and allied crafts, mural painting.	11,500 (incl. 2,500 pamphlets)	256
Hammersmith College of Art and Building, Lime Grove, Shepherd's Bush, W.12.	Art and crafts, architecture, building, structural engineering and surveying.	10,000	113

		Books	Periodi-cals
Schools of Art—continued.			
St. Martin's School of Art, 109 Charing Cross Road, W.C.2.	Painting, drawing, advertising and commercial design, illustration, modelling and sculpture, fashion and dress design, millinery and machine embroidery, silkscreen printing.	4,000	80
Colleges of Commerce:			
Balham and Tooting College of Commerce, Tooting Broadway, S.W.17.	Accountancy, banking, company, office and public administration, commerce, economics, management, language studies, legal studies.	7,500	130
Catford College of Commerce, Plassy Road, Sangley Road, Rushey Green, S.E.6.	Accountancy, advertising, banking, commerce, economics, grocery, insurance, languages, librarianship, management, public administration, salesmanship, secretaryship, shipping, transport.	3,500	30
City of Westminster College, Francis House, Francis Street, S.W.1.	Economics, sociology and professional studies, languages, business training, arts and general studies, science.	5,000	90
Holborn College of Law, Languages and Commerce, Princeton Street, W.C.1. (Moving to new premises in Red Lion Square in 1961.)	Law, languages, commerce.	3,750	65
Literary Institute:			
City Literary Institute, Stukeley Street, Drury Lane, W.C.2.	A wide variety of classes in the arts and the humanities.	12,000	24

The Education Library at County Hall arranges inter-library loans for these libraries, and also for the libraries of day schools, and maintains a union catalogue of the periodical holdings of all maintained and aided colleges.

CHAPTER XII

THE UNIVERSITY OF LONDON LIBRARY

By J. H. P. Pafford

Goldsmiths' Librarian, University of London

THE UNIVERSITY AND ITS LIBRARIES

THERE were many projects for the formation of a University of London at least from the latter part of the sixteenth century but it is strange that London, almost alone among the capital cities of Europe, did not in fact establish a university until the early nineteenth century since it had been an important seat of learning from early times.[1] The beginnings of the University as we know it are to be seen in the opening of University College in 1828 and of King's College in 1831. Neither of these – the foundation colleges of the University – obtained a charter to grant degrees although the former used the title of 'London University' until 1836. In that year the University of London[2] was established as a separate body to examine and award degrees to students of the two foundation colleges, and although many other colleges and institutions became associated with the University, this remained little more than an examining body until the end of the century. It was not until the University was reconstituted after the University of London Act of 1898 and again after the Act of 1926 that the central organisation came to take the vitally important part in academic and financial matters affecting all the colleges which it has held ever since.[3] But the group of colleges and schools which, with the central organisation, form the University, had even by 1900 become very large and is larger still today. The University now comprises some seventy-four colleges, schools and institutions which together form easily the largest university in the country. In 1958–59 there were over 25,000 full-time as well as many part-time internal students and there were over 24,000 registered external students. The immense size and range of the University is also clearly brought out simply by listing some of its schools and colleges – University and King's Colleges, the London School of Economics, the Imperial College of Science and Technology,

Queen Mary College, Birkbeck College, the famous colleges which are primarily for women (Bedford, Westfield, Royal Holloway and Queen Elizabeth College), the great medical schools at Guy's, St. Bartholomew's, St. Mary's, St. Thomas's, etc., and the many specialist medical institutes associated within the British Postgraduate Medical Federation. And then there are the very important non-medical specialist schools, as of Oriental and African Studies, Slavonic and East European Studies, Historical Research, Education, Art, Law, Archaeology, Commonwealth Studies, Classical Studies, Germanic Studies, etc. These and many others make up that unique and mighty organisation known as the University of London, which, like any other university, is continually developing, assuming new responsibilities – as with the Colleges in special relation in Africa and the West Indies – embracing new studies and incorporating new colleges and institutions.

Every university has its own characteristics and London certainly no less than any other. These are often easier to appreciate than they are to define but it is perhaps right to say that London has always been marked by a certain liberal outlook, a wish to promote the study of all branches of knowledge and a desire that what it has to offer shall be offered as fully, as widely and as freely as possible. And so we see in London a pioneer, for example, in the non-requirement of religious tests for entering a university, a pioneer in the admission of women to degrees, a pioneer in granting external degrees to students not only in the British Isles but throughout the world, particularly in the Commonwealth, and one of the first in the field of extension and tutorial classes. London was also the first to recognise English as a suitable subject of study for a university degree and the first to found a faculty of science.

With all this growth there has naturally been a steady development of libraries. Every institution in the University has a library primarily for the service of its own members, and some of these libraries, with the institutions to which they belong, are older than the University itself. And there is also the University Library[4] which, although it has developed chiefly during the present century, can trace its origins almost back to the year in which the University was established. Together these libraries make a very impressive group indeed; they contain well over three million volumes covering all subjects studied in the University and, for many subjects, have research collections of outstanding, even of national, importance.[5]

There is no central authority in any way controlling these libraries and they are also independent of each other. Nevertheless, there has always been co-operation between them; there have been projects and achievements in the field of union catalogues[6] and an index to special collections was made as long ago as 1908 by the first Goldsmiths' Librarian of the University in what is still the finest book on the libraries of London.[7] Libraries have, on the whole, avoided the unnecessary collection of specialised material which would more properly be in the library of a special school or institute or in a well-known special collection in one of the general libraries. The special schools and institutes clearly show from their titles at any rate certain subjects in which their libraries are strong, and the whereabouts of some other special collections are well known. Furthermore, there are actual co-operative schemes in force such as that whereby, with certain reservations, the University Library collects economics before 1851 for the Goldsmiths' Library and the British Library of Political and Economic Science collects later material; several libraries divide the field of law between them, and there are other agreements concerning certain branches of history. A committee of librarians of the University[8] is now engaged on developing this co-operation still further and has already begun to compile an index of special collections. One obvious problem which must become acute for libraries in such a big city is that of space, and an important step is now being taken which will go some way towards a solution. That is in the erection of a depository library in the grounds of Royal Holloway College at Egham. The building was started in the autumn of 1959 and the first part should be ready for use in 1961. The first stage will accommodate about 250,000 books and have a small reading room: the completed building will take about two million books and there is room for even further expansion. To this depository all libraries in the University will be able to send books which are not frequently needed and this will undoubtedly reduce, although it will not eliminate, the need for further expansion of some library buildings in London.

THE UNIVERSITY LIBRARY

The University Library is a general library with over 700,000 books and 4,000 current periodicals. Centrally situated and open for long hours it gives a reference and lending service, and is freely available to every member of the University, the teaching staff, students, internal and external, and all graduates. It is particularly strong in arts subjects but it has collections of growing importance in the sciences, particularly in periodicals, and it has a strong collection of medical periodicals.

History

The history may be divided into four periods which more or less coincide with moves to different buildings: 1838–70, 1870–1906, 1906–45 and 1945 onwards.

1838–70: The first indication that some sort of library did exist is the record of a gift of books in 1838 when the University headquarters were in Marlborough House, but there is no specific mention of the University Library until 1846 and little more is heard of it until 1870 when the University established its headquarters in Burlington Gardens.

1870–1906: This was a period of great acquisitions and of great difficulties for the library since it was inadequately provided with money, staff, space and equipment. In 1871 Mr. (later Sir) Julian Goldsmid gave £100 for each of the next ten years to buy classics (Greek and Latin) in order to establish "a first-class University Library, which . . . will not only improve the position of the University, but also be of great service to its students and graduates". In the same year Baron Overstone bought the mathematical library of Professor Augustus de Morgan – 4,000 volumes of old and rare works – and presented it to the University "in the hope that it may prove the first fruits of a library which shall ere long become in all respects such as the University of London ought to possess"; and also in 1871 the University received by bequest the library of 7,000 volumes of George Grote the classical historian.

In the same year the first regular Library Committee was appointed which directed the Registrar to have a catalogue compiled. The Senate also resolved that "in the first selection of books to be purchased for the Library the requirements of members of the University who are already Graduates be kept chiefly in view". In 1873 successful application was made to the Treasury for £100 a year for the maintenance of the library.

It is interesting to note that in 1872 the Senate specified that the library was to be chiefly for graduates and clearly had the intention to establish a library primarily for research. In 1876 a catalogue was printed of which an uncorrected version with shortened entries, but brought up to 1897, was issued in 1900.

The likelihood that the library had been little used until this time is shown by the fact that it was not until 1877 that it was formally

opened to readers. In 1879 rules were drawn up and put into force
whereby members of the Senate and members of Convocation and
others recommended by them could borrow from the library. In the
same year the library of the British Association was presented and in
1880 the library received a collection of Russian books from the widow
of Sir John Shaw-Lefevre.

In 1893 the Senate asked the Library Committee to report on "the
best means of increasing the facilities for borrowing books from the
University Library" and at the reconstitution of the University in 1900
the library was transferred from Burlington Gardens to South Kensington. Here the library, then consisting of about 30,000 books, was in a
disordered condition, some of the books being stacked on the floor
owing to lack of shelves. This naturally provoked criticism and there
were even suggestions that the library should be dispersed. This was
strongly opposed by Convocation in 1903 and many others followed
Convocation's lead and determined that the library should be properly
established. These included Sidney Webb who wrote to the Principal
on 14th January, 1904, saying that he hoped that the University might
soon have "a really efficient organisation of a University Library
worthy of London and covering the whole field and work of the
University as a whole with an adequate salary for a Chief Librarian of
organising capacity and high standing" and in February 1904 L. W.
Haward was appointed as 'Acting Librarian' and in 1905 as 'Librarian'
at £150 a year with R. A. Rye as assistant. Haward resigned in
November 1906 and Rye succeeded him as 'Goldsmiths' Librarian' at
£175 a year with one assistant and a boy. On 26th October, 1906, the
Chancellor, the Earl of Rosebery, reopened the library after its
reorganisation by Haward and Rye.

During this last period, in 1903, the library received the magnificent
gift from the Goldsmiths' Company of the great collection of early
works on economics formed by Professor A. H. Foxwell and known as
the Goldsmiths' Library. This contained 30,000 volumes, immediately
doubling the size of the library, and there is no doubt that its acquisition
was the chief reason for the appointment of a full-time librarian.

1906–38: The third period opens with the library firmly established
thanks to its great benefactions, to Convocation, to certain distinguished
members of the University including Sir Edward Busk, Sir William
Job Collins, the Hon. William Pember Reeves, Professor Sylvanus
Thompson and Sidney Webb, and to the work of Haward and Rye.
And since that time – largely due to the able and devoted service of

R. A. Rye – the library has suffered no further crisis – apart from the alarm caused by the abortive proposals in the Haldane Report of 1913 – and has made remarkable progress. At first development was slow. In 1907, on the proposal of Professor Sylvanus Thompson, it was decided to create a strong bibliographical section and this has become a particular and very useful feature of the library. It was then also decided to print Accessions Lists and produce Annual Reports, both of which have appeared regularly ever since.

1910 saw the beginning of the Travelling Libraries, now called the Extra-Mural Library, which started at the request of the University Extension Board by an agreement to house and administer in the library sixty books purchased for issue to Tutorial Class students. In less than fifty years those sixty books have grown to a library of over 85,000 volumes which issues 40,000 books a year to Tutorial Classes and Extension Courses.

In 1911 the staff had grown to eight; about £800 a year was spent on books, periodicals and binding and minor activities, and over 5,000 books were lent. But in that year the Senate cut the library vote by £200 and economies had to be made which included abandoning a project for a union catalogue of University College, King's College, London School of Economics and the University Library. In 1912 the library received from Lady Welby some 2,500 volumes on philosophy, economics and theology; and then, naturally, development was retarded by the First World War.

The position of all university libraries has been greatly strengthened by the University Grants Committee which has always strongly advocated library development. In its report of 3rd February, 1921, the Committee said that "the character and efficiency of a University may be gauged by its treatment of its central organ – the Library". The fullest provision for library maintenance was regarded by the Committee as the "primary and most vital need in the equipment of a University". This report was probably one of the causes leading to further increases of staff and to the consideration of the needs of the library for new accommodation.

In 1924 it was resolved to establish a music library, as being important "not only to the student who is making music his special study, but also to all members of the University interested in the subject". The music library today is one of the finest of its kind in the country. In 1929 the Teachers' Guild of Great Britain presented the library of R. H. Quick – about 1,000 early books on education including school books, and some other educational works, and in 1931 the library received the Durning-Lawrence Library, a very important collection of about 7,000 volumes largely of seventeenth-century literature containing one of the best collections in the world on Sir Francis Bacon and valuable collections on Shakespeare and Defoe. In 1936 the library received on deposit the Harry Price Library of 15,000 volumes on magical and occult subjects which became a bequest on the death of Mr. Price in 1948.

The growth of the library made the acquisition of new premises a matter of extreme urgency. When the new buildings in Bloomsbury were first projected, a separate building for the University Library was envisaged. Many will feel that a great opportunity was missed when this was abandoned. But the library was glad indeed to move in 1938 into its present fine buildings designed by Dr. Holden.

Then came the second war and further dislocation of the library. In 1940 the new buildings suffered from air-raids, the tower and three stack rooms were heavily damaged but only about 200 books were lost. Unfortunately about fifty were valuable early books some of which cannot be replaced. The Goldsmiths' Library was then evacuated to the Bodleian and other books were sent to the University Museum of Archaeology and Ethnology, Cambridge. The library continued its services during the war, being controlled during the illness of Mr. Rye by Miss M. S. Quinn the sub-librarian. Mr. Rye retired in 1944 after forty years' service and Miss Quinn in 1949 after thirty-one years. It is difficult even to appreciate and much more to express the great debt which the University owes to those two devoted librarians and their staff, some of whom are happily still with us.

1945–: Mr. Rye had brought a fine library to the new buildings and after the war its development was rapid. This was but the natural result of having, for the first time, adequate premises and increased funds and staff, and the great increase in the numbers of students and staff in the University. There was general expansion throughout the University and the library, too, was carried along on the crest of that wave.

The most notable developments have been the establishment of a Bindery (1948) and a Photographic Department (1948); the setting up of an Open Access Lending Library in 1952 – hitherto nearly all books except reference books and music, had been housed in the closed stacks – the giving of much greater freedom of access to the stacks and the increase in provision of seats for readers – in 1946 the library could seat 268 readers, now it can take 500. In 1946 permission was obtained from the L.C.C. to use the whole of the tower – previously, because of fire risks, the part above the eighth floor could not be used. All the extensive war damage was repaired and several other structural alterations made. Shelving was installed throughout the library, micro-film readers and other items of special apparatus were obtained and provision made for typing and other special needs of research workers. The Sterling Library room was a special construction opened in 1956 and the north-east wing, designed as a periodical reading room and stack, was built and opened in 1959. With all this there has been a great all-round increase in the use of the library and an increase in staff to cope with the rapidly growing work of serving readers and building up and cataloguing the collections.

There have also been many notable acquisitions since the war – the Elzevir collection and the Eliot-Phelips Spanish Library both received from the Guildhall, the Austin Dobson Library from Mr. Alban Dobson, the Shorthand Library of Mr. W. J. Carlton, the deposit on permanent loan of the fine library of periodicals belonging to the British Psychological Society and of the libraries of the Plainsong and Medieval Music Society and the Royal Musical Association, and the similar deposit by the Church Commissioners of the library of Bishop Porteus of about 4,000 volumes. An outstanding gift is that by the late Sir Louis Sterling of 4,000 rare and valuable books in English literature – of which further mention is made below – with an endowment of £5,000, and the Goldsmiths' Company have continued their benefac-tions by setting up an endowment fund of £5,000 for the Goldsmiths' Library. Mr. Troup Horne, who during his lifetime gave considerable sums for the purchase of books in memory of Sir Edwin Deller, bequeathed his own books to the library at his death in 1953 and a fund of £2,100 to continue purchases for the Deller Memorial Library.

It can surely be agreed that the growth of the library in the last fifty years has been remarkable. From a collection of 30,000 books, housed inadequately in rooms some of which were used as administrative offices, without adequate shelving, many books being stacked on the floor, inadequately catalogued and in disorder, with a staff of one part-time lady clerk and an annual expenditure of about £100, has developed a library of 700,000 volumes, 4,000 current periodicals and a considerable collection of manuscripts, with a staff of sixty-nine librarians, five binders, five photographers, fifteen attendants and ten part-time staff for evening duties, with an expenditure on books, periodicals and binding alone (and entirely excluding the Extra-Mural Library) of over £34,000, housed in a building which can take a million volumes, having over 12,500 registered readers and lending over 140,000 volumes a year.

Services and Collections

The library's policy is to cover all subjects studied in the University but to build up research collections only in certain arts fields. It is a policy which would naturally develop when the library at South Kensington was near to the Science Museum: but even if that had not been so, it is obviously desirable with many sciences that their libraries should be closely associated with laboratories. But there are signs that teachers in the University would like to see a strong collection of periodicals in the University Library in all subjects and the library is already strong in medical and mathematical periodicals. Indeed the periodicals department is of very great importance and will become increasingly so. The University Library acts as a central agency to libraries of the University in many ways – for example, in giving bibliographical information, in lending books, in taking a leading part in the compilation of union catalogues of periodicals and of incunabula, and in disposing of duplicates – but the work of the periodicals department in the supply of bibliographical information, including the locating of periodicals in other libraries and in the compilation of union catalogues of periodicals, is outstanding in this service.

But although the library has always been primarily for the postgraduate, it has also always accepted the task of providing a service for undergraduates. There are general principles which govern the needs of these two groups of readers which are common to all university libraries[9] and, if the dangers of over-simplification are accepted, it is not difficult to define them. The undergraduate requires a well-chosen, well-arranged, non-specialised modern collection in all subjects in which there should be two or more copies of a comparatively few books in most fields. He also needs a well-equipped and well-furnished library which is easily accessible and open for long hours. His books must be on open access and many must be available for loan and there must be good catalogues. He will, in many subjects, have little need of periodicals at least until his third year, but should be able to see the chief periodicals in his field. He also needs the service of a library staff which is able to guide him at any rate in the elementary principles of using a library and of using reference books.

It is obvious that the undergraduate must expect that his needs will primarily be met by his college library. He must spend most of the day in his college and his college lecturers recommend books which may not always be those recommended in the same course in another college. The college libraries are naturally the undergraduates' first and main sources of supply. Nevertheless, partly because the needs of the internal undergraduates are so great and partly because the University Library also serves the external students, the University Library does provide as a part of its service precisely the kind of library which has been indicated. The reading rooms contain some 40,000 books on open access of which many of the general reference books are of great value to undergraduates. These may not be borrowed but the rooms are staffed with librarians who can give guidance in the use of the library and of reference books. There is also the Open Lending Library with, on open access, some 60,000 books obtainable with no delay, which is another part of the library to browse in, in addition to the reading rooms. There are perhaps 250,000 more books in the library which are available for loan. There is also the Periodicals Room where current numbers of some 2,500 periodicals can be seen, and the Periodicals Stack with 31,000 volumes of back numbers which is on open access to all readers. There is a detailed author catalogue to the library as a whole, there is a subject catalogue of books added since 1942 and there are many special catalogues.

But while all these services are well used by undergraduates they are also extensively used by postgraduates; and, just as the main library needs of undergraduates can be summarised, so can those of postgraduates. The research worker requires first of all a good general working library in all subjects. After that he must have in his field all the main basic works, the essential reference books, bibliographies and catalogues, series, standard editions and monographs, and periodicals: and the collection of periodicals must be extensive with complete runs of the chief journals. All this is essential, but after this the research worker cannot predict his needs: he may require anything. This demand obviously cannot be met in advance by any single library, but a large library can specialise and collect minor literature in a few subjects, and this, of course, opens up a fruitful field for co-operation with other libraries. For the rest, a library providing for the research worker must be ready to supply an information service, not only in making its own resources fully known but also in directing an inquirer to other libraries likely to be useful to him, in obtaining bibliographical information for him, in borrowing on his behalf from other libraries and in providing or obtaining photographic and Xerographic copies. This will include the obtaining of special material, such as university theses, microfilms and microcards. Furthermore, the library should provide special facilities for the research worker – carrells or special tables, typing rooms, microfilm readers, quick copying processes and recording and tape and disc playing equipment. All these things the library provides and its service is steadily increasing in value to research workers. Since 1946 it has appointed senior members of its staff to take responsibility for the main sections of the library, to become familiar with them and see that they are developed; and these assistants are able to help with bibliographical inquiries. In addition to the catalogues mentioned above, the library issues every two months Accessions Lists, grouped by subjects and it has also issued special bibliographies and the union catalogues of periodicals which have been mentioned.

Collections. But important as all these services are, the main thing for the research worker is that a library shall have the right books. The University Library has made and continues to make the strongest possible effort to meet the research worker's first need – to provide the basic reference and source books in most arts subjects; and it has a special strength in dictionaries, encyclopaedias and bibliographies.

As to the collections of particular importance, the special strengths in primary and secondary literature, the library has some research material of this kind in almost all arts fields and even in some others. Certain of these collections are of outstanding importance, others are less so and some are hardly more than small 'pockets' of interesting material. It is impossible to give a detailed account even of the chief of these but the following list shows some of the more interesting. Those collections which are of major importance are marked with an asterisk and further details of some of them are given below:

Agriculture, early works on	*Bibliography and bibliographies
Archaeology	Bimetallism
Architecture	Broadsides and proclamations
Art	Classical literature
Astronomy, early works on	Conjuring
*Bacon, Sir Francis	*Defoe, Daniel
Bank notes	*Dobson, Austin
Bibles	*East India Company

*Economics, early works on
*Education, early works and university
Egyptology
Elzevir Press books
Emblem books
*English literature
Finance and currency, early works on
France, Revolution and Napoleon
French language and literature
Italian language and literature
*Leibniz
Liberia and the slave trade
*Linguistics
*Local history and topography
*London
*London University
*Magic, early works on
*Mathematics, early works on
*Medical periodicals
*Music
Napoleon
Oastler, Richard
*Owen, Robert

*Palaeography
Papyrology
*Parliamentary papers (British)
Private presses
*Psychical research
*Psychology (particularly periodicals)
*Railways
Rastrick, J. U., and H.
Rationalism
*Shakespeare
*Shorthand
Short stories, particularly in English
*Slavery
Spanish books (of the fifteenth and nineteenth centuries)
Switzerland, history of
Temperance
*Theses (of London and of foreign universities)
Theses, bibliographies of
Transport
University calendars and magazines
Witchcraft and demonology
World War 1914–18

But a central university library naturally builds up research collections and in many other fields the library possesses material which, in a smaller library, would be regarded as special collections.

Of the special collections mentioned, the Goldsmiths' Library of Economic Literature is of outstanding importance. This great collection, now of about 70,000 volumes, was presented to the University Library in 1903 by the Worshipful Company of Goldsmiths. Its main strength lies in English works on economics and allied subjects but it also contains many foreign publications, and every attempt is made to add to the collection, particularly of books printed before 1851. There are many books in the Goldsmiths' Library printed since that date but, normally, additions of books later than 1850 are confined to certain special topics, e.g., slavery, transport and the City companies, in which the collection is very strong. The collecting in a comprehensive way of economics since 1850 is carried out by the Library of the London School of Economics. Next in importance for university study in the

special 'strengths' mentioned above is the collection of English literature and particularly Shakespeare. English literature is a vast subject
and no doubt the library only possesses a fraction of all the books in the
field, but of the important books it owns a very large fraction and of
the secondary literature its holdings are considerable. An acquisition
which greatly strengthened the English literature section was the
Sterling Library presented by Sir Louis Sterling in 1956, of which a
catalogue had been published in 1954. This contains many of the
treasures of English literature including a set of the Shakespeare folios
and three quartos. The library already possessed one set of the Shakespeare folios in the Durning-Lawrence Library. But the Sterling
Library brought so many fine books, as well as some important manuscripts, to the library that it is impossible to give any detailed account
of it here. It must be enough to say that it ranks high among outstanding
gifts of literary treasures received by any British library in modern
times.

The Shakespeare material in the University Library must, after the
'Copyright' Libraries and the Birmingham Public Library, be one of
the finest if not the finest in the country. It is true that the library is not
very strong in one important element in a Shakespeare library – viz.,
a large collection of contemporary Elizabethan literature – but even
here its resources are far from negligible: the library appears, for
example, to have more English books printed before 1640 than any
English university library outside Oxford, Cambridge and Durham.[10]
In editions of Shakespeare since the seventeenth century, and
in critical works it is believed that the library has few serious gaps and
it is strong in secondary Shakespearian material. It is also strong in
general literary and dramatic history and criticism, in linguistics and
philosophy and other fields which may be required by a student of
Shakespeare.

The Austin Dobson collection was presented by the poet's son, Mr.
Alban Dobson, in 1946 and has been added to, chiefly by Mr. Dobson,
since that time. It is as nearly a complete collection of printed works by
and about Austin Dobson as it is possible to gather and it includes
letters and other manuscripts.

But the collections in English literature are strong in so many fields –
the drama is one – and individual authors that further details cannot
be given. There are good collections in most modern western literatures and languages and in philosophy and branches of theology. The
library is rich in much material not only as the result of gifts but from

carefully selected purchases made over many years in carrying out its policy. And so in the Middlesex North Reading Room the library has on open shelves one of the finest collections of bibliographies in the country and in the Palaeography Room a very fine collection, also on open shelves, of catalogues and facsimiles of manuscripts and of monographs on palaeography and archives as well as periodicals dealing with these subjects.

In book selection the library has the indispensable help of the teaching staff of the University and it is particularly indebted to the Library Advisory Sub-committees of the Boards of Studies which have given such valuable service since the war.

Of manuscripts the library has only a small collection. Among the few medieval manuscripts, the *Life of the Black Prince* in Anglo-Norman French of about 1385, *Robert of Gloucester's Chronicle* of about 1440 and a *Piers Plowman* of a little earlier are the most notable. There is a fairly large collection of manuscript material of the sixteenth to eighteenth centuries in the Goldsmiths' Library; there are some interesting literary manuscripts – including manuscripts of Burns, Byron, Hogg, Scott and several writers of the twentieth century – in the Sterling Library, there are the Austin Dobson manuscripts and a large collection of manuscripts of Lady Ritchie (Anne Thackeray) and the library possesses over 4,000 letters chiefly of literary but with a few of musical interest – most of the latter having been presented by Miss Harriet Cohen – as well as other miscellaneous manuscript material.

Psychical research, magic and the occult are strongly represented in the library bequeathed by Mr. Harry Price; mathematics and astronomy in the library of Augustus de Morgan, which is rich in valuable early books in these fields. The library is also strong in modern mathematical periodicals. Psychology is well represented in the library's own collections but the library also houses on permanent deposit the library of the British Psychological Society which is one of the finest collections of psychological periodicals in the country. Mr. W. J. Carlton is in course of presenting his great library of books in and about shorthand. There are over 14,000 items in all, most of which have already been received.

Buildings. The building is part of the headquarters of the University of which the original architect was Dr. Charles Holden and the whole block comprises not only the Senate House, administrative offices and library but also certain colleges and schools of the University and the University Union. The library as planned before the war was, in fact, almost completed when war broke out, but the final part, the periodicals wing, was built only in 1959. Most of the reading rooms and the administrative offices are on the fourth floor, there is an open lending library on the second and third floors, there are special rooms on the fifth floor which also includes the library bindery and the Music Library, and the book stacks are on the sixth floor – which runs the whole length of the building and takes nearly 200,000 books – and in the tower. The photographic department is in the basement.

The reading rooms are built out round a central catalogue and book service hall and exhibition halls. The Goldsmiths' Room housing the main part of the Goldsmiths' Library seats sixty-eight readers and has eight carrells. The two Middlesex Rooms (North and South) each seat eighty readers and each have eight carrells – and the library would wish to miss no opportunity of expressing its gratitude to the Worshipful Company of Goldsmiths and to the Middlesex County Council for these fine rooms. The Middlesex South contains about 8,000 reference works in all subjects except law, music, palaeography and bibliography: the North also has 8,000 books which are mostly bibliographies but include general legal reference books. The Palaeography Room contains books on its subject and adjoins the Rare Books Room which was built for the Sterling Library. There is also the Periodicals Room seating ninety readers which has already been mentioned. The library is now completely shelved but, although all parts of the tower are in use, it will be some years before the building is full since there is room for about a million books. There are arguments for and against towers for book storage, but in a large city like London where ground space is very costly such overhead methods of storage are essential on grounds of economy. Given adequate lifts, a tower also offers easy access to books since there are as yet no mechanical devices for speedy horizontal travelling comparable to vertical lifts. London also provides arguments in favour of reading rooms on a floor well above ground level. In a smaller town, where a library can be built away from the sound, sight and fumes of traffic and away from other buildings, there would be an advantage in having reading rooms on the ground floor which do not have to be approached by lifts or stairs, but in London it is worth climbing a little to have the advantages of quiet, airiness and an unimpaired natural light which might not be possible on a ground floor.

Services. The library has over 12,500 currently registered readers and is available to all present internal staff and students, to all external students and to all graduates of the University. Other readers may be admitted in special circumstances. Both reference and lending services are given, and of the 140,000 books lent in 1958–59 about 10,400 were sent by post and the remainder borrowed by readers in person. The main special departments of the library are the Goldsmiths' Library, the Periodicals Room, the Palaeography Room and the Music Library, together with the general reference works and bibliographies in the Middlesex Rooms and the collections of parliamentary papers and of maps.

In addition to the main catalogues of the library mentioned above, the library regularly issues printed accessions lists of its additions and it has published a number of special catalogues and bibliographies of which the most recent are the catalogue of periodicals issued in 1956 and of the Robert Owen exhibition published in 1959: some other publications are mentioned in the *Guide to the Use of the Library*. The library is a centre for bibliographical inquiries of many kinds because of its great wealth of bibliographical material, and it receives from personal calls and by telephone and post numerous inquiries from libraries and other organisations, including many which are not associated with the University. Among other special services must be mentioned the microfilm and microcard readers and the very busy photographic department. The latter supplies, every year, large quantities of microfilms, photostats and other photographic copies of books and documents chiefly for members of the University and university institutions overseas.

In the future no doubt the library will become used even more for the deposit of small libraries and other collections of books and manuscripts. It is to be expected that its purchasing power will increase and that there will be gifts of books and manuscripts, and certainly the collection of material, printed and manuscript, relating to the University will grow extensively. It is certain, too, that the library's services will grow in extent and kind and that it will take an increasing part in the compilation of union catalogues, especially of periodicals, and other co-operative enterprises. The special collections naturally attract gifts and will continue to do so, and the library would take every opportunity of expressing gratitude to its great benefactors, particularly the Goldsmiths' Company, Sir Edwin Durning-Lawrence and Sir Louis Sterling, and its indebtedness to the devoted work of the first Goldsmiths' Librarian, R. A. Rye, and his sub-librarian Muriel S. Quinn.

Enough has been said to show that the University Library is developing on certain well-defined and normal lines in building up collections of books, periodicals and manuscript material, in supplying services and information and in co-operating with other libraries particularly within the University. A brief description of its growth and of some of its contents and activities has shown that something has been achieved; but there can naturally be no complacency, for there is much still to do and, in the nature of the task, that will always be the case. It can only be said that the development of the library has been rapid and extensive and that there is every sign that this development will continue.

NOTES AND REFERENCES

1 For notes on the proposals for establishing a university in London, reference may be made to WILSON, S. G.: The University of London, 1923; University of London. The historical record, 1926; University of London: Calendar "Historical Note' in current issue , and the first edition of the present work, pp. 125–127.

2 A slight difficulty in terminology may be noted here. 'The University' is sometimes used, at any rate for the nineteenth-century period, for the central organisation as distinct from the colleges. But in general use (as subsequently in this chapter) the term naturally refers to the University as a whole, the colleges and schools together with the central authority and its activities.

3 For the history of the University since 1836 reference should be made to LOGAN, D. W. The University of London, an introduction, 1955, and to the works noted above.

4 In this chapter the University Library is sometimes referred to simply as the library.

5 For accounts of other libraries in the University see Chapters XIII, XIV, XV.

6 WILKS, J., and LACEY, A. D. Catalogue of . . . Western palaeography 1921 (Univ. Library, Univ. College, King's College). Various union catalogues of periodicals have been published (A General Supplement to BUCOP, American History, Psychology, Law, Classics, Germanic Studies, Medicine, Botany, and Mathematics) some of which include libraries outside the University, and others are in preparation (Romance Studies and Theology) and a catalogue of Incunabula is almost ready for the press.

7 RYE, R. A. The students' guide to the libraries of London. 3rd edition, 1927.

8 The Standing Conference of Librarians of the Libraries of the University of London (SCOLLUL) was established in November 1955. There had previously been committees of librarians.

9 These needs were also set out in a lecture to Convocation of the University of London on 10 January, 1959.

10 RAMAGE, D. A finding list of English books to 1640. 1958.

CHAPTER XIII

THE LIBRARY OF UNIVERSITY COLLEGE LONDON

By J. W. Scott
Librarian

HISTORY AND DEVELOPMENT

THE Library of University College London in Gower Street has had an unbroken history since it was first opened to students on 19th January, 1829. Although its history has been admirably told already by Professor H. Hale Bellot and R. W. Chambers in Chapter 13 of Hale Bellot's *University College London, 1826–1926*,[1] and also by Reginald Arthur Rye in his *Students' guide to the libraries of London*,[2] it may be worth setting out in full the first detailed statement made on the library:

LIBRARY.

"A collection of Books, amounting to more than 6000 volumes, was laid open for the use of the Students on the 19th of January [1829]. The Rev. Dr. Cox, who was appointed Librarian in July 1827, but without salary until his services should be required, entered upon the duties of his office as soon as a room was ready for the reception of the books, and he attends daily from ten in the morning to four in the afternoon. By carefully watching opportunities, a considerable number of books have been obtained upon very moderate terms. The great object has been to confine the purchase to books most useful for the purposes of education. The vicinity of the British Museum, and the facilities of access to the noble collections in that establishment, render it unnecessary to buy rare and very expensive works; so long, at least, as the funds of the University are inadequate to the accomplishment of objects of more immediate importance.

"The University Library at present consists of 6500 volumes, of which 5340 have been purchased, the remainder being donations. A commencement has also been made of a Collection of such Maps, Plans, &c. as may be useful in the several branches of study, and more especially in the Latin and Greek classes.

"Dr. Cox has nearly completed one Catalogue, and is preparing others, in order to provide every practicable facility for consulting the books. The Council have not yet been able to do more than frame temporary Regulations for the management of the Library: they are, however, particularly anxious to render it as extensively useful as may be found consistent with the security and preservation of the books, and with this view are endeavouring to form a plan by which the books may be lent to the Students for use at their own houses.

"A large proportion of the Law Students being engaged professionally during the early part of the day, and it being inexpedient on many accounts to open the general Library in the evening, a separate room has been allotted for Law Books, to be open from five to nine each evening." [Later in 1829 a separate Medical Library was opened near the Anatomy Theatre.]

Dr. Francis Augustus Cox who held office as Librarian until only 1831 is probably the only librarian to be summarised in the *Concise Dictionary of National Biography* as "Baptist Minister: a wealthy man:". As a minister of religion he was not able to hold a place on the Council of the College but was appointed Librarian instead. Fortunately the catalogue which he himself wrote out has been traced with certainty. The two earliest manuscript catalogues still existing are his alphabetical catalogue of the General Library in two volumes kept up to date until about 1849, and a separate manuscript catalogue of the Law Library which was commenced in December 1849 and finished in April 1850 by William James Champion.

Other sources which still exist for the history of the library are the Minutes of the General Library Committee from Friday, 7th May, 1852, until 5th April, 1876, although from a resolution of their meeting on 5th December, 1859, where we read "that Mr. Foster's letter be referred to the Medical Library Committee", it can be inferred that there had been since 1829, a separate committee for the Medical Library. The minutes, however, are extremely brief, and for many years there was only one meeting of the committee and indeed in certain years it never met at all. It is indeed no surprise to read the resolution of 2nd November, 1857: "That the Library Committee as at present constituted does not work well. – Carried unanimously." A report of the Senate on the appointment and duties of the Library Committee, laying down regulations for the holding of their meeting and the conduct of their business, was adopted by the College Council on 7th July, 1877, and from that date until May 1920 the minutes of the committee were written in substantial quarto ledgers which still exist in the library (with the exception of No. 3 for October 1903 to June 1909). It is interesting to note here, however, that the retention of manuscript minutes until 1920 was obviously the maintenance of tradition rather than resistance of innovation, for we read in the minutes of 3rd March, 1887 "with reference to the preparation of the supplementary catalogue Mr. Horsburgh reported for Professor Goodwin and himself that after examining various specimens of type-writing they had decided to entrust the work of type-writing the entry slips to Misses McLachlan and Lock who had undertaken to do the work at the rate of 1s. per 1,000 words".

A third source for the history of the Library is a series of manuscript accessions registers. The first five volumes cover the years 1830 to 1889 completely; volumes VI and VII cannot be traced, but volume VIII takes the series from January 1912 without any further break to the present day. Volume II and the first seven pages of Volume III record, under the date 1st February 1833, the gift of 4,000 books and sixty-one pamphlets from Jeremy Bentham who had died the year before. A separate volume records donations to the Medical Library between 17th February 1837 and 10th March 1875.

A fourth source is a series of large folio letter-books of documents bearing upon the library from 1910–28, after which time such documents were embodied in a modern filing system. A similar separate letter-book for the Mocatta Library Committee covers the period 1906–25. Finally, there is a "Professor's suggestion book" (although it is sad to notice that even here the apostrophe is misplaced) which covers the period from 19th November, 1877 to 1907.

The descriptions of the library by Chambers[1] and Rye[2] mentioned above are still the fullest and best, for the brief list of principal collections in the library compiled by Luxmoore Newcombe, 1927,[3] adds little to them, or to the list which currently appears in the *Calendar* of University College London. Newcombe did, however, compile a detailed history of the library up to 1926[3] which though never published can be only briefly summarised here. Dr. Cox was Librarian from 1827, with an assistant Joseph Gimson from October 1830. Unfortunately in December 1831 Cox fell a victim to urgent economies so Gimson continued alone. On his resignation, John F. Kennel was appointed Librarian from 12th November, 1834, at £60 per annum. Kennel resigned on 22nd July, 1841, and William James Champion, a student of the Schoolmasters' class was chosen as sub-librarian of the General Library. In October of the same year H. B. Tuson was appointed sub-librarian of the Medical Library. After Champion's resignation in 1850 no more sub-librarians were appointed and both libraries were run by beadles for nearly twenty years. In 1858 Council considered appointing a librarian, but waited until January 1868 before appointing Arthur Henry Bleek as Librarian to superintend all College libraries. In April 1871 Adrian Wheeler, after experience in New College, London, and at the Royal Society was also appointed to arrange the Graves Library. From 1st August, 1871, Bleek was not re-engaged and Wheeler became Librarian. In 1901, Raymond Wilson Chambers (Librarian 1901–24, Professor of English Language and Literature 1922–41) was appointed Librarian, and (as he himself says[1]) "was fortunate . . . in being able to collect round him a group of energetic and scholarly young men, fresh from school, who mostly worked for their degree simultaneously with their library work". These young men were Luxmoore Newcombe, later Librarian of University College London 1924–26 and of the National Central Library 1926–45, Richard Offor, Librarian of the University of Leeds 1919–47, Wilfrid Bonser, Librarian of the University of Birmingham 1929–52, and John Wilks who remained in the library all his working life, serving as Librarian from 1926 to 1954. Recent papers by two of this group add interesting personal notes of the history of the library. The first is the Chambers Memorial Lecture of 1953 delivered by John Wilks, [4] which incidentally records the lovely remark made by A. E. Housman to Chambers when he was appointed Librarian: "Ah, Chambers, now you will be like the Devil. On thy belly shalt thou go and dust shalt thou eat all the days of thy life." The second is an article by Richard Offor, entitled *Reminiscences of a University Librarian*[5] which shows how apposite was Housman's remark, for the dust which had settled on the library uninterruptedly for three decades from 1871 seems to have been one of Chambers's greatest problems. At least the remarkable bibliographical finds which Dr. Offor and his colleagues discovered beneath that dust are still in the library to this day, and one of them indeed, the *Nuremberg Chronicle*, had been in the library since 1833, for it is recorded in the 1833 accession register amongst the books presented by Jeremy Bentham. It is no exaggeration to regard Chambers as a creator of the library as we know it today: for he gave it a well-trained staff, open access, considerable physical expansion, [6] the card catalogue, the nucleus of the collection of medieval manuscripts, four of its printed catalogues and five of its deposited libraries.

Turning to the development of the library in terms of the space it has occupied in College, it is sad to see that at the very outset the Great Library was never completed as originally planned and in 1828 the General Library was instead housed in the Small Library, and a separate Medical Library was established in 1829. The General Library, as it has long been known, running out from west to east behind the main building of the College was designed in 1848 by Professor Thomas Donaldson, who then held the chair of architecture in the College. It contained everything except the Medical Library until 1873 when the original Small Library was again taken over under the name of the South Library.

Chambers gained the seminar libraries he had long advocated[7] in 1907 when University College School and the School of Advanced Medical Studies both left the College to become independent, autonomous bodies. The library was then able to expand down the steps of the General Library along the length of both corridors leading out of the Flaxman Gallery, for the whole length of the first floor of the main building. The next major addition to library space was the opening of a medical sciences library in the new Anatomy building erected in 1923 by a gift from the Rockefeller Foundation. The opportunity was taken to commemorate Sir George Thane who had held the chair of Anatomy from 1877 to 1919 by calling it the Thane Library. A photograph and description of the building occur in a paper by Sir Grafton Elliot Smith,[8] the then professor of Anatomy. Finally, in 1938 the Foster Court Science Library was opened in a building in the southern part of the College and was described in a paper[9] by the Librarian, John Wilks.

At the outbreak of the 1939–45 war, the manuscripts and rare books were evacuated to Aberystwyth to join the treasures of many other libraries and galleries in the solid rock cellars beneath the National Library of Wales; any who ever saw those amazing Aladdin's Caves filled with manuscripts, pictures and rare books will never forget the sight. The Medical Library was evacuated to Leatherhead in 1940 when the Faculty of Medical Sciences reassembled there after its initial evacuation to Cardiff and Sheffield. On 24th September, 1940, the library to the north of the Dome and the Gustave Tuck Library were burnt out with heavy losses of books in the Science Library, the English, German, Scandinavian, Phonetics and Advanced Arts Libraries and the Mocatta Library of Anglo-Jewish history, estimated in the College report of 1940–41 to involve nearly 100,000 books and pamphlets in all. In August 1940 College administration had been established at Stanstead Bury, Stanstead Abbotts, and the library was ultimately removed there, before the air raid on 16th April, 1941, when the main block south of the Dome and the Dome itself were burned out.

The return of all the evacuated books was finally completed in session 1948–49 when the manuscripts and rare books were returned from Aberystwyth. At the end of session 1953–54 Sir Albert Richardson's reconstruction of the main building was completed, although the new Gustave Tuck Theatre and Mocatta Library were now at the south of the College and not the north; the library's only additional space to its pre-war holding was in Nos. 24, 25 and 26 Gordon Square for its collections in History and Political Economy. Finally, in session 1955–56 the library acquired storage space for some 100,000 volumes in the basement of Flaxman House in Flaxman Terrace.

The College Library which now holds some 660,000 books and pamphlets is housed as follows: the first floor of the main building holds the Physical Sciences Library in a two-storey building at the north end; six Arts Libraries in the corridor leading to the Flaxman Gallery hold collections in Philosophy, Hebrew, Linguistics, Phonetics, Italian, Classics, French, Ancient History, and Archaeology (Yates Library); the General Library (or Donaldson Library) leading out of the Flaxman Gallery holds the Law Library, the Scandinavian collection, the Arts Libraries of Architecture, Fine Art and Psychology together with a general reference section; the southern corridor leading from the Flaxman Gallery to the South Junction houses a room for the display of current periodicals in the arts subjects, a small room for the Ogden Library, administrative rooms for the library staff together with a small strong room, and the main issue desk and catalogue hall. In the South Junction are the Library of the Folk Lore Society, the German Library, and the English Library, which is known as the Chambers Memorial Library. Directly above, on the second floor of the main building is the reconsituted Gustave Tuck Lecture Theatre and Mocatta Library.

The History and Political Economy collections are housed in the four houses in the north-west corner of Gordon Square which house the departments of these subjects. The Biological Sciences Library (including Geography and Geology) is in the library on the first floor of the Foster Court building which was originally opened in 1938. The Thane Library of Medical Sciences is still in the rooms which were allotted to it in the Anatomy building in 1923; departmental collections under the control of the College Library exist in the departments of Anthropology, Architecture, Egyptology (Edwards Library), Librarianship and Town Planning.

Stack books are housed in a store above the Arts Libraries, in the basement of the Gordon Square houses, a mezzanine stack in the Thane Library, and in Flaxman House.

CATALOGUES

In addition to the fragmentary manuscript catalogues already mentioned above, the following printed catalogues have been issued by the library:

1. Catalogue of books in the library belonging to the Medical Society of University College. London. 1843.
2. Catalogue of books in the General Library, etc. 3 v. 1879.
3. Supplement to the catalogue, 1879, etc. [containing additions to the year 1886]. 1897.
4. Catalogue of books in the Medical and Biological Libraries, etc. 1887.
5. Additions to the libraries during 1887–(1900). 1888–(1901).
6. [T. Whittaker]. Report on the Bentham MSS. at University College London, with Catalogue [1892].
7. R. A. Rye. Catalogue of the printed books and manuscripts forming the Library of Frederic David Mocatta. 1904.
8. R. W. Chambers. Catalogue of the Dante collection. 1910.
9. L. Newcombe. Catalogue of the periodical publications. 1912.
10. J. Wilks and A. D. Lacey. Catalogue of works dealing with the study of Western palaeography in the libraries of the University of London . . . and at University College and at King's College. 1921.
11. W. Bonser. Catalogue of the geological books in the library . . . , including the library of the Geologists' Association. 1927.
12. Dorothy K. Coveney. A descriptive catalogue of manuscripts in the library of University College London. 1935.
13. A. Taylor Milne. Catalogue of the manuscripts of Jeremy Bentham in the library of University College London. 1937.

The card catalogue originated by Chambers in his 1901 reorganisation has now developed as follows: the catalogue hall in the main building contains an author catalogue of the complete holdings of the library compiled on the dictionary principle, together with a classified catalogue which has been in process of compilation since the task of classifying the library was first undertaken in 1950. The original cataloguing rules were based on those of the British Museum, but modifications from the Anglo-American code were adopted over the years. The rules were considerably revised to bring them more into line with the code and any probable revision of the code in 1955 and again in 1959. The changes made in 1955 were described by A. E. Tooth at the time,[10] and a paper on the changes of 1959 by the same author has now been published. The classification of the library begun in 1950, follows a classification scheme devised by Kenneth Garside[11] (Deputy Librarian at University College 1947–58 and now Librarian of King's College London). The sectional libraries of Physical Sciences, Medical Sciences, Biological Sciences, and History and Political Economy, have card catalogues of the books in their sections copied from the entries in the main card catalogue. Similar catalogues of copied entries exist in the departmental libraries in Egyptology, Anthropology, Architecture, Town Planning and Librarianship. Two interesting union catalogues have been compiled in sheaf form; one is a Swedish Union Catalogue giving details of Swedish books and books of Swedish interest in the libraries of the British Museum and the library of University College; the second is a similar union catalogue of the Norwegian books and books dealing with Norwegian language and literature in the libraries of the British Museum and of this College. A handlist of scientific periodicals in the library was duplicated for internal library use in 1954 and a little earlier a list of German periodicals was duplicated. Although it is obvious that additions to the library have rendered the majority of the printed catalogues mentioned above out of date, the library still maintains up-to-date annotated copies of the catalogues of the Bentham manuscripts, of the Dante collection, and of Miss Coveney's manuscript catalogue. and hopes in the future to issue revised editions of these three catalogues, and also catalogues of several of the special collections such as the Graves Library, the Mocatta Library, the Ogden Library, the Chadwick Papers, and the Landsdowne Tracts.

THE MANUSCRIPT COLLECTIONS

There is no doubt that the most interesting and important group of manuscript material is that which bears upon the social, educational and political reform movements of the beginning of the nineteenth century of which movements, of course, the very buildings of the College are to some extent a physical expression. This group consists of the following five blocks of letters and papers: 75,000 sheets of Jeremy Bentham manuscripts; 50,000 letters and papers addressed to Lord Brougham; over 250 boxes of the papers of Sir Edwin Chadwick; the Minute books, Letter books, correspondence, etc., of the Society for the Diffusion of Useful Knowledge; and finally, the official correspondence of the College itself during the first fifteen years of its existence from 1825 to 1840.

Bentham

Jeremy Bentham in his will of 30th May, 1832, of which a draft is still preserved in the Bentham manuscripts, left all his papers to his young colleague John Bowring whom he appointed as his executor "for the better enabling him to publish a complete edition of his works". After Bowring had completed the eleven volume edition published by William Tait in Edinburgh in 1843, he retained the papers for only a few years more before handing them over to the College. A minute of the College Committee dated 31st January, 1849, records Bowring's gift to the College of 148 parcels and cases of manuscripts of Jeremy Bentham. Unfortunately the manuscripts were not opened for many years, and it was not until 1887 that Adrian Wheeler, the then Librarian, made the first list of them. Some fifteen years later concern was still felt in the College over the difficulty of making full use of the Bentham papers and on 13th January, 1892, the Committee of Management of the College recorded that a letter had been received from Mr. J. Power Hicks, a Life Governor of the College, suggesting that the condition and accessibility of the manuscripts should be investigated. He further offered a sum of £50 towards any expenses the Council might think it desirable to incur in examining, copying or type-writing the manuscripts in question. After inquiring into the position through Professor Croom Robertson, who as Professor of Philosophy held the list made some years previously by the Librarian, it was decided to accept Mr. Power Hicks' generous offer and use the money to engage a "competent scholar" to make a detailed catalogue and report. Professor Croom Robertson recommended one Thomas Whittaker, formerly sub-editor of the periodical *Mind*, and these recommendations were accepted. It is interesting to note that these early minutes are signed by Professor W. P. Ker who was at that time the Chairman of the Library Committee.

One of the first direct results of the appearance of the catalogue in 1892 was a request from Professor Elie Halévy some years later to study the Bentham manuscripts. Thomas Whittaker notes at the end of his catalogue a supplementary catalogue of boxes, numbered 149 to 155, which held Bentham papers from the Chadwick manuscripts which had arrived during the arranging and cataloguing of the original 148 boxes. A note in the handwriting of R. W. Chambers dated 1907 in the library's copy of Whittaker's report records the further addition of boxes 156 to 168 which had been found in the College in 1903, and later additions to the Bentham manuscripts which now fill 177 boxes include a box presented by Miss Ruth Butler in memory of her brother, Professor H. E. Butler, Professor of Latin in this College from 1911 to 1943. Finally, in 1953, the arrival of the Ogden Library in the College added thirty-three more Bentham letters, and a most unusual group of eight from Bentham's father to Richard Clark, together with two letter-books of Sir John Bowring with various letters to or about Jeremy Bentham. In 1932 when C. K. Ogden was invited to deliver an address[12] to mark the centenary of the death of Bentham, he closed his remarks as follows: "I offer three concrete suggestions for those who desire this Centenary to have some practical outcome." Of which the second suggestion in his own words, was:

"By the courtesy of the Library Committee, I and others have had access to them, but until Professor Halévy decided to sacrifice himself, no one had actually read more than a few pages; and they have never been studied at all from the point of view of symbolic theory.

"They were officially catalogued many years ago, but the collation was not sufficiently circumspect to prevent the re-interment of two parts of one complete unpublished work in two quite different sarcophagi.

"They may be safe from fire and theft; but they enjoy no immunity from Acts of God, or of the King's Enemies, or from the still more maleficent ravages of Time. The last risk is the most serious, because certain of the inks employed by Bentham and his amanuenses are fading rapidly, and many of the pencilled notes are already undecipherable.

"They will, however, be fortunate to survive the next War; in which, if science continues to be applied chiefly for destructive purposes, one single bomb should be more than sufficient to blow the entire British Museum a *kilometre* into the air.

"The cost of duplicating the 5000 most promising sheets – by photostat or other methods – need not exceed £100. The other 70,000 could then be vicariously exploited during the next decades, by such documentary adventurers as American enthusiasm will undoubtedly supply – if only as a result of the present Celebrations."

As a result of this, it was decided to ask Mr. A. Taylor Milne to ensure that each document was numbered and adequately preserved, to prepare a detailed catalogue,[13] and to add a subject catalogue and index to correspondents. Since its appearance in 1937 this proved a most effective key by which scholars can make their first entry into this mass of manuscript material.

Following the works published by Professor Halévy in 1901–04,[14] Professor C. W. Everett, of Columbia University, commenced work upon them in 1926 and has continued doing so since, producing a number of books[15] which embody considerable transcriptions from the manuscripts. Other manuscripts have been transcribed in books edited by Dr. William Stark[16] and by the late C. K. Ogden.[17] In 1959 Lord Cohen, Chairman of the College Committee, accepted the chairmanship of a National Bentham Publications Committee to publish a complete edition of the works of Jeremy Bentham, in which any of the manuscripts still not edited will be able to take their place, whilst others will prove invaluable in the re-editing of Bowring's edition.

Brougham

The collection of 50,000 letters addressed to Lord Brougham came to College in 1953 as the most important single section of the Ogden Library. The late C. K. Ogden had published a description of some of the main points of interest within the Brougham papers in his own periodical *Psyche*.[18] When the letters arrived in College they were still to a considerable extent tied up in the same bundles with the legal red tape which had been tied around them by Sir Denis Le Marchant who acted for so long as Brougham's secretary. Professor Aspinall of Reading University was the first scholar to use the Brougham papers after their purchase by Ogden at Sotheby's on 15th May, 1938, although unfortunately not until some time after he had published his book on *Lord Brougham and the Whig party*. Although he was only able to see them briefly under the difficult conditions of war-time storage, he produced two most interesting papers[19] on problems of dating in Brougham's life and memoirs, and Le Marchant's reports. The most intensive work on the collection was carried out in 1956 by Professor Chester W. New, Emeritus Professor of History from McMaster University, Canada, who examined the whole collection in the preparation of his definitive biography of Lord Brougham. The papers are now being indexed in the College Library and an individual card giving the full name of the correspondent, the date of the letter, a brief summary of its contents, and a number by which the letter can be quoted is being made for each letter. At the time of writing some 33,000 letters have been dealt with and some twenty or thirty scholars from various parts of the world have already made use of the collection. It is hoped that ultimately a catalogue giving at least the correspondents in alphabetical order of name will be published by the College. The

Brougham letters include material on the trial of Queen Caroline, the anti-slavery question, on the development of London University, the Society for the Diffusion of Useful Knowledge, the Mechanics' Institutes, and other educational activities, a considerable number of legal papers with letters on legal reform and many letters and papers connected with the National Association for the Promotion of Social Science. Amongst the many correspondents are: Lords Denman, Grey, Holland, Lyndhurst, Murray, Normanby, Lord John Russell and Lord Wellesley; George Birkbeck, Thomas Coates, Sir David Brewster, Gladstone, M. D. Hill, Francis Jeffreys, Augustus de Morgan, Joseph Parkes, Zachary Macaulay, William Shepherd, William Wilberforce, Sir John Eardley Wilmot; Brougham's step-daughter Lady Malet, Miss Louisa Octavia Hope, Madame Blaze de Bury, Guizot and two Americans, Edward Everett and Charles Sumner.

Chadwick

The letters and papers of Sir Edwin Chadwick, the sanitary reformer and disciple of Bentham, were given to the College in 1898 through Sir Benjamin Richardson and supplemented in 1905 by a further collection of 500 of his books and pamphlets. The collection consists of correspondence with Chadwick, together with memoranda, reports, pamphlets and newspaper cuttings covering the period 1828–90. They are at present arranged in a series of 268 boxes in which they are roughly grouped by alphabetical order of subject. The subjects include such items as cholera, deportation, education, electoral reform, the improvements of London 1856, local government, police, poor law, railways and sanitation; and amongst the correspondents are to be found such names as Prince Albert, the Empress Victoria of Germany, Disraeli, Gladstone, J. S. Mill and Lord John Russell. In 1952 there appeared two books on Chadwick by scholars who had worked through the Chadwick collection in University College: S. E. Finer's *Life and times of Sir Edwin Chadwick*[20] and R. S. Lewis's *Edwin Chadwick and the public health movement*.[21] The library looks forward to the day when it may issue a detailed catalogue of the Chadwick papers, but in the meantime finds that the two books mentioned above are the most effective ways of making use of the collection.

S.D.U.K.

In 1848 the manuscript minutes, letter and account books of the Society for the Diffusion of Useful Knowledge together with letters, papers and receipts were deposited in University College Library by Thomas Coates who at that time was Secretary to the Society and had also been Secretary to the College until 1835. It is, however, rather sad to read in his letter of 10th October, 1860, to Lord Brougham "it was a great mistake in me to part with the archives of the Society. They exist and are obtainable; but are in a cellar in University College and are difficult of access." The papers were studied in considerable detail for a Ph.D. thesis presented in 1932 by Miss Monica C. Grobel.[22] The thesis (in four volumes) contains in an appendix a detailed description of the papers which forms the best index to them, as well as a prefatory description of the collection.

College correspondence

The archives of the College used by Professor H. Hale Bellot in writing the history of the College in 1926 were listed by Miss H. Raven Hart in 1927;[23] unfortunately most of these archives were lost in the destruction of the Records department during the recent war. However, one group which had already been transferred to the library was preserved; this is the correspondence of the College during the period 1825–40, now arranged in a series of sixty-nine boxes, each letter being numbered consecutively from 1 to 4,864. A card index in the library gives the names of the principal correspondents, many of whom were active both in the College and in the Society for the Diffusion of Useful Knowledge which was so closely linked with the College; the following are represented by twenty letters or more: Professor A. Amos, Lord Auckland, Professor J. Austin, Dr. George Birkbeck, Lord Brougham, Professor J. Conolly, Professor Samuel Cooper, Dr. F. A. Cox, Professor Augustus De Morgan, Professor John Elliotson, Professor R. E. Grant, Joseph Hume, Professor T. H. Key, Professor John Lindley, Professor J. R. McCulloch, Professor Henry Malden, Sir Anthony Panizzi, Professor G. S. Pattison, Professor Richard Quain, the Duke of Somerset, Professor Anthony Todd Thomson, William Tooke.

It is remarkably appropriate that the five collections of manuscripts described above should have all come together from different sources into the library of University College, to form a composite whole in the very building where the auto-icon of Jeremy Bentham is still to be found. The detailed and accurately documented story of how the auto-icon of Jeremy Bentham was originally prepared and how it came to rest in this College has been fully told by Charles Marmoy, the Librarian of the Thane Library.[24]

Medieval manuscripts

Apart from an odd isolated gift such as the lovely twelfth-century Latin Bible presented to College by William Steere as early as October 1859, the bulk of the medieval manuscripts added to the library before 1900 had been those in the Graves collection of mathematics and early science. Of these Graves manuscripts eleven are of the fourteenth to fifteenth century and forty are of the seventeenth and eighteenth centuries. The eleven early Graves manuscripts form a most interesting group, as astronomical, astrological, mathematical and medical manuscripts of this date are so much more rare than theological or liturgical manuscripts. Two of them, Mss. Lat. 16 and 17, embody excellent *volvelles* displaying orbits of the planets, signs of the zodiac, and other information bearing upon the construction of calendars. There is also a manuscript of the *Tractatus de sphera* written by Johannes de Sacrobosco at the very beginning of the fourteenth century, which is not included in the list of known manuscripts set out by Lynn Thorndike in his recent book on Sacrobosco.[25] Another Graves scientific manuscript of the fifteenth century is delightfully illuminated with a series of coloured ink drawings for the occupations of the month and for the signs of the zodiac. Professor Priebsch, Professor of German 1898–1931, took a great part in developing the study of palaeography in the College, and with the help of Chambers and Dr. Seton, the Secretary of the College, succeeded in persuading friends of the College from time to time to make purchases of manuscripts, as, for example, the fifteen medieval German manuscripts bought with contributions totalling £408 at the Phillipps sale in April 1911. The disappointing story of the complicated negotiations between College and the German Government and Emperor in connection with other Phillipps manuscripts has been told by Mr. A. N. L. Munby.[26] Amongst manuscript fragments bought at Bonn in 1921 is the earliest manuscript in the library: a part of one folio of a seventh-century uncial manuscript of St. Mark's Gospel. The manuscripts were fully described and catalogued by Miss Dorothy K. Coveney in a catalogue published in 1935, at which date the collection totalled ten fragments and 203 manuscripts: of which nine fragments and fifty-seven manuscripts were written before 1600. Four of the most interesting are:

a thirteenth-century lectionary on uterine parchment with minia-
tures and capitals in gold, red and blue;

a thirteenth-century manuscript of Rabanus Maurus' commentary
on St. Matthew's Gospel from Pontigny;

a large fifteenth-century illuminated manuscript of translations into
German of *Alexander the Great* together with Guido delle Colonne's
Historia Troiana;

and the Auchinleck manuscript of Hector Boece's *Hystory of Scotland*
translated by John Bellendene.

Since that date seventeen manuscripts have been added to the collection, particularly on 28th July, 1927, when six fifteenth-century
manuscripts were bought at Sotheby's sale of the manuscripts of the
British Society for Franciscan Studies and of Walter Seton. These
additions to Miss Coveney's catalogue have been catalogued by Mr.
Neil Ker of Oxford, under the co-operative scheme for recording
uncatalogued manuscripts organised recently by the Standing Conference of National and University Libraries. It can be seen therefore from
the above notes that Rye's mention in 1927 of ninety-six manuscripts
"earlier than the year 1500" should have been "earlier than the year
1800".

Charters

There is in addition to the medieval manuscripts a small collection of
charters in the College Library of which the earliest is Roger Morti-
mer's charter of 1199 to the Abbey of Cwmhir in Radnorshire which
was presented to the library by Mr. G. E. Walker of the College
Committee in January 1957. A collection of eighteen German charters
of the fourteenth to sixteenth centuries was presented to College in
1912 by the German Emperor as part of the recompense for those
Phillipps manuscripts which he and the German Government had
retained.

Professorial collections

The collections of letters and papers bequeathed by former professors
of the College form an interesting group of manuscripts. They include
Robert E. Grant (Anatomy 1828–74), Augustus De Morgan (Mathematics 1828–31), Thomas Graves (Jurisprudence 1838–43), F. C. Montague

(History 1893–1927), W. C. Clinton (Electrical Engineering 1926–34), A. F. Murison (Roman Law and Jurisprudence 1883–1925), Sir William Ramsay (Chemistry 1887–1913), W. P. Ker (English 1889–1922), Arthur Platt (Greek 1894–1925), Sir Ambrose Fleming (Electrical Engineering 1885–1926), F. G. Donnan (Chemistry 1913–37), and R. W. Chambers (English 1922–41). The majority of these professorial collections include manuscript notes of lectures and articles. A most amusing link between two professors is found in a manuscript of forty-six leaves by Professor J. T. Graves giving 2,862 anagrams on the name of Augustus De Morgan in English, Latin, French and German. Professor Murison left manuscript editions of texts of Theophilus and Justinian. The Ramsay papers include the actual laboratory notebooks in which he and his colleagues recorded the details of their experiments on the rare gases. The Fleming collection includes a series of most interesting manuscript notebooks describing the historical and exciting story of the first transmission of wireless signals from Professor Fleming's research station at Poldhu in Cornwall. The W. P. Ker papers contained sufficient unpublished material for a posthumous book on modern literature to be edited by Professors James Sutherland and Terence Spencer.[27] Similarly from the manuscripts and papers left to the library by R. W. Chambers, Professor George Kane has been able to draw considerable help for his work on Piers Plowman.[28]

Mocatta

The two most important manuscripts in the Mocatta Library are a _Haggadah for Passover_, heavily illuminated in gold and colour, probably executed in the fifteenth century, and a _Mahzōr for the whole year_ according to the Italian rite also illuminated with gold and colour, probably executed in the early part of the sixteenth century. The Lucien Wolf collection bequeathed in 1931 included fifty-three boxes of manuscript or typescript notes on Jewish genealogy dealing largely with the middle period of the history of Jews in England between the expulsion and the resettlement, including some material on the genealogy of medieval Spanish Jewry. Finally, the Myer David Davis collection comprises some 340 exercise-books of notes on names of Jews extracted from Calendars of State papers and other published historical sources such as the Rolls series and the Camden Society publications. They deal largely with Jews living in England prior to the expulsion of 1290. The notes formed the basis of a number of papers by M. D. Davis which are listed in Cecil Roth's *Magna Bibliotheca*.[29]

Ogden

Just as the fifty-one Graves manuscripts provided the start of the manuscript collection, so the Ogden collection made the greatest single addition by adding thirty-one individual manuscripts written prior to 1700, and the Bacon-Tottel collection of fifty-four volumes almost entirely in manuscript. Unfortunately, an adequate description of the manuscripts must await the publication of a separate paper on the Ogden Library, just as a full description of the Ogden collection must await some form of descriptive handlist or catalogue which it is hoped to issue. However, one may mention briefly here a fourteenth-century annotated manuscript Ovid, and a most important group of seventeen Elizabethan and Jacobean manuscripts with considerable interest for Bacon and Shakespeare scholars. This includes an early manuscript of *Leicester's Commonwealth*, the Earl of Northumberland's manuscript copy of Grimaldus' *The Counsellor*,[30] a manuscript *Chronicle for 1569–74*, a manuscript entitled *Historie of actiones done in England concerning Essex, Carr, Northampton and Overbury*, and a manuscript dated 1577 of William Lambarde's *Nomina Saxonica*, supported by four copies of the printed edition of 1581. Bacon is represented not only by a manuscript of *The controversys in the Church of England*, but also by the important Bacon-Tottel collection. This was discovered by Marcham at Shardeloes in forty-eight volumes, which have since been increased to fifty-four. Both the content of the manuscripts themselves, and the form and style of the marginal annotations, reveal problems of ownership of the greatest interest. The books contain several passages copied from the works of Bacon, and those numbered 9–10 and 12–38 are commonplace-books with entries revealing very close links with both Bacon and Richard Tottel. Amongst later manuscripts in the Ogden Library the forged catalogue of Shakespeare's Library made by W. H. Ireland is the most interesting item in a small Ireland collection. There are also 826 letters of John Bright covering the period 1847–78, as well as sixty-seven letters of Emile Zola to Marius Roux written between 1864 and 1885. Coming to the twentieth century we find a most important Arnold Bennett manuscript collection of over 2,000 letters from Arnold Bennett to the firm of Pinker who acted as his agent, together with the author's corrected manuscripts of *The man from the*

north and *Body and soul*. The collection includes a manuscript original
of *Women today and tomorrow*, 1919, and eleven letters from Joseph
Conrad, nineteen from Roger Fry, and forty-four from André Gide,
to Bennett.

BOOK COLLECTIONS

In the early years the individuals who had been principally concerned
with the foundation of the College gave considerable help to the
library. A gift of about 4,000 books came from Jeremy Bentham himself as early as 1833. In 1837, three years after the death of Robert
Morrison, a missionary who had translated the Bible into Chinese,
College accepted the splendid Chinese Library of 15,000 volumes which
he had left on condition that the appointment was made of a professor
of Chinese for five years at a salary of £60 a year. Samuel Kidd, who
had been professor of Chinese in the Anglo-Chinese College which
Morrison had founded in Malacca, was appointed to the chair. After
Kidd's early death in 1843 the appointment lapsed for some time, and
ultimately the library was transferred to the School of Oriental and
African Studies. The Ricardo fund, which was subscribed by the public
in 1839, has from the very outset been of great importance in building
up the Ricardo Library of Political Economy. In 1828, and in later
years, Lord Chief Justice Denman presented sets of the *Journals* of the
House of Commons and of the House of Lords together with other
parliamentary papers. In 1847 the law library of William Blackburne
(2,500 volumes) was presented by his sister, and in 1855 the large
parliamentary collections of Joseph Hume came to the library. In 1850
Edward Home of Manchester presented a collection of some 10,000
volumes and 5,000 pamphlets and in 1869 James Morris presented some
8,000 volumes principally on the classics and humanities. The Morris
collection has been reassembled since the 1939–45 war and, together
with the Hume tracts, is now the only one of these book collections
presented in the first forty years of the library's life to be retained as a
separate collection.

The large majority of the bequests of books in the latter part of the
nineteenth century were from the professors of the College; indeed it
is well worth repeating the words of Chambers himself:[1] "Our
library, in very large measure, is the kindly bequest of the men who
taught in the rooms where their books are now stored: not only the
donors of the larger collections enumerated above, but others: men
like George Fownes, T. H. Key, M. J. M. Hill, Ernest Starling, Vaughan

Harley, or Arthur Platt." Between 1870 and 1894 the following ten science collections were bequeathed by former professors:

> J. T. Graves (Mathematics, 1870)
> W. Sharpey (Physiology, 1874)
> R. E. Grant (Comparative Anatomy, 1874)
> Sir Richard Quain (Clinical Surgery, 1877)
> E. A. Parkes (Clinical Medicine, 1877)
> T. Graham (Chemistry, 1879)
> W. K. Clifford (Mathematics, 1879)
> J. Morris (Geology, 1883)
> M. Beck (Surgery, 1893)
> Sir John Eric Erichsen (Medicine and Surgery, 1894)

During this period the Quain Law Library, and the Yates Library of Classical Antiquity and Archaeology, were both presented in 1876. In 1892 Miss Amelia B. Edwards followed her generosity in endowing a chair of Egyptology by leaving her library to become the Edwards Library of Egyptology. The thirteen collections of books enumerated above, ten of them in the Faculties of Science and Medical Science, two in the Faculty of Arts and one in the Faculty of Laws, have been embodied into the working collections of the various subjects taught in College, and in a number of cases have always formed the larger part of that collection.

Sharpey-Grant Library

Two stand out as deserving a more detailed description: the collections of Professor William Sharpey and of Professor Robert Edmund Grant formed for a considerable period the nucleus of the Medical Library. Sharpey had always been a book collector, and in addition to his own working library of works on physiology he had added many interesting early printed medical books, including such rarities as the first edition of William Harvey's *De motu cordis* of 1628 and his *Exercitationes de generatione animalium*, printed in London, of 1651. Professor Sharpey persuaded his friend Grant to leave his library of 4,000 volumes to the College with his personal estate to endow it. Sharpey himself made the first catalogue of the combined Sharpey-Grant Library which was the basis of the printed catalogue of the Medical and Biological Libraries published in 1887. The Grant fund, which to this day still brings in a welcome income of £80 a year, has since 1874 played a most important part in adding to the library's holdings of foreign scientific literature.

Graves Library

The second outstanding collection from professorial gifts listed above is the magnificent library which College received in 1870 by bequest from Professor John Thomas Graves. Indeed it would be true to say that the three outstanding collections in the library are the Graves Library, the Rotton collection which came in 1926, and the Ogden collection which came in 1953. Graves had been professor of jurisprudence from 1838 to 1843 and had been able throughout his life to keep alive his interest and his work in the three separate studies of law, classics, and mathematics. His varied publications are listed in his obituary notice in the *Proceedings of the Royal Society*,[31] of which he was elected a Fellow in 1839 for his researches in mathematics. Many of his articles on classical subjects were published in Smith's *Dictionary of classical antiquities*, his papers in mathematics appeared over a number of years in the *Proceedings of the Royal Society*, the *Philosophical magazine*, and the *Transactions of the Royal Irish Academy*, whilst his articles on legal subjects can still be consulted in the *Encyclopaedia metropolitana*.

He was a book collector himself for the whole of his life, and the splendid library which he left to his College now contains well over 14,000 items, principally devoted to early mathematics, but also embracing the history of physics, applied mathematics in all its branches, and to a lesser extent chemistry and the biological sciences. The fifty-one manuscripts in the Graves collection have already been mentioned and to some extent described. The collection of some 180 incunables in the College Library owes a debt of equal magnitude to the Graves Library, for seventy-five of them are distinguished by the bookplate of the Graves collection. Equally the 1,020 books printed before 1640 in the College Library include many which originally came with the Graves Library.

The Graves Library has not remained a closed collection since it was bequeathed but has been steadily supplemented by purchases. The creation in 1925 of the Rouse Ball fund from a sum of money left to College by W. W. Rouse Ball, a Fellow of the College, especially provides an opportunity for making regular additions of early mathematical works. The most important single collection within the Graves Library is the Euclid collection which now comprises well over 260 items and contains eighty-three of the editions of works by Euclid printed before 1640; indeed of the twenty-six earliest editions of Euclid listed in Thomas Stanford's bibliography[32], the College Library now holds all the first nineteen from the *editio princeps* published by Erhard Ratdolt at Venice in 1482, to the edition in 1574 of Accolti at Rome, and four of the remaining five: the only three desiderata being the variant of the *editio princeps*, Johann Steinmann's Leipzig edition of 1577, and the Cologne edition of 1600. Amongst the complete translations are found the first into any modern language, the Italian of 1543, the first German translation (1562), the first French translation (1564), John Day's edition of the first English translation with John Dee's preface of 1570, the first edition in Arabic (1594), as well as later translations into Turkish, Chinese, Persian, Hebrew, Finnish and other languages. A most interesting association item is Karl Pearson's annotated copy of Euclid.

A collection of treatises by Sacrobosco, of which the Graves Library holds a fourteenth-century manuscript, are represented by eight incunables and a number of early printed versions. Indeed, as Professor Douglas McKie indicated in his recent inaugural lecture[33], the wealth of the Graves collection is so great that a fuller and more detailed description should certainly be published. It includes such famous books as first editions of Newton's *Principia* and *Opticks*, Thomas Salusbury's *Mathematical collections* of 1661–65, a most interesting inscribed copy of Galileo's *Il Saggiatore* dated 1683, first editions of the works of Priestley, Boyle, Kepler, Galileo and Napier, important runs of early periodicals, such as a complete set of the Philosophical Transactions of the Royal Society from its first volume in 1665 and of the Transactions of the Royal Irish Academy from Vol. 1 (1787) onwards. French scientific periodicals are equally strong: the Académie des sciences is represented almost completely with *Histoire* from 1699–, *Mémoires* from 1816–, and *Comptes rendus* from 1835–; the rare periodical *Observations sur la Physique* (title varies) edited by l'abbé Rozier from 1771 to 1793 is almost complete and from then onwards as *Journal de Physique* it is complete. Standard mathematical journals are complete such as:

Journal de Mathématique, 1836–.
Journal für die reine und angewandte Mathematik, 1826–.

The publications of the German academies beginning with *Histoire* de l'académie royale . . . de Berlin, Vol. 1– 1745– are strong. The runs of periodicals in Graves Library also contain:

Commentationes soc. reg. scientiarum Gottingensis. 1751–1837.

Commercium litterarium ad . . . scientiæ naturalis incrementum. Norimbergae. 1–15. 1731–45.

Opuscula omnia actis eruditorum Lipsiensibus inserta. 1–6 (1682–1729). 1740–46.

Association copies of great historical interest are constantly to be found in the Graves Library such as Henry Cavendish's own copy of Pascal's *Traitez de l'equilibre de liqueurs* of 1663. Graves had not only a book collector's eye for a good copy, but also the means to procure good copies, many of which he himself put into splendid bindings of leather or vellum.

Throughout the early part of the present century individual libraries and special collections continued to come to College. In 1903 the library of classics and philosophy (2,580) collected by Dr. Frederick Septimus Leighton was presented by the wish of his children, Mrs. Sutherland Orr, Mrs. Matthews, and the painter Lord Leighton. In 1905 Mrs. Strong presented the Oriental library of her late husband who had been professor of Arabic in the College from 1894 to 1904. This collection of about 1,000 Oriental texts and grammars was retained in College when the other Oriental collections were transferred in 1922 to the School of Oriental Studies. Since 1905 the Librarian of the College has sat daily at a handsome desk which was presented together with the books of Professor Arthur Strong.

The Whitley Stokes collection of Celtic literature, folk literature, and comparative philology presented to the College in 1910 by his daughters, is still retained as a separate collection kept up to date and increased by regular additions. The original 3,500 volumes have now been increased to 4,000 and subscriptions are maintained to seven periodicals. Apart from the many scarce books, the most interesting feature of the collection is the quantity of autograph letters inserted in the books from Whitley Stokes himself and Dr. Kuno Meyer, who taught Celtic in the College between 1908 and 1913, and from philologists such as W. O. E. Windisch, A. Bezzenberger, M. H. d'Arbois de Jubainville, G. I. Ascoli, V. Henry, H. Zimmer and F. Max Muller. Here again is a specialist collection of such quality as to justify the publication of a separate catalogue.

Rotton Library

When Sir John Francis Rotton died in 1926, after serving on the College Committee from 1869 to 1906, he left to the College the splendid library of over 30,000 volumes which he had collected during the last twenty years of his long life. The subjects represented are the literatures and history of England, France, and Italy, the classics, economics, law and fine art. Its strongest period is undoubtedly the eighteenth century and some of the early editions of the works of Pope are of considerable rarity. Sir John Rotton was a careful book collector who always preferred the good copy to a bad copy and also saw to it that most of his books were handsomely bound. This collection has, in the same way as the Morris collection and the Whitley Stokes collection, been reassembled since the war and is now separately housed. It forms one of the four or five special collections which it is hoped to house adequately in separate rooms as soon as development of the present library buildings will allow.

Other major gifts to come to the library after the Rotton Library either followed the traditional pattern of former professors and members of the College leaving their books to the library, or were acquired in the vigorous reconstruction of the library carried out by John Wilks between 1945 and his retirement in 1954. In the former category Professor Edmund Gardner, professor of Italian from 1925 to 1934, bequeathed his library in 1935 including not only additions to the Dante collection but an interesting collection on the Arthurian legend. Similarly in 1936 some 2,000 books on German philology were presented by the widow of Professor Karl Pearson, to which his son Professor Egon Pearson later added a a number of books on applied mathematics from his father's library.

Post-war reconstruction

Two collections presented in the years 1941–42, immediately after the war-time disasters, when so many friends of the College presented their books, almost completely re-formed the libraries of philosophy and psychology. Professor G. Dawes Hicks, who had held the Grote chair of Philosophy of mind and logic from 1904 to 1928, bequeathed in 1941 his library of 3,929 books and 408 pamphlets; in the following year the extensive psychological library of 1,300 volumes of Dr. A. Wohlgemuth, who had been a research student in the College, was presented by his widow. A collection of the books of R. W. Chambers, including valuable material on Sir Thomas More, was given by his sister in 1943 and supplemented in the same year by a bequest from his late colleague, Dr. Elsie Hitchcock. Similarly in 1945 Lady Fleming presented a most interesting collection of 500 volumes from the library of Sir Ambrose Fleming who had held the Pender chair of Electrical Engineering from 1885 to 1926. In 1955 Professor J. P. Hill, the Jodrell Professor of Zoology from 1906 to 1921 and Professor of Embryology from 1921 to 1938, left his outstanding collection of 6,000 embryological reprints including a specialised section on marsupial embryology which is virtually comprehensive.

Two book collections acquired by John Wilks in his rebuilding of the library were the library of the former Anglo-German Academic Bureau purchased in 1945, and a collection of 1,000 books on recent German history purchased from the library of Rudolf Olden in 1947. The purchase of 1945 of the palaeontological library of Sir Arthur Smith Woodward was the first major step in re-forming the Zoological Library. Sir Arthur Smith Woodward during his years as Keeper of the Geology Department of the British Museum (Natural History) had collected a library of some 400 monographs, over 100 bound volumes of periodicals, and 10,000 reprints which was described in a letter at the time by Dr. Marie Stopes, who had been a reader in palaeontology in the College, as "world famous, unique and irreplaceable, including pamphlets on veterinary palaeontology which include almost every one of the older and rarer works now difficult or impossible to obtain". Dr. Marie Stopes herself very generously assisted College in the purchase of this important collection. Six years later in 1950 it was possible to add a collection of 5,000 offprints in the specialist field of protozoology collected by Dr. Clifford Dobell.

But Mr. Wilks's greatest achievement in rebuilding the library was his work on the Scandinavian collections. He himself undertook two tours of Norway, Sweden and Denmark, as a result of which generous gifts of both money and books were made by the Danish, Norwegian and Swedish Governments and from learned institutions, publishers and individuals in all three Scandinavian countries. The Danish section was described by Wilks[34] in a short paper published in 1947. The Icelandic section of the Scandinavian Library was by its nature the most difficult to replace, but in 1953 it was found possible to purchase 2,200 volumes (particularly the early books) from the library of Herra Snaebjörn Jónsson, of Reykjavik. The generous help displayed by Iceland and the three Scandinavian countries in helping to replace the library's losses is still being offered and helps considerably the further extension of the Scandinavian collections. These now total well over 14,000 volumes, and must, with the Scandinavian collections at the Universities of Leeds and Cambridge, be included in the three most important

Scandinavian Libraries in the country. The success with which they were rebuilt in the ten years following the war to an extent far greater than the pre-war collections goes some way to alleviate the regret at the destruction within the former Scandinavian Library of the John Daulby Icelandic collection presented in 1861 by the widow of William Caldwell Roscoe, and the loss of all the gift of 1,201 Scandinavian books from the library of Professor W. P. Ker with the 128 Danish books from the personal collection of Her Late Majesty Queen Alexandra.

Dante

The important Dante collection in the College, of which a printed catalogue was issued in 1910, owes its origin to the bequest in 1876 by Dr. Henry Clark Barlow of his Italian library containing his important Dante collection. At the same time he endowed the Barlow Memorial Lecture on Dante. The collection was supplemented by any editions of Dante which had come in the previous year with the Morris Library, or which came in 1906 in the Mocatta Library, or in 1910 in the Whitley Stokes collection. These differing sources are shown in the Dante catalogue published in 1910, which also indicates editions of Dante in the library of Sir John Rotton which eventually was bequeathed to the College in 1926. It has been further supplemented by gifts from Sir Herbert Thompson in 1921, whose valuable collection of early Italian books included two Dante incunabula, and by Huxley St. John Brooks, whose collection of 1,500 books, mainly on Dante, had been deposited in the College Library and was purchased by the College on his death in 1949. Finally, the library has been able to make modest though steady additions to the Dante collection from endowments such as the Rotton fund. The collection as a whole now numbers over 5,000 items and is over twice the size of the collection which was catalogued in 1910. The thirty-six editions of the *Divina Commedia* in the collection printed before 1600 commence with two incunables, printed by Vendelin da Spira, Venice 1477, and the first illustrated edition printed by Nicholas di Lorenzo, Florence 1481, and also include two copies of the first Aldine edition of 1502 together with five later Aldine editions. Amongst the many sixteenth-century editions is that of 1544, which first included the commentary of Alessandro Vellutello and for which a delightful series of three full-page woodcuts for each cantica, and one smaller one for each canto were cut.

Castiglione

The gift of books made by Sir Herbert Thompson in 1921 not only provided considerable additions to the Dante collection but also brought into the College one of the most complete collections of editions of Castiglione's *Il libro del cortegiano* known to exist. The collection ranges from the Aldine *editio princeps* of 1528 to the translation by L. E. Opdycke which appeared in a limited edition in 1902 with an exhaustive bibliography of the editions of the work.[35] In addition to the 1528 edition the other four early editions of Aldus of 1533, 1541, 1545 and 1547, are all present. Indeed, of the 110 editions of the work listed by Opdycke as appearing before 1640, this collection contains sixty-one, and also an edition of 1557 published in Paris by E. Graulleau not known to Opdycke. The collection now comprises 102 separate editions of this book of which seventy were published before 1800, including the first English version translated by Thomas Hoby, printed in London by William Seres in 1561, together with nine other English editions printed before 1640. This collection is still maintained as a separate collection to which additions are made whenever possible.

History Library

The History Library housed in Gordon Square contains a strong collection of early parliamentary papers from 1731 to 1850. The early volumes from 1731 to 1800 known as the Abbot collection is of outstanding interest containing over twenty individual papers which can now be regarded as unique. Professor and Mrs. Ford[36] have told how Speaker Abbot had made up four sets of pre-1800 parliamentary papers in 110 volumes: one for the Speaker's Gallery, one for the British Museum, a third for the Clerk of the Journals, and a fourth to be kept by the Clerk for the use of the house. The set now in College, the Speaker's own set, was very generously deposited on loan by the Controller of His Majesty's Stationery Office in 1906, as a result of the initiative of Professor Pollard.

The History Library also holds three important series of bound volumes of tracts. The first is the Hume collection which was included in the parliamentary collection of Joseph Hume presented in 1855. The Hume Tracts (over 5,000 items) comprise 352 bound volumes of tracts printed between 1810 and 1850 on economics, politics, education, religion and social reform. Many are presentation copies inscribed by the author to Joseph Hume. Each tract is individually catalogued in the library catalogue but there is no doubt that a published handlist would increase the usefulness of the collection; for many of the items are extremely rare, and some unique.

The other two series, the Halifax Tracts and Lansdowne Tracts were deposited in the library in 1918 by the London Institution when its library was broken up, and both are described in the preface to volume II of the London Institution's catalogue.[37] The Halifax Tracts (3,582 items originally in 145 volumes) were bought by the London Institution as lot 1748 at Sotheby's sale of the library of George Montague Dunk second Earl of Halifax (1716–71) on 21st November, 1806; they cover the period 1559–1749 including many originally collected by Walter Yonge, M.P. (1581?–1649) and the Royalist supporter Fabian Philipps (1601–90). The Lansdowne Tracts (2,024 items in 247 volumes) were bought by the London Institution as lot 1051 at Sotheby's sale of the Bibliotheca Lansdowniana Pt. II on 5th May, 1806; they cover the years 1679–1776 and have a double link with this College. For Jeremy Bentham had been a close friend of William Petty, second Earl of Shelbourne, and later first Marquis of Lansdowne, since his visit in 1781 to Bowood, Lord Shelbourne's Wiltshire house; and secondly, Etienne Dumont, Bentham's collaborator and translator, had added many items to these tracts whilst he was employed as tutor to Lord Lansdowne's sons.

In the History Library are special collections of American history, Latin American history and London history, for the College has chairs of the first two subjects, and a readership in the third. The American History Library, which now holds some 6,000 volumes owes a great deal to Professor H. Hale Bellot who, as the first professor of American history from 1930 to 1955, gave great help in building up the collection. Professor R. A. Humphreys was appointed the first professor of Latin American history in 1948; a grant of $2,000 was made by the Rockefeller Foundation towards the library and in the following session 800 volumes were received in the bequest of Professor C. H. Huberich. The Latin American History Library now holds over 3,000 volumes and receives about twenty-five periodicals. The London History Library has developed from the collection of 2,000 volumes left by Captain Ward in 1872 and augumented in 1945 by a large collection of books and pamphlets from the library of Miss E. Jeffries Davis who was Reader in London History from 1914 to 1940.

Ogden Library

Of the three great book collections in University College – the Graves (1870), the Rotton (1926), the Ogden (1953) – the Ogden is probably the greatest. It was purchased with a generous grant made by the Nuffield Foundation to encourage research work in the field of communications. C. K. Ogden himself described his library as "an Orthological library of 50,000 volumes with universal English as a solution to the international problem of Debabelization, and the educational problem of Word Magic as its focus". From this library he sold in 1953, the Brougham papers and the individual manuscripts described above, a background collection of 3,500 volumes to the Bentham-Brougham group including 152 early Bentham items, and about 1,500 volumes (including 21 incunabula and 394 *S.T.C.* books) of carefully built special collections of rare books in fields related to his interests. He once listed the special interests of his collecting as "semantics, meaning, word magic, supplemented by subsections of sign systems, symbol systems and non-verbal notations (including cryptography and shorthand), universal language, translation and simplification". Many of these interests are supported by author rather than subject collections. The special collections of the Ogden Library (with the number of items in brackets) deal with: J. V. Andreae, the author of *Turris Babel* (9), Bacon (41), Boyle (35), Chaucer (6), Coleridge (16), Comenius (15), Halliwell Phillips (237), Ben Jonson (9), Kircher (19), Milton (23), Minsheu (34), Shelley (22), Bishop Wilkins (22), annotated books (300), cryptography (21), emblems (85), and shorthand (13). It is impossible to mention briefly more than the nine outstanding of these.

The Bacon collection, supplementing the Bacon manuscript and the Bacon-Tottel manuscripts mentioned above, includes an annotated copy of Castiglione's *Courtier*, 1561, inscribed "JB", and first editions of *Novum Organum*, 1620, *Apophthegmes*, 1625, the rare *Memoriae* of 1625, and several annotated first and early editions of *Sylva Sylvarum*, 1627, and *Resuscitatio*, 1657. Obviously the collections listed above frequently interlink, as for example in the copy of Bacon's *Declaration of the . . . treasons . . . of Essex*, 1601, in which Ireland forged three Shakespeare signatures.

The Boyle collection adds to the Boyles already in the Graves Library a further thirty-five first and early editions including the copy of his first work *Seraphic love* (1659) bound for his sister the Countess of Warwick to whom it was dedicated.

The Jonson collection includes no less than five books printed between 1537 and 1615 from Jonson's Library inscribed on the title-page "tamquam explorator" at the head, and "sum Ben Jonsonij" at the foot; two of them, the Vitruvius (1586) and Despautere's *Commentarii grammatici*, 1537, have underlinings and annotations, whilst his copy of Otto van Veen's *Amorum emblemata*, 1608, has a verse added in Jonson's handwriting. Three of these books are listed by Herford and Simpson in their edition of Ben Jonson.[38] Finally, this unusually interesting Jonson group contains the annotated copy of Greneway's 1598 translation of Tacitus discovered by Israel Gollancz and described in detail in *The Times Literary Supplement* in 1928.[39]

The Milton collection includes a first edition, first state of *Paradise lost*, 1667, also three copies of the eighth state of 1669, together with two copies of the first edition of *Eikonoklastes*, 1649, and first and early editions of several of the English prose works.

The Minsheu collection with its many notable first and early editions of the 1617 *Guide into tongues* has been described by Professor Franklin B. Williams[40] who considered it "the world's most remarkable Minsheu collection".

The Shelley collection includes a three-page letter, including a poem of two verses, written 16th March, 1814, to T. J. Hogg; his autographed marked copy of Petrarch, the corrected proofs of his *Ode to Naples*; and ten copies of the first editions of six of his works.

The 300 annotated books naturally interlink with the other special collections for they include some of the manuscripts, all the incunabula and a remarkable range of books annotated before 1640. The most remarkable is Sir George Buc's copy of John Hayward's *Life of Henry IV* with his note on the trial of Hayward and its unique title-page. Some have been already mentioned, others are annotated association copies of great interest, such as Coleridge's copies of Kant (1795), of W. C. Well's *Two essays* (1818) and of Bentham's *Not Paul but Jesus* (1823), all with considerable manuscript annotation; a copy of *Astronomicon* of Firmicus Maternus (1533) with 500 manuscript annotations by Dr. John Dee, together with his annotated copy of Johannes Werner's book on the sphere (1522); Constable's copies of the memoirs of Sir Joshua Reynolds, 1813, and Wright's *Life of Richard Wilson*, 1824; and Richard Bentley's Virgil published by the firm of Wechel in 1683.

The cryptography collection is comprised entirely of rare and interesting books from the first edition in 1518 of the *Polygraphy* of Johannes Tritheim, supported by four copies of its translation into

French by Collange in 1561, through three copies of the *Cryptomenytice* published in 1624 by Duke Augustus II of Brunswick-Luneberg under his pseudonym of Gustavus Selenus, including Falconer's *Cryptography* of 1685 and *Mercury, or the secret messenger* written by Bishop Wilkins in 1641.

Finally, the shorthand collection[30] includes one of the rarest books in the Ogden Library, Timothy Bright's *Characterie* of 1588 (STC 3743): Mr. Ramage's[41] recent finding-list of *S.T.C.* books did not reveal any further copies of this work than those known already at the Bodleian and Magdalene College Cambridge (Sir Geoffrey Keynes has reported copies in the Rosenbach and Crawford Libraries); there is also a set of the miniature (2½ in. by 1¾ in.) edition New Testament and Psalms in the shorthand system of John Rich, and a manuscript of the Bible in the shorthand system of John Willis dated 1622.

Libraries deposited

The libraries of ten learned societies have been either presented to, or deposited in, the library during the last seventy-three years, giving considerable strength by adding specialist collections to what might have remained a general bookstock.

Philological Society. The library of the Philological Society was presented to the College in 1887, bringing with it at the time a most useful system by which the Philological Society exchanged their publications for those of similar societies and academies throughout Europe. The College Library benefited for many years by the addition of periodicals brought in by this exchange scheme.

Mocatta Library. The splendid collection of printed books and manuscripts formed by Frederick David Mocatta was catalogued for its owner in 1904 whilst it was still in his possession by Reginald Arthur Rye, the Librarian of the University of London. Rye states in his preface "Mr. Mocatta hopes that his collection will one day form the nucleus of a Jewish library which shall in a large measure contain works dealing with the Jews and their history". The Jewish Historical Society of England and University College rapidly took the necessary steps to turn Mr. Mocatta's hope into reality, after he left his library in 1905 to the Jewish Historical Society on condition that a home had to be found for it within two years of his death. The full story of the arrangements made between the Jewish Historical Society and University College London was set out in detail in 1930 by Sir Hermann

Gollancz,[42] at that time the Professor of Hebrew in the College. Friends of the Jewish Historical Society and of the late Mr. Mocatta, particularly Sir Isidore Spielman and Mr. Gustave Tuck, generously formed an endowment fund for the Mocatta Library, which for the next twenty years, with the constant help of the Jewish Historical Society, steadily increased the holdings of the Mocatta Library.

In 1924, Sir Hermann Gollancz, on his retirement from the chair of Hebrew, presented his own important library to the College to be housed as a separate collection within the Mocatta Library. This included a collection of tracts on the Jews in England containing some extremely scarce and valuable items as early as the mid-seventeenth century. In 1925 the Anglo-Judaica from the library of Israel Abrahams were added as a third section of the Mocatta Library. Similarly, on the death of Lucien Wolf in 1931 his large library of books, pamphlets and manuscripts which he had bequeathed to the Jewish Historical Society, was housed as another separate collection in the Mocatta Library. The original Mocatta Library was now more than full, so that College were extremely fortunate that Mr. Gustave Tuck spent his first year of office as Chairman of the Jewish Historical Society in 1929, organising an appeal for the Mocatta Library. After Mr. Tuck suffered the loss of his wife in July 1930, he decided at once to construct and equip a new Mocatta Library and Gustave Tuck Theatre as her memorial. The new library was completed and dedicated on 13th December, 1932. The whole development of the Mocatta Library and Gustave Tuck Theatre was described by the Reverend Ephraim Levine,[43] a member of the Council of the Jewish Historical Society, in 1933.

The many books which had been added since Rye originally catalogued the library of Frederick David Mocatta in 1904, are all included in the revised edition of Jacobs' and Wolf's *Biblioteca Anglo-Judaica* which was produced by Dr. Cecil Roth in 1937.[29] Such was the historic and important collection so tragically destroyed in 1941, when only the manuscripts, the Lucien Wolf collection and the early editions of Josephus, which had been evacuated to Aberystwyth, were saved. Once again, however, the Jewish Historical Society, and the many friends of the Mocatta Library, under the Chairmanship of the late Owen Mocatta, actively began to re-form the Mocatta Library. The splendid collection of Anglo-Judaica formed by the late Asher Myers was acquired and with the support of generous gifts of books from the late Professor Cyrus Adler, the Guildhall Library, and many members and friends of the Society, a re-formed Mocatta Library was on the shelves when the new Gustave Tuck Theatre and Mocatta Library, admirably designed by Professor Sir Albert Richardson, was re-dedicated by the Chief Rabbi in September 1954. The library has been further enriched by the presentation of the library of the late Albert Hyamson by the Jewish Historical Society, and by the deposit of the important collection of letters and papers of the late Moses Gaster. The library now holds some 5,946 books and 5,000 pamphlets and receives currently twenty-nine periodicals. It is the intention of the Mocatta Library Committee to re-issue a catalogue of the new Mocatta Library and this project is already receiving active consideration.

Geologists' Association. In 1907 the library of the Geologists' Association came to the library bringing with it not only a valuable collection of books and pamphlets but a most flourishing exchange scheme which at present brings into the College Library 258 periodicals.

Folk-Lore Society. The library of the Folk-Lore Society,[44] deposited in the College Library in 1911, has developed into one of the principal folk-lore collections in the world, consisting now of well over 12,000 volumes and holdings in at least 254 periodicals relating to the study of folk-lore; 101 periodicals are currently received by exchange of the Society's publications.

London Mathematical Society. In 1929 the library of the London Mathematical Society was deposited in the College Library and has during the last thirty years grown considerably as a result of the exchange system organised by the Society. In the union list of mathematical periodicals in London compiled at the University of London Library[45], the London Mathematical Society are shown to have holdings in 254 of the 627 separate titles listed. In all 280 periodicals are regularly received under the Society's exchange scheme.

Malacological Society. The library of the Malacological Society, of which a printed catalogue had been compiled in 1927,[46] was deposited in the College in 1930. This includes the early eleven-volume corpus *Systematisches Conchylien-Cabinet* edited by F. N. W. Martini and J. H. Chemnitz between 1769 and 1788, and also a copy of Baron Cuvier's *Anatomie des mollusques*, 1817, with Cuvier's own woodblock library stamp, and an inscription that Cuvier presented it.

Viking Society for Northern Research. In 1931 the Scandinavian collections were enriched by the library of the Viking Society for Northern Research, the bulk of which was unfortunately destroyed along with the heavy losses inflicted by the war on the Scandinavian collection. However, the exchange system operated by the Society is now bringing into College fifty-three periodicals, and is thereby giving great help to the rebuilding of the Scandinavian collection.

Hertfordshire Natural History Society. In 1935 the Hertfordshire Natural History Society deposited their library in the College which, in addition to a large number of periodicals and an exchange scheme which brings in forty-seven current periodicals, also contained a copy in original binding of the important tenth edition of Linnaeus *Systema naturae*, 1758.

British Society for Franciscan Studies. In 1938 the British Society for Franciscan Studies deposited its books in the College Library and disbanded the Society. The Society had printed a catalogue of its library in 1904[47], of which the library holds a copy with additions to the library up to 1938 noted largely in the hand of Chambers.

Huguenot Society. Finally, the library of the Huguenot Society was deposited by the Governors of the French Hospital in 1957. The Society uses its own publications as an exchange medium to bring in other periodicals, and its holdings of some 3,000 books and 200 volumes of periodicals related to the Huguenots must make it one of the principal collections of this literature in this country. The Huguenot Library also contains an interesting collection of manuscript ledgers connected with the administration of the Royal Bounty made to Huguenots, as well as the important collection of manuscript notes on the genealogy of 900 Huguenot families compiled by the late Henry Wagner.

The presence of these ten specialised libraries, each originally gathered together by a learned society, naturally provides a most important supplement to the broad general character of the working collections in the various academic subjects taught in the College. In the experience of the library, all the ten agreements made between College and the Societies have proved to be of mutual benefit to the College and to the individual Society concerned. The various exchange schemes operated through the publications of the Societies bring a welcome stream of additional periodicals into the collections; and members of all the Societies have the full use of the College Library, just as members of the College may use the libraries of any or all of the Societies. In broad terms this type of agreement between an established academic library of some size, and learned societies, may very well become more frequent in the future, for it prevents the break-up of an important collection which has been gathered together over a number of years by specialists in that field.

These notes on the book collections of the College attempt to give some indication of the range and quality of the special collections.[48] Little has been said of the normal working collections in academic subjects which one would assume to find in such a library; but it is impossible to describe the book collections of University College London without stressing its great wealth of periodical holdings in all subjects. For the library currently receives 4,368 periodicals by gift, exchange and purchase and has holdings in about 6,500 different titles, many of which are complete.

ADMINISTRATION

The Librarian is responsible through the Library Committee to the College Committee for the administration of the College Library. The Library Committee consists of five members of the Professorial Board elected by the Board together with five representatives elected by the Faculties of Arts, Laws, Science, Medical Science, and Engineering which cover the whole range of teaching in the College. To these ten members the Provost of the College and the Librarian are added as *ex officio* members of the committee; as in most academic libraries, the Librarian also acts as secretary to the committee. The committee meets six times a year (unless there is insufficient business to warrant a meeting) and normally holds two meetings in each term. At the beginning of each session the committee submits an annual report on the work of the library in the previous session through the Professorial Board to the College Committee.

The Library Committee formulates its budget for each session which normally follows a straightforward pattern. Funds are established for such known commitments as periodicals, work in continuation, binding, equipment and expenses, part-time employment, and exchanges; the remainder of the library's annual vote is then divided between a general reserve fund and allocations for the academic departments. It is the policy of the Library Committee that these departmental allocations are not fixed grants, but rather guides to ensure that the library develops equally on all fronts. Moderate over-spending of the departmental allocations can always be tolerated and supplementary allocations can be made by the library in the course of the session from the general reserve fund. The general reserve fund is also available to meet any expensive purchases beyond the means of the departmental fund, and to fill gaps in the sets of periodicals and major research sets.

The staff of the College Library which now totals forty-two is made up as follows: Librarian, Deputy Librarian, eleven assistant librarians and a secretary of the library (of a status equal to the assistant librarians), four senior library assistants, eight library assistants, thirteen junior library assistants and three graduate student-assistants appointed annually for one year's library experience before proceeding as students to the School of Librarianship in the College. Probably the most unusual feature of the staff organisation is that the eleven assistant librarians (whose level is that of good honours graduates with professional library qualifications) are regarded primarily as subject specialists, and only secondarily are they deployed by any function of librarianship. This bears a close resemblance to the organisation of German academic libraries, and offers an interesting coincidence in a library where Chambers first managed to introduce open access by extolling the virtues of German seminar libraries. The whole range of subjects in the bookstock of the College is shared out amongst the assistant librarians, with close attention to the academic subjects which they themselves had studied, and also to any additional subjects in which they have developed an interest. Within the subjects allotted to them, each assistant librarian is expected to be responsible for as many routine processes as possible from book selection and ordering to cataloguing and classification. Obviously, certain aspects of library work must be centralised, such as responsibility for the standard of the catalogue, and the organising of the order and accession department, and these are carried out as secondary duties by the assistant librarians. As the College Library maintains four separate sectional libraries, each maintaining its own catalogue, borrowers' register and current periodicals, the supervision of the work carried out in these libraries, together with similar work in the general library, provides the secondary functional task for five of the assistant librarians. Of the six remaining assistants, one is responsible for the catalogue, a second for the order and accession room, a third for the libraries housed in departments, a fourth for the exchange of duplicates with other libraries, a fifth for the co-ordination of the classification, and a sixth for the organisation of the special collections within the library. Theoretically, of course, this system of subject specialists is no more than a logical development of every academic library's practice of appointing a medical librarian and sometimes as well a science librarian; in University College, each section of the library has its own assistant librarian. Out of the many advantages two are particularly worth mentioning: in the matter of book selection, which is always a two-way process of receiving suggestions from the academic staff and equally keeping the academic staff informed of publishers' announcements and second-hand book-sellers' catalogues, the contacts between the College and the library are considerably increased; secondly, the system goes a long way towards removing the feelings of frustration often created in individuals by over-departmentalisation, for the normal response of each assistant librarian is to shoulder such full responsibility for his section of the library that he virtually becomes a librarian in his own right. As far as the writer is aware, this subject specialisation system has been described so far only by A. J. Loveday,[49] who was himself for six years on the staff of the College Library.

The College Library is maintained primarily for the members of the College at the three different levels of teaching staff, research workers, and undergraduates; but in addition, it offers facilities to all appointed teachers (i.e., professors and readers) and examiners of the University of London. Because of its historic links with University College Hospital, it also offers facilities to members of the teaching and administrative staffs of the Medical School, and of the medical staff of the hospital. All members of the ten learned societies who have deposited their libraries in the College are automatically admitted as readers in the College Library and following the practice of academic libraries, members of the staff of universities throughout the world are normally offered library facilities, as are any other bona fide students who need to use the library.

The library takes a full share in the national system of inter-library loans as organised through the National Central Library, and also takes a full share in the direct loaning and borrowing between British libraries which has been so stimulated and developed by the appearance of the third edition of the *World list of scientific periodicals* and by the recent completion of the *British union-catalogue of periodicals*. The trend for increased direct borrowing is being maintained: 75 per cent of the inter-library loans in 1959–60 were in response to direct requests, contrasted with 71 per cent in the previous session. The College Library normally lends to other libraries three or four times as many books as it borrows.

The College Library takes its share in the co-operative library schemes now organised by various bodies in this country. The weekly list of accessions to the library, which is circulated regularly to all Heads of Departments, members of the Library Committee, and to any other individuals on the academic staff who desire to receive it, is also sent to the National Central Library. Information on the holdings of periodicals has been sent to the *British union-catalogue of periodicals* for its forthcoming supplement, and this information will be transmitted to the *World list of scientific periodicals* for inclusion in its fourth edition. Lists of subscriptions to new periodicals are sent both to the *British union-catalogue of periodicals* and to the Standing Conference of National and University Libraries for inclusion in the Conference's bulletin. The library's holdings of books printed before 1640 were sent to Mr. Ramage of the University of Durham for inclusion in the finding-list[50] published in 1958; copies of these lists were also at the same time sent to Professor W. A. Jackson of Harvard University, and the National Central Library: supplementary lists are sent of additions to the library collection of *S.T.C.* books. Annual returns are sent to the National Register of Archives of additions to the manuscripts and letters in the College Library. Finally, information on the theses presented by postgraduate students of the College is forwarded to Aslib for inclusion in their annual list of theses.

A bindery, established in 1957, has now been developed to a staff of six: a journeyman forwarder, a journeyman finisher, three sewers and an apprentice. Already it is producing more than half of the library's annual binding. It is hoped to develop the bindery until it can cope with the whole binding of the library. Although the bindery already shows economic saving over the charges of commercial binders, this is by no means the most important advantage. The two great gains from the library bindery of higher quality binding, and of direct control ensuring speedier return, are advantages of far greater value.

In the summer of 1959 Dr. Mees, a Fellow of the College, very generously presented an American Kodak microfilm camera to carry out the double task of photographing all the early College records, and putting on to microfilm the library's important manuscript collections such as the Bentham and Brougham papers. The microfilm camera is operated by one of the library's junior library assistants, and the necessary processing of the film is done outside College. The library holds three microfilm readers and one reader for microcard and microfiche.

NOTES AND REFERENCES

1 CHAMBERS, R. W. The Library [forms Chapter XIII, pp. 417–426 of H. Hale Bellot's University College London, 1826–1926. University of London, 1929].

2 RYE, R. A. The students' guide to the libraries of London. 3rd edition. University of London, 1927. [University College, 194–200.]

3 NEWCOMBE, L. University and college libraries of Great Britain. 1927. [U.C.L., 138–142.]
—— The Library of University College London 1826–1926. [Typescript – unpublished.] 1926.

4 WILKS, J. The influence of R. W. Chambers on the development of university libraries. University College London, 1953.

5 OFFOR, R. Reminiscences of a university librarian. *Lib. World* 51 (1) 1949, 138–141.

6 CHAMBERS, R. W. The modern language library at University College. *Mod. Lang. Q.* 6 1903, 13–15.

7 CHAMBERS, R. W. The library of University College London. *Lib. Assn. Rec.* 11 1909, 350–358.

8 SMITH, Sir G. E. University College London. Department of Anatomy. N.Y., Rockefeller Foundation, 1924.
Also see MARMOY, C. F. M. The Thane library of medical sciences. *First International Congress on Medical Librarianship Congress handbook* 1953, 27–28.

9 WILKS, J. Foster Court Science Library, University College London. *Lib. Assn. Rec.* 39 1937, 205–209.

10 TOOTH, A. E. Cataloguing rules and practice: changes at University College London. *J. of Doc.* 12 1956, 88–93.
—— Cataloguing rules and practice: further changes at University College, London. *J. of Doc.* 16 1960, 71–79.

11 GARSIDE, K. The basic principles of the new library classification at University College London. *J. of Doc.* 10 1954, 169–192.

12 OGDEN, C. K. Jeremy Bentham 1832–2032: being the Bentham Centenary Lecture, delivered in University College London, on June 6th 1932. University College, 1932, p. 45.

13 MILNE, A. T. Catalogue of the manuscripts of Jeremy Bentham in the library of University College London. University College, 1937.

14 HALEVY, E. La formation du Radicalisme philosophique. 3 vols. Paris, Alcan, 1901–4.

15 EVERETT, C. W. Anti-Senatica: an attack on the U.S. Senate sent by Jeremy Bentham to Andrew Jackson. *Smith College studies in history* 11 (4) 1926.
—— A comment on the Commentaries. Clarendon P., 1928.
—— The education of Jeremy Bentham. N.Y., Columbia U.P., 1931.
—— Bentham's Limits of Jurisprudence defined. N.Y., Columbia U.P., 1945.

16 STARK, W. Jeremy Bentham's economic writings. 3 vols. Allen & Unwin, 1952.

17 BENTHAM, J. The theory of legislation, ed. by C. K. Ogden. Kegan Paul, 1931.

—— Bentham's theory of fictions, by C. K. Ogden. Kegan Paul, 1932.

18 OGDEN, C. K. Useful and entertaining knowledge: the Benthamic tradition. *Psyche* 18 1938–52, 127–204.

19 ASPINALL, A. Le Marchant's reports of debates in the House of Commons, 1833. *Eng. Hist. Rev.* 58 1943, 78–105.

—— Lord Brougham's '*Life and Times*'. *Eng. Hist. Rev.* 59 1944, 87–112.

20 FINER, S. E. Life and times of Sir Edwin Chadwick. Methuen, 1932.

21 LEWIS, R. A. Edwin Chadwick and the public health movement. Longmans Green, 1932.

22 GROBEL, M. C. The Society for the Diffusion of Useful Knowledge. London Ph.D. Thesis, 4 vols., 1932.

23 RAVEN-HART, H. A list of the archives of University College London for the period 1825–1907. *Bull. Inst. Hist. Res.* 5 1927–28, 77–82.

24 MARMOY, C. F. M. The 'Auto-Icon' of Jeremy Bentham at University College London. *Medical History* 2 1958, 1–10.

25 THORNDIKE, L. The *Sphere* of Sacrobosco. University of Chicago P., 1949.

26 MUNBY, A. N. L. Phillipps studies no. 5. Cambridge U.P., 1960, p. 36.

27 KER, W. P. On modern literature: lectures and addresses, ed. by Terence Spencer and James Sutherland. Clarendon P., 1955.

28 LANGLAND, WILLIAM. Piers Plowman: the A version, ed. by George Kane. Vol. I. Athlone P., 1960.

29 ROTH, C. Magna bibliotheca Anglo-Judaica. New edition revised. Jewish Hist. Soc. of Eng., 1937.

30 OGDEN, C. K. The Orthological Institute: from Bentham to Brougham. *Psyche*, 18 1938–52, 371–386.

31 *Proceedings of the Royal Society*, 19 1871, Obituary notices, xxvii–xxviii.

32 THOMAS-STANFORD, C. Early editions of Euclid's elements. Bibliographical Society, 1926.

33 McKIE, D. Science and history. Lewis, 1958, p. 15.

34 WILKS, J. Danish libraries in Britain, I. University College London. *Denmark* (Sept.) 1947, 6–7.

35 CASTIGLIONE, B. The book of the courtier by Count Baldesar Castiglione (1528), translated and annotated by Leonard Eckstein Opdycke. Duckworth, 1902.

36 FORD, P., and FORD, G. A guide to parliamentary papers. Blackwell, 1955, p. 53.

37 LONDON INSTITUTION. Catalogue of the library of the London Institution. Vol. II The tracts and pamphlets. 1840, p. xi-xii.

[38] JONSON, BEN. Works, ed. by C. H. Herford and Percy Simpson, 11 vols. Clarendon P., 1925–52. "Books in Jonson's library", Vol. I, App. iv, 250–271, and Vol. XI, 593–603.

[39] *Times Lit. Supp.* 1928, 10 May, p. 355 and 21 June, p. 450 and p. 468.

[40] WILLIAMS, F. B. Scholarly publication in Shakespeare's day: a leading case. [John Minsheu's *Guide into the tongues.*] Washington, Folger Shakespeare Lib., 1948. Joseph Quincy Adams: Memorial studies, 755–773, 1948.

[41] *Times Lit. Supp.* 1960 10 June, p. 369.

[42] GOLLANCZ, Sir H. A contribution to the history of University College London. Privately printed, 1930.

[43] LEVINE, Rev. E. The origin and growth of the Mocatta Library, Museum and the Gustave Tuck theatre, University College London. Spottiswoode, 1933.

[44] BONSER, W., and GARSIDE, K. The classification of the library of the Folk-Lore Society. *Folk-Lore*, 66 1955, 267–281.

[45] UNIVERSITY OF LONDON LIBRARY. Union list of periodicals on mathematics and allied subjects in London libraries. University of London Library, 1958.

[46] MALACOLOGICAL SOCIETY OF LONDON. Library catalogue (Radley Bequest). 1927.

[47] BRITISH SOCIETY OF FRANCISCAN STUDIES. Catalogue of the library. 1904.

[48] WILKS, J. Research material in the library of University College London. *Stechert-Hafner Book News* 10 1956, 105–108.

[49] LOVEDAY, A. J. University College London: a study in administrative subject specialisation. *Library Association of Malaya and Singapore. News letter* 3 (3) 1959, 16–19.

[50] RAMAGE, D. A finding list of English books to 1640 in libraries in the British Isles. Council of Durham Colleges, 1958.

Chapter XIV

THE BRITISH LIBRARY OF POLITICAL AND ECONOMIC SCIENCE

By G. Woledge

Librarian

I

THE British Library of Political and Economic Science (known till 1925 as the British Library of Political Science) is peculiar among British libraries in that it was designed for two functions, which it continues to carry out to their mutual advantage; it is at the same time the working collection of the London School of Economics (the country's largest centre of social studies) and a national collection of materials for research. Its scope, like that of the School, is not restricted to economics and politics, but embraces the social sciences in the widest sense; and it is believed to be the largest library in the world exclusively devoted to them.

It was established by public subscription in 1896 on the initiative of Sidney Webb (afterwards Lord Passfield), the leader of the group who had founded the School in the previous year; the reflection of his own methods of research can be seen in the appeal for funds, with its emphasis on the need for collections of official publications, pamphlets, and privately printed reports and documents such as were available neither in the British Museum nor in any special library in the country, as a basis for the comparative study of such subjects as local government, poor relief, railway rates, and co-operation. The School would no doubt in any case have collected a library, but in fact the scope of the library and the scale on which it was planned bear indelibly the marks of Webb's mind. His active support of the library continued for more than half a century, and since Sir Thomas Bodley refounded the Oxford University Library, no British library has owed so much to the mind and work of one man.

After six years in adapted quarters in Adelphi Terrace, the library moved with the School to a new building on part of the present site in

Clare Market and Houghton Street. It had already a large collection of
materials, though scarcely yet, nor for many years to come, well
enough chosen or sufficiently organised to be called a valuable collection. Much of the material needed – privately printed reports and the
like – could only be obtained by gift from the bodies producing it,
and they responded well to requests for help. Private collectors, too,
were generous; Webb gave his unique collections on English trade
unionism, and Sir William Acworth made the first of his gifts of books
on transport. But little money was available for the many types of book
which had to be bought, and for some years the library was woefully
short of many essentials.

Shelf-room was also insufficient, and books were kept in locked cases
outside the library, stacked in piles on the floor and even tied up in
bundles. Staff was short, unskilled, and constantly shifting; there was
no subject catalogue, and the author catalogue was restricted to certain
categories of material, excluding those in which the library was richest,
which were incidentally the most difficult to trace.

The first librarian (till 1909) was John McKillop; but the greater part
of his time was taken up by his collateral duties as secretary of the
School, and for a great part of her service from 1903 to 1918 Miss Mary
F. C. Stuart was *de facto* librarian with the title of 'Hon. Curator of
Documents'.

In 1910, the first full-time librarian was appointed, B. M. Headicar
(1875–1958), formerly district librarian in the Southwark public
libraries. In the twenty-four years of his energetic librarianship much
progress was made. The stock continued to increase; collections of
manuscripts and rare books were given or bought, and the Fry Library
of International Law and the Schuster Library of Comparative Legislation were deposited. A subject catalogue, which Headicar had from the
first insisted on as an essential, was prepared and published with
financial help from the Carnegie Trust and the Rockefeller Foundation.
New premises were built (1925, 1933) with benefactions from Mr. and
Mrs. Cobden Unwin and from the Rockefeller Foundation, and other
extensions were adapted from other parts of the School premises; they
were equipped with a lavish variety of ingenious experimental equipment; the library was one of the first in the country to install a book-
conveyor (since discarded) and a photostat.

The librarian from 1933 to 1944 was W. C. Dickinson, formerly
assistant secretary of the School and subsequently Professor of Ancient
(Scottish) History at Edinburgh. Under his librarianship, the library

strengthened its stock and greatly improved its organisation. Amongst special collections received may be mentioned those on the book trade and the Spanish Civil War, and the Cannan and Bonar collections; further details of all these are given below; the Schuster Library was presented outright, and brought up to date by extensive purchases. Perhaps even more important was the systematisation of the library's day-to-day purchases of current and older literature under an acquisitions officer and with the help of an acquisitions committee. The cataloguing department was organised under a senior cataloguer, new routine methods were devised, and the very imperfect author catalogue was revised throughout and nearly completed. The problem of space again became acute; it was solved for the time partly by the adaptation of more of the School premises, partly by internal re-arrangements.

From 1939 to 1945 all of the School except the library was evacuated to Cambridge. After some months when the library was used by the Ministry of Economic Warfare (which then occupied the whole of the building), it was virtually closed through these years, and a much reduced staff was mainly concerned with making such acquisitions as were possible under difficult conditions, and overtaking arrears of cataloguing; some 150,000 volumes were evacuated for safety to different parts of the country, but in the event the library was only very slightly damaged by bombardment.

Since 1945, progress has been steady but less spectacular; the premises have been extended, chiefly by the adaptation of existing buildings, and special arrangements have been made for the collections of early books (up to 1850), of Russian and East European publications, and of overseas government publications.

II

The scope of the library – wider than is often realised – is the social sciences in the fullest sense of that term. For parts of its field it does not aim at being more than a working library, though a good one, for a teaching institution; this is notably the case with geography, anthropology, general history, philosophy, and psychology, though particular aspects of all these subjects are collected more fully. There are other topics falling within its field where the existence of more narrowly specialised libraries makes exhaustive collecting unnecessary; and in one particular field, that of law, the library takes part in a comprehensive scheme of inter-library co-operation. It is hoped that fuller knowledge of the country's book resources will make it possible to extend yet further this kind of co-operative book collection. With these exceptions, the aim of the library is to collect all the materials likely to be needed for research within its field. It need hardly be said that this aim is achieved with varying success in different subjects, and never completely.

The library does not collect books in non-European languages, but it does attempt to cover all European languages, though it no doubt tends to fall short in books from the more remote or inaccessible countries and in the less familiar languages. An inquiry[1] made in the 1930s showed that in collecting foreign material it had been very successful as compared with other great libraries, much less so by any reasonable absolute standards.

Since 1946, the collection of Russian (and other East European) material has been organised as a distinct department of the library's work; as well as in current publications, it is rich in revolutionary literature produced in Russia and abroad since the beginning of the nineteenth century.

The library collects books of all dates. It is already rich in early works, but it is naturally far from complete in them, more particularly in minor works which, unimportant individually, may collectively form essential source material for research; it must be admitted that this is true in many directions even for books published for some years after the foundation of the library. Here again, gaps are continually being filled, but very much preliminary bibliographical work still needs to be done. By arrangement with the University of London Library, the responsibility for a comprehensive collection of minor early English writings on economics is left to the Goldsmiths' Library there, and unnecessary duplication of other materials in that collection is avoided.

A more detailed account of some of the richer parts of the collections follows.

The library is naturally strong in government publications. For the United Kingdom, it is almost complete, even for the earlier years, though it does not now acquire current scientific and technical publications which do not bear on the social sciences. It has been a depository library for U.S.A. 'documents' since 1903, and has a very full set of them from 1873, as well as a large selection of more recent 'processed' documents not included in the deposit; it has also a representative selection of the documents of individual states. For other countries, though very few are entirely unrepresented on the library's shelves, the collections vary much in completeness, and very much work remains to be done in assessing and acquiring them.

With these may be grouped the publications and documents of inter-governmental organisations – the United Nations and its specialised agencies, the League of Nations, and numerous others; most of these are received as gifts from the bodies which produce them.

Publications of local government authorities are collected less exhaustively, but the library has representative documents of about 150 of those in Great Britain, and a small selection from many other countries.

The collection of statistics is naturally full. Many of them are govern-ment publications, but the library has also the chief collections published in other forms. A reading room devoted to them contains on open access the chief current statistics for all parts of the world, and a selection of those for earlier years, particularly for Britain and the U.S.A.; the main collection is in the reserve stacks.

In economics, the library is perhaps richest in theoretical books; it acquires currently all important treatises from all parts of the world, and most of the academic periodicals; there are still gaps in its collection of the earlier literature, but they are filled as opportunity arises. The literature of descriptive economics, more extensive and of very un-equal value, is acquired more selectively, but the library attempts to acquire all academic works of any importance, and a good selection of those produced for practical purposes, including periodicals, annuals, and reports relating to different aspects of trade, industry, and com-merce. There is a particularly full collection of bank reports from all parts of the world, most of them not published. The collection of works on Transport, the nucleus of which was given by Sir William Acworth and which is kept up to date by the library, contains much historical material and an extensive collection of reports of transport under-takings; there is also a collection of manuscript and printed materials on land and water transport in Scotland in the late eighteenth and early nineteenth centuries. Another special collection is that on the book trade, the nucleus of which, given by Mr. A. D. Power, has been much increased by other benefactors, notably Sir Stanley Unwin, Mr. Geoffrey Williams and Mr. J. G. Wilson, and by purchase. In trade unionism, the Webb collection, as has already been mentioned, was one of the earliest benefactions to the library; the reports and periodicals it contains are kept up to date. Business archives are not collected extensively, partly because it is felt that they are more valuable in the locality to which they relate; but the library has a good deal of miscellaneous material of this kind from the seventeenth century onwards. Of printed histories of individual firms, the library acquires all it can; but many of them are printed for private distribution, and some no doubt escape notice. The library has large selections from the private libraries of Edwin Cannan (including his manuscripts and correspondence) and James Bonar.

For politics and public administration, one kind of primary source material is the government publications which have already been mentioned. The library contains many special collections of the material of political controversy, amongst which may be mentioned one of tracts from the time of the English Civil War, one of ephemeral material from the Spanish Civil War, and the Hutchinson collection on Socialism, which contains comprehensively writings for and against it.

In the field of law, the library's policy is defined by an agreement with the Institute of Advanced Legal Studies and certain other libraries, by which each is responsible for certain groups of material. Those falling to this library include the law of Germany and those countries that follow the German civil code, the law of Eastern European countries, and the law (in any country) of certain topics, such as commercial law, administrative law, copyright and patent law. The basis of the collection of foreign law is the Schuster Library of Comparative Legislation, the nucleus of which was collected by Dr. E. J. Schuster and given to the library by the Society for Comparative Legislation. In all these areas, the collection of current and recent materials is strong. The Fry Library of International Law, formed in memory of Sir Edward Fry, is the property of independent trustees, but is housed in the library and administered by its staff. It covers public international law and private international law (conflict of laws), and is probably the fullest collection of books on these subjects in the country.

Amongst other subjects in which the library attempts to be in some measure exhaustive may be mentioned sociology (theoretical and descriptive), criminology and penology, demography, some aspects of colonial affairs, economic and social geography, social and economic history, and international relations. There are also strong collections on general and political history, anthropology, philosophy, and psychology. Enough has probably been said above to indicate the general lines on which these are collected.

Of the manuscript collections some fall easily into these subject groups. The raw materials, topographically arranged, of the Webbs' history of local government, the files of political organisations, or the private papers of Courtney or Lansbury, are obviously relevant to politics; the many sets of private accounts, to economics; the recently acquired papers of Malinowski, to anthropology. But it is less easy to classify the records of other social research (such as the Webbs' notes on trade-unionism in the collection already mentioned or the material collected by Charles Booth for *London life and labour*), the letters of British emigrants to the United States, and the bulk of the private papers, whether those of John Stuart Mill, Frederic Harrison, the Webbs, Graham Wallas, E. D. Morel, Lord Beveridge or Bernard Shaw. It will be apparent that most of the library's holdings, a fuller account of which has been published elsewhere,[2] are quasi-archival, but it contains also a number of literary manuscripts, including a large part of those of John Francis Bray, the early Socialist.

The library has over 17,000 periodicals and other serials, of which over 8,000 are received currently. Its total contents amount to about 400,000 bound volumes, together with materials not yet bound. The total number of items is not known exactly, but is well over one million.

III

The main body of the users of the library consists, of course, of the staff and students of the School, including 700 higher degree and research students; but that hospitality to unattached scholars which in general characterises British university libraries is in this case part of the library's *raison d'être*, and it welcomes all research workers who need its resources. Pressure on space makes it necessary to exclude those whose needs can be satisfied elsewhere, including (except during the School vacation) undergraduate and similar students. It may be added that for persons engaged in academic and non-profit-making research, the fees are usually remitted.

The library lends books extensively to other libraries through the National Central Library and direct. It tries to answer bibliographical and to some extent other inquiries addressed to it either by callers or through the post; many of these come from abroad, and some of them involve a good deal of research, though care is taken to avoid doing work that the inquirer can be expected to do for himself.

The library occupies the lowest three floors of one end of the

School's main building. It is entered by way of a room which contains the catalogues, some reference books (mainly bibliographical), and the counter where inquiries are answered and books issued and received. A great part of the conversation incidental to the transaction of library business is thus kept out of the reading rooms, and the points of contact between readers and the library staff are as far as possible concentrated. It is believed that this was the first such room to be provided in any British library, though they were already common in the United States. This is the most noteworthy feature of premises that (except in detail) are the result of unpremeditated growth rather than of deliberate planning.

There are thirteen reading rooms: eight devoted to particular subjects or groups of subjects, one for current periodicals, one for the use of manuscripts and other rarities, two for research students, and one for the teaching staff. This sub-division is due to historical accidents, and though some of the rooms are finely proportioned, it would be more convenient if they were fewer and larger.

There are places for some 670 readers, and at busy times every place is occupied. The reading rooms contain an open-shelf collection of some 40,000 volumes – except in the case of one or two subjects, a select collection chosen for the purpose. A smaller open-shelf collection might be sufficient and in some ways better, were it not that it is impossible to allow readers any access to the stacks. It is arranged on a modification of the Library of Congress classification.

There is a series of study-rooms attached to most of the teaching departments of the School, open to specialist undergraduates; they are provided by the library with small duplicate working collections of books but are administered by the departments concerned. Some of these must necessarily be physically near their departments – that in geography, for instance, is used in connection with the large map collection in that department; but it is proposed to move the others to rooms which can be brought within the library enclave, where they will be both more accessible and more secure.

The reserve stacks, which contain the rest of the library's collections, ramble underground beneath the reading rooms, beyond them and round a basement courtyard, and come up to the surface again beyond; a reminder that the library stands near if not on the site of the Magpie and Stump where Mr. Pickwick met Mr. Lowten, which announced that it had 500,000 barrels of double stout in its cellars, leaving the mind in a state of not unpleasing doubt and uncertainty as to the precise direction in the bowels of the earth in which this mighty cavern might be supposed to extend. The reserve stacks, though extensive in several directions, are not extensive enough. There is not room enough to maintain a regular subject order, and the books, other than special collections, are arranged in the following groups: government publications (arranged by country); serials (each having an arbitrary running number); pamphlets (bound separately if of particular age or importance, otherwise several in one volume, and arranged by a broad subject classification); and 'treatises' – i.e., all other books (arranged by size and running number). This is felt to be a serious defect, and it is proposed to remedy it in the near future by removing a sufficient number of books to make it possible to arrange those that are retained by subject, and then giving readers access to them.

The books removed, together with several thousands already stored away from the main library premises, will be sent to the university's library depository; and it is also proposed to provide for the growth of the collections in the immediate future by sending there from time to time sections of less heavily used books equal in bulk to the accessions.

There is a good suite of work rooms for the library staff, opening conveniently off the space behind the counter; it is not, however, large enough to house all of the staff.

It is hoped that in the not very distant future it will be possible to house the library in a completely new building in which, amongst other improvements, it will be possible not only to give research workers better access to more books but also to give better and more tempting facilities for undergraduates, who are at present provided for partly in the main library, partly in the separate lending library described below.

Of the library's two principal catalogues, one is of particular importance as a published contribution to international bibliography. This is the subject catalogue, published as *A London bibliography of the social sciences*. The first four volumes contain the library's stock in 1929 (as well as relevant holdings of some other libraries), the fifth to eleventh the acquisitions of 1929–55. In the meantime, the continuation up to date is available on cards in the library. It is arranged in dictionary form, with subject-headings based on those of the Library of Congress. Though it has many defects and is not always easy to use – or at any rate to get the fullest use out of – it is the most comprehensive and in many ways the fullest guide to the literature of the social sciences, and is all the more valuable because that literature is in general very inadequately sign-posted.

The other principal catalogue, the Author (General) Catalogue, calls for little special comment. It is on cards, according to the Anglo-American code. It is still incomplete for certain materials of minor importance, and British parliamentary papers and U.S.A. Government publications are excluded, since they have adequate printed catalogues.

Select lists of recent additions, classified under broad subject-headings, are stencilled and issued monthly.

The library publishes a leaflet of *Notes for readers* and a *Guide to the collections* which gives a fuller account of its contents and arrangement.

The library does not in principle lend books to individuals; but members of the School staff can use books in their own rooms, and they and research students can borrow certain classes of books for home reading. There is a lending library, separately organised but under the same general administration, which provides so far as possible all the books likely to be needed by undergraduates, other than those which they can be expected to buy for themselves; books in great demand are provided in multiple copies.

In 1940, Mrs. Bernard Shaw gave the School a sum of money to establish a library of books not related to its regular studies; the Shaw Library is kept up from the regular funds of the School, and now forms a good general library in which art, music and literature are perhaps the most prominent subjects. It is kept in an informally furnished room apart from the main library, used also for concerts and exhibitions.

IV

The library has a staff of fifty-three (including six porters). Eleven of these are in senior grades for which a degree is normally required, including the librarian, the deputy librarian, and three sub-librarians responsible respectively for acquisitions, for processing, and for services to readers. Non-graduates (who are generally recruited as school-leavers) are encouraged, and indeed expected, to undertake highly skilled work.

In book-selection, the library benefits much from the teaching staff and its wide contacts with public affairs in many directions, and from the many research workers amongst its readers; these are particularly valuable in bringing to notice current materials outside the book trade or suggesting channels for their acquisition, and in locating collections of earlier materials which have not come into the regular second-hand market. The librarian has, however, a wide responsibility for book-selection, and in fact the library's intake is so large in relation to the field covered that for normal and straightforward acquisitions, whether of current or earlier material, it cannot rely to any extent on proposals from teachers and other readers, though these are encouraged and always welcomed.

Current English and American publications are in the main selected from announcements and ordered on (or before) publication. For foreign books, where the acquisitions are more select, more use is made of reviews, but announcements are also used; full use is also made of the too meagre opportunities afforded by the book trade for personal inspection of new foreign books.

A good deal of the library's intake of current material consists of reports and the like which are not regularly published; much of this can only be traced through press reports of conferences and the pro-ceedings of official and unofficial bodies, or by private inquiries, and can only be obtained by writing to the body responsible.

Second-hand books are chosen from catalogues in the usual way.

A small and informal acquisitions committee, consisting of members of the teaching staff with the librarian and the acquisitions officer, meets at frequent intervals to decide on doubtful cases – both those in which the value of a particular book is uncertain, and those which involve a decision on policy; although the general lines of the library's acquisitions policy are, of course, already settled, questions of the latter kind are still surprisingly frequent. Perhaps even more valuable than any decisions on specific points is the discussion of the library's needs between its officers and its users; such discussion does, of course, take place profitably on many occasions, more and less formal, without any such organisation; but it is found that the continuity of regular meetings adds greatly to its value.

Of the processes of acquiring books, once it has been decided that they are needed, there is little that calls for particular comment except the visible index system of recording the receipt of current periodicals, which has been fully described by Dr. Plant, the deputy librarian.[3]

The draft catalogue entries are written by the cataloguers on work-cards, from which the entries are prepared by cataloguing-typists; in addition to the cards for public use and duplicates of subject catalogue entries for printing, carbon copies of main entries provide a shelf-list in sheaf form.[4]

[1] WAPLES, D., and LASSWELL, H. D. National libraries and foreign scholarship: notes on recent selections in social science. University of Chicago P., 1936.

[2] ALLEN, C. G. Manuscript collections in the British Library of Political and Economic Science. *Journal of the Society of Archivists* 2 (2) 1960, 52–60.

[3] PLANT, M. Periodicals procedure in a university library. *Coll. and Res. Libs.* 3 (1) 1941, 57–63.

[4] PLANT, M. The statistical treatment of accessions. *Lib. Assn. Rec.* 40 (8) 1938, 407–412.

Chapter XV

OTHER LIBRARIES OF THE UNIVERSITY OF LONDON

By D. T. Richnell

Librarian, Reading University

INTRODUCTION

THE library provision of the University of London is highly complex. Unkinder words have sometimes been used. But it should be understood that the complexity arises from the nature of the University itself and is the result of its historical development. If the library provision could be planned *de novo*, it could possibly be fashioned nearer to the librarian's heart's desire, but any radical re-fashioning of the libraries would involve the re-fashioning of much more besides – the administrative and academic structure of the University itself. As it stands, the library provision represents the present stage in a process of organic growth which has dictated a pattern that, if difficult to grasp at first, nevertheless corresponds in most ways to the practical needs of the University. To say this, however, is not to suggest that it is incapable of improvement.

The purpose of this article is to describe the libraries of the University other than those which are dealt with in other chapters. In order to place these libraries in their setting and to understand their purposes and functions, it is necessary to know something of their origins and relationships with one another. This is not the place for a historical sketch of the growth of the University, but this chapter will be easier to understand if read in conjunction with Sir Douglas Logan's *The University of London: an introduction* (1955), and with the chapters in this volume on *The University of London Library*, *The Library of University College* and *The British Library of Political and Economic Science*.

Sir Douglas Logan opens his historical survey thus:

"The University of London was founded by Royal Charter in 1836 ... [It] concerned itself solely with examining for the first sixty-four years of its existence and it was not until 1900 that it could be said to have become a University in the fullest sense of the word. By that time a number of institutions in London had already built up an established reputation in the field of higher education and the important innovation introduced by the reconstruction of 1900 was to bring those institutions into a federal relationship with the University. They nevertheless remained independent bodies on the shoulders of which the main burden of providing undergraduate teaching rested and, indeed, still rests. In a sense, therefore, the University of London is an *ex post facto* rationalisation of the major facilities for higher education existing in the metropolis at the end of the nineteenth century. This is not, of course, the whole truth, for a federation is more than the aggregate of its individual members."

Federal in nature the University is, and since the teaching and research is carried out in a number of constitutionally and geographically separated institutions, the library provision is also constitutionally and geographically separated. Moreover, since the functions of these institutions vary widely, the nature of the libraries required to carry out these functions shows a similar variety. In considering the libraries of the various institutions it must always be remembered that the University Library, which only came into prominence following the reconstruction of the University in 1900, is available to all the members of all the institutions, as a supplement to the resources of their own libraries. No more will be said about it here, but its important role in the provision of reference and loan material must not be left out of the picture.

THE INSTITUTIONS OF THE UNIVERSITY

The number of institutions comprising the University has greatly increased since 1900, and they go by a bewildering diversity of names, but they fall into certain categories which are relevant to the library provision (although these categories may not correspond with the classification used for other official purposes in the University Calendar). The first of these categories may be termed the general Colleges, that is, those institutions in which research and teaching in a number of faculties and subjects is conducted at both undergraduate and postgraduate levels. The second category comprises those in which the research and the teaching at both undergraduate and postgraduate levels is limited to a group of related subjects in one or more faculties. The third category is those institutions in which the research and teaching is confined to staff and postgraduate students in a clearly defined subject field. The fourth category is those institutions which, whilst preparing undergraduate and postgraduate students for University examinations, are not primarily or entirely devoted to University studies.

These categories can be better appreciated in concrete than in abstract terms and it is, therefore, desirable to list the institutions in each. It is possible at the same time to give certain information relevant to their libraries in tabular form:

1. *General Colleges*

	No. of Vols. *	Seats for Readers *	Annual Expendi- ture (1957–58) * £	No. of Internal Students (Sept. 1958) †
University College, Gower Street, W.C.1 . . .	470,500	680	62,000	2,759
King's College, Strand, W.C.2 .	189,500	817	28,220	2,140
Bedford College, Inner Circle, Regent's Park, N.W.1 . .	113,600	201	17,155	831
Birkbeck College, Malet Street, W.C.1	70,200	92	15,457	1,433
Queen Mary College, Mile End Road, E.1	61,800	419	12,731	1,297
Royal Holloway College, Engle- field Green, Surrey . .	51,500	144	8,964	393
Westfield College, Kidderpore Avenue, N.W.3 . . .	41,500	88	4,476	289

2. *Special Colleges*

London School of Economics and Political Science, Houghton Street, Aldwych, W.C.2 .	391,800	625	56,656	1,995
School of Oriental and African Studies, W.C.1 . . .	[220,000]‡	159	28,910	196§
Imperial College of Science and Technology, Prince Consort Road, S.W.7 . . .	73,100	175	16,220	2,228
School of Slavonic and East Euro- pean Studies, W.C.1 . .	56,200	60	6,345	78
Royal Veterinary College, Royal College Street, N.W.1 . .	15,900	99	4,120	367
Queen Elizabeth College, 61–67 Campden Hill Road, W.8 .	11,500	62	3,991	133
Wye College, nr. Ashford, Kent	12,000	50	3,485	226
Courtauld Institute of Art, 20 Portman Square, W.1 . .	24,100	108	25,174	90

2. Special Colleges—continued

	No. of Vols. *	Seats for Readers *	Annual Expenditure (1957–58) * £	No. of Internal Students (Sept. 1958) †
School of Pharmacy, 29–39 Brunswick Square, W.C.1 and 17 Bloomsbury Square, W.C.1	[2,500]	[52]	[1,892]‖	156
New College, 527 Finchley Road, N.W.3	[25,000]	[22]	[134]¶	42
Richmond College, Richmond, Surrey	[15,000]	[12]	[150]¶	73

The thirteen Medical and Dental Schools, also, may be considered as belonging to this group, but they are not included here, since they are dealt with in the chapter on *London's Medical Libraries*.

3. Postgraduate Research Institutes

	No. of Vols. *	Seats for Readers *	Annual Expenditure * £
Institute of Historical Research .	80,600	99	6,529
Institute of Education . .	66,400	150	9,028
Institute of Archaeology . .	12,900	24	3,620
Warburg Institute . . .	107,300	63	13,677
Institute of Advanced Legal Studies	54,000	144	5,562
Institute of Commonwealth Studies	23,300	60	2,980
Institute of Germanic Languages and Literatures . . .	13,400	56	1,848
Institute of Classical Studies .	4,000 [+31,000]	40**	2,285

* The figures in these columns, with the exception of those in square brackets, are taken from the University Grants Committee *Returns from Universities*, 1957–58. [Cmnd. 832. 1959.] The figures for expenditure comprise salaries, books, periodicals, binding and sundries, but they do not include expenditure from endowments, or sources of income other than the Treasury Grant.

† The figures in this column are taken from the *University of London Calendar*, 1959–60.

‡ This figure, supplied by the Librarian, includes not only books, but certain special categories of Oriental material.

The fifteen institutes federated in, or associated with, the British Postgraduate Medical Federation, also, may be considered as belonging to this group, together with the London School of Hygiene and Tropical Medicine and the Lister Institute of Preventive Medicine. They are excluded here for the reason given in the case of the Medical Schools.

4. *Institutions with Recognised Teachers*

It is unnecessary to give a list of all the institutions with recognised teachers, since the libraries of these institutions do not fall within the framework of the University. They are of such varied nature as colleges of technology and polytechnics, colleges of music, colleges of education and so on. For the most part the libraries are no more than basic collections for students and staff and need not receive further notice. Since, however, they do not fall under the other chapters of the present volume, some reference will be made to the libraries of those institutions which may be considered to have importance as sources of research material, or to be in process of development as major centres of scientific and technical literature.

THE LIBRARIES OF THE GENERAL COLLEGES

The first category of general colleges may be said very broadly to constitute those which came to be associated with the University in the earlier (i.e., pre-1900) phase of its growth. This is only an approximate truth, since the admission to the University of some of these colleges dates from early in the present century, and some of the specialised schools were admitted long before. It is useful for the present purpose only as an indication that the conception of general colleges with libraries administering to the needs of staff and students is rooted in the traditions of the federal University. But it is not tradition alone that determines the continuation of separate library provision in each of the colleges. It will be seen that they are dispersed over a wide area; there are two mainly residential colleges (Royal Holloway and Westfield) and one partly residential (Bedford); and there is one (Birkbeck) in

§ The figure for full-time, part-time, and intercollegiate students for 1958–59 is over 500.
‖ These figures, supplied by the Librarian, are for October 1958. See p. 220.
¶ These libraries have no full-time staff.
** See pp. 224-5.

which the first degree courses are provided for evening and part-time students. The libraries, therefore, have to serve the local and special needs of the college members, and their individual existence and control is a matter of necessity as well as tradition.

The dispersion of the colleges and the disparity in their nature are of less significance, in considering their library provision, than the disparity in their size and history. The range of the subject fields covered varies from University and King's Colleges, at which teaching is conducted in nearly all faculties, to Westfield College, in which it is confined to two.[1] It will be seen from the figures quoted above that there is only the remotest relationship between the numbers of students in the colleges and the size of their libraries. These factors make generalisations about the libraries of limited value.

It is possible to say, however, that the college libraries exist almost exclusively to serve the needs of their own college members, whether students or staff; that their reading rooms and bookstocks must be adequate for the reference needs of their students and provide as many books for loan as possible; and that the research collections are developed for and by the teaching staff for their own specialised needs as far as financial resources permit. In the past the requirements of the teaching staff in the colleges have led to the creation of departmental libraries, but the present tendency is towards the integration of these with the general library collections.

The amount of money available for the development of specialised research collections is necessarily proportionate to the size of the book funds. This means that the largest college libraries, which have the largest funds, and which are also those with the longest history, have accumulated very considerable research collections which make them of consequence to research workers outside as well as inside the colleges. University College Library is the most outstanding example of this, as will be seen from the chapter devoted to it. King's College Library, though much smaller, is the next in importance.

The 200,000 volumes in the library of **King's College** are at present deployed in the general library and in a large number of departmental libraries. The general library is not only a collection of works of reference, general periodicals, and so on, but also comprises the main working collections in a number of the humanities. Owing to lack of space in the main building, the collections in other subjects are in the departmental libraries, until such time as the collections in all the humanities can be brought together in a new library building. In general, the collections are of internal significance only, catering for the undergraduates, postgraduates and the special needs of the staff. In some cases, however, the collections are sufficiently large to be ranked among the most important in London. King's College is, for example, the centre of Portuguese studies in the University, and the main research collection of Portuguese materials, recently strengthened by the purchase of the library of Professor E. Prestage, is to be found here. Other collections of special importance include Imperial History, Military Studies, Modern Greek, Spanish and Theology.

In this library, as in most others, it is the special collections that contain the material of greatest importance for research workers outside the college. To a large extent, the acquisition of special collections is bound to be fortuitous, resulting from gift or bequest, but usually such acquisitions fit naturally into the pattern of academic teaching and research, arising as they often do from former members of the staff or others associated with the work of the College. The special collections in King's College Library excellently demonstrate this point. The English Library incorporates the libraries of Professor W. W. Skeat, Dr. F. J. Furnivall and Professor A. W. Reed; the Marsden Library, containing some unique and rare editions of works dealing with languages, was bequeathed by Dr. William Marsden, one-time Secretary to the Navy;[2] the Wheatstone Library, consisting of books of historical interest on electricity and kindred subjects, was bequeathed by Professor Sir Charles Wheatstone; and there are a number of other similar examples. Such bequests form the basis on which important collections can be built. The Ronald Burrows Library of Medieval and Modern Greek, dealing with Byzantine history and with the language and literature of modern Greece, has since been enriched by the gift from Dr. William Miller of 800 volumes from his own collection, and these gifts, together with the library's acquisitions by purchasing, constitute this a primary source in London for medieval and modern Greek materials.

There is one collection of similar stature at **Bedford College** – the Dutch Studies Library, which is the main collection on Dutch language and literature in the University. The other special collections in this College library, the Morton Sumner bequest of books and works of art, the Oliver bequest, the Herringham collection, Professor Spurgeon's Library, and books from the libraries of J. C. Robertson, Marshall Griffith and Dr. Margaret Macdonald, consist for the most part of good working copies of books, in many cases duplicates, for use in the general library. Only one of them, the Herringham collection, is housed as a separate entity under the terms of the bequest. In Bedford College Library a high proportion of the books is in the general library, and the number of departmental libraries, mainly in the Science Departments, is correspondingly small.

The same in varying degrees is true of the other general college libraries. None of them claims to have special collections of major importance, though in each will be found sections or items of particular interest – an increasingly strong collection in Engineering at **Queen Mary College,** the Lyttleton family letters at **Westfield College,** a general section of books on the Fine Arts at **Royal Holloway College,** and the R. C. Trevelyan Memorial Library at **Birkbeck College.** The last is worthy of special mention. This collection of over 5,000 volumes was formerly the private library of R. C. Trevelyan and was purchased for the College after his death. It is separately housed and is intended as "a library in which students of the College and members of the staff can come and browse and read with pleasure and with profit. . . . It is also likely to gain in significance over the years as marking the tastes of a man of letters in his period."[3]

It will be seen that this collection differs from most other special collections as being one intended for general cultural and recreational reading rather than as a research tool. It will be found that there is an increasing tendency to make such book provision in the libraries of university institutions.

THE LIBRARIES OF THE SPECIAL COLLEGES

The special colleges belong in the main to the second phase of the University's development, the period from 1900, which was one of ever-increasing diversity and specialisation in University studies. The libraries of these colleges present an entirely different picture from those of the general colleges. There are, naturally, some features in common, since the libraries exist primarily to cater for the needs of undergraduates, postgraduates and staff. But the differences are far more marked, since the specialised nature of the teaching and research inevitably calls for libraries that far exceed, in depth, the provision that can be made in most general college libraries. The difference can best be seen in a comparison between the library of the School of Oriental and African Studies (about 220,000 volumes) in an institution with about 500 students (including part-time and inter-collegiate students) and the library of Queen Mary College (62,000 volumes) with 1,233 internal students.

The disparity in the size and nature of the libraries within this group, however, is even more marked, and they are dispersed over a wider area. Generalisation is thus rendered even more difficult than in the case of the general colleges, and it is wiser to concentrate on the particularly interesting features of each. The largest and most important library in the group is that of the London School of Economics and Political Science, but since this is the subject of a special chapter, there is no need to deal with it here.

The next in size is the library of the **School of Oriental and African Studies.** This is situated on the central University site, and "is open not only to students of the School but also to scholars and others interested in Oriental and African studies".[4] As this statement suggests, it is a research library of the first importance in the fields which it covers.

It is the largest library of its kind in the country which provides lending facilities and the comparatively large size of its inter-library loans (approximately 500 volumes a year) testifies to its value. "Teaching is provided in the languages, history, law, religions and customs of Oriental and African countries, and in phonetics and linguistics. The academic work of the School is organised in nine departments: India, Pakistan, and Ceylon; South East Asia and the Islands; the Far East; the Near and Middle East; Africa; Phonetics and Linguistics; History; Law; Cultural Anthropology."[4] With such a wide area of studies to cover, it is little wonder that the library is relatively large in proportion to student numbers.

So important a library could not have been assembled in so short a time without a co-operative effort on the part of other institutions and individuals, which illustrates not only the generosity of libraries and benefactors, but also the rationalisation of resources which has taken place within the federal University and which must be a continuing process in its growth.

"[The library's] nucleus was formed by the oriental books previously belonging to the London Institution [whose premises were taken over by the School at its foundation], by large donations from the India Office, the British Museum, and private persons, and by the transference from the University Library and the libraries of University College and King's College of their oriental books in exchange for the non-oriental books of the London Institution Library. Among the collections so acquired was the oriental portion . . . of the library . . . belonging to William Marsden . . . which was presented by him to King's College in 1835." [5]

From the beginning there has been a steady growth, much accelerated by the great activity of the School during the Second World War and the subsequent implementation of the recommendations of the Scarbrough Report. [6]

In addition to the books acquired by purchase, there have been further transfers of books from other libraries of the University. For example, the Far Eastern Art collection, which had been built up by Professor W. P. Yetts at the Courtauld Institute of Art, was transferred to the School Library in 1957. This included many lantern slides and photographs, which now form an important part of the collection of these materials. The collection of slides on Oriental Art and Archaeology now numbers over 10,000. Other noteworthy additions include the Martin Hartmann collection of many hundreds of pamphlets on Islamic subjects – as yet uncatalogued – and the Auboyneau collection, purchased in 1949, which includes many early printed books on the Near East. Mention must also be made of the valuable library of books in Western languages and Chinese on Far Eastern ceramics and art, which forms part of the Percival David Foundation of Chinese Art – though this library is separately administered as part of the Foundation's collections. [7] It should be noted that the resources of the library are in some fields remarkably wide. The Department of Phonetics and Linguistics is not confined to Oriental languages and aims at universal coverage. This has led, for example, to the provision of a collection of books on American Indian languages. It should also be noted that there are a number of departmental libraries in the School, the contents of which are not included in the main catalogue of the library. These departmental libraries, which come under the general supervision of the Library Committee, present a diversified picture of book provision. Some are in the nature of seminar libraries, containing research material, while others contain extra copies of standard works and textbooks for the undergraduate students.

The library of the **School of Slavonic and East European Studies,** although very much smaller, is comparable in the scope of its coverage and the purpose which it serves. Although the status of this School is somewhat different, being a University Institute with a Council appointed by the Senate as governing body, its role in relation to Slavonic and East European studies is essentially the same. The origin of the library, also, is the same, since it was "founded out of books from the General Library of King's College, London, from the Marsden Collection, the Barton Collection (principally Western and Southern Slav), the London Institution and various private sources. It has been continually enriched by gifts from the governments of the Slavonic and East European countries, by exchanges with academic and cultural institutions in those countries, by purchase, and by private gifts and bequests."[8]

The growth of the library has been most rapid since 1945, partly as a result of the Scarbrough Report. Not unnaturally the Russian collection is the strongest, and it contains a considerable proportion of older (pre-1917) works, notably source materials for Russian history. It has recently been enriched by the permanent loan of the library of the Russian Orthodox Church in London, which contains many eighteenth-century items. The Roumanian collection has similarly been greatly strengthened by the acquisition of the library of Dr. M. Gaster, which is strongest in nineteenth-century material. The library of Professor W. J. Rose has helped to form a good Polish collection, and sections on all the other Balkan countries (with the exception of Greece) are being developed. The Baltic languages, also, are well represented.

One of the difficulties facing any library in these fields is the impossibility of obtaining copies of many essential works, and the library has undertaken a fairly large-scale project of microfilming. This is being carried out by the University Library Photographic Department. There is another form of co-operation with the University Library. Personal loans to members of the University who are not members of the School are arranged through the University Library. This ensures that material not available elsewhere in the University is at the disposal of any members who may need it, whilst it prevents the unnecessary use of the School Library for more common Slavonic items. The School Library makes its resources available for inter-library loans through the National Central Library.

The Courtauld Institute of Art, which also has the status of a University Institute, has a library of considerable significance. There is, of course, a library of books, mainly on Western art, of some 25,000 volumes, but there are, in addition, two libraries of a special type – the Witt Library of reproductions of paintings and drawings from the fourteenth century onwards, presented by Sir Robert Witt, and the Conway Library of photographs and reproductions, the nucleus of which was bequeathed by Lord Conway of Allington. The latter covers European architecture, sculpture, manuscript illumination, tapestries, and so on, of the Christian Era.

There is a group of three specialised colleges, of which the libraries are similar in size and function. These are Queen Elizabeth College (formerly King's College of Household Science), Royal Veterinary College, and Wye College (Agriculture and Horticulture). The libraries are adequate to serve the needs of the students in their specialised fields, and the current research needs of the staff, but are not, as yet, of a size to give them great significance as research collections. The **Royal Veterinary College Library,** however, contains a collection of books of historical interest, many of which are the property of the Veterinary Medical Association of the College on permanent loan to the library, and the other colleges are gradually acquiring such material relevant to their subjects. **Queen Elizabeth College** has an attractive new library reading room, and Wye College can claim to have by far the oldest library building in the University. This is part of the original fifteenth-century foundation of the College of St. Gregory and St. Martin, the reference library occupying the north side of the quadrangle. **Wye College,** situated fifty miles from the central University site, provides the extreme example of the need for self-sufficient library provision. Part of the library of the Royal Veterinary College has to be kept at its field station for the same reason.

The **School of Pharmacy** is similar in size and specialised function to these colleges, but its library provision illustrates another aspect of the diversity that exists within the University as a result of its history and development. This School was founded by the Pharmaceutical Society of Great Britain in 1842, but was not admitted as a School of the University until 1925. Although since then it has been taken over from the Pharmaceutical Society, there has been, until very recently, no library provision, since students have free access to the library and museum of the Society. This is a fine collection of over 30,000 volumes, with manuscripts and a historical collection which includes many early pharmacopoeias, English and foreign herbals, and the Hanbury Library containing many rare illustrated botanical works. This special arrangement obviated the need to build up a separate library for the School for many years, but the time has now come when special provision for students has been found necessary. A reading room has been provided, and the nucleus of a collection formed from books in the departments of the School. It is hoped that there will be a rapid increase in the number of volumes.

Similar considerations are responsible for the unorthodox nature of the library provision for the **Imperial College of Science and Technology** which is an institution or group of associated colleges at South Kensington, including the Royal College of Science, the Royal School of Marines and the City and Guilds College. This is, in terms of student numbers, the largest of the specialised colleges in the University (and is still in process of very rapid expansion), but the number of volumes in the libraries (70,000) is in no way commensurate with its size. These volumes, however, represent only the contents of the series of departmental libraries housed in the respective departments. The main research collection used by staff and students is the **Science Library,** which is housed in the Imperial Institute Road building which also accommodates the Chemistry and Physics Departments of the College.

"The presence of the Science Library in its midst has made it unnecessary for the Imperial College to develop a large central library of its own. . . .

"Each Department of the Imperial College has its own library for reference and loan. . . . In the City and Guilds College, library facilities are centred on the extensive Unwin Library. . . .

"The Haldane Library, at present a collection of some 6,000 books, based on the former Union Library, exists to encourage wider reading. . . . The collection is being rapidly expanded and is intended within a few years to form an important part of the library facilities of the College.

"Plans for the new College building to be erected in due course on the central site include provision for the main part of the Science Library. Linked to it the College plans to have a central Imperial College Library, which will co-ordinate the services of the departmental libraries, and will adjoin the expanded Haldane Library."[9]

This quotation serves to illustrate the complexity of library organisation that can develop within a single college, or amalgam of colleges, and the process of rationalisation that must accompany the expansion of teaching and research facilities. The institution of the Haldane Library is an interesting development in line with the College policy of extending the students' training beyond the limits of purely scientific and technological subjects. The Haldane Library may be compared with the R. C. Trevelyan Memorial Library at Birkbeck College and the Shaw Library at the London School of Economics.

The two remaining colleges to be considered in this category are theological colleges – New College (primarily Congregational) and Richmond College (Methodist). (King's College Theological Department prepares students for Holy Orders in the Church of England, but the Department's library forms an integral part of the College Library.) The library of **New College** contains over 21,000 books, and since it is an old foundation (1673) it includes an important collection of seventeenth-century Puritan and eighteenth-century deist literature. The library of **Richmond College,** which was opened in 1843, is well provided with Biblical, theological, and Methodist literature. None of the three theological teaching establishments is in receipt of grants from the University Grants Committee (*see also* pp. 280–1).

THE LIBRARIES OF THE POSTGRADUATE RESEARCH INSTITUTES

To say that the Postgraduate Research Institutes and their libraries belong entirely to a third phase in the development of the University is to oversimplify the picture. They are a growth parallel to that of the specialised colleges, and result from the same tendency towards specialisation in university studies. But whereas the specialised colleges, such as the School of Oriental and African Studies and the School of Slavonic and East European Studies, embrace both undergraduate and postgraduate teaching and research in fields peculiarly their own, the institutes are conceived as centres of postgraduate teaching and research in fields of study that are common to a number of institutions of the University.

"The base on which the typical institute concerned with the humanities rests is a research library, highly selective in its intake, which requires relatively limited accommodation in the University Precinct. Because of the central situation of such an institute, the teachers of the University concerned, though still fulfilling their obligation to provide undergraduate instruction at the various Schools to which they are attached, are able to use the institute for their own work, for seminars and for the supervision of postgraduate students. Developments on such lines might well be possible in mathematics or theoretical physics, but not in the experimental sciences, where the laboratory and not the library is the heart of the matter."[10]

The first institute to be founded, and the one which has to some extent become the model for others, was the **Institute of Historical Research.** It was established through the efforts of Professor A. F.

Pollard and others in 1921, and has built up a library of over 80,000 volumes in its thirty-eight years' existence. The policy of the library has been to concentrate on the printed source material of historical research.

"It consists of a series of seminar libraries, equipped with books containing or describing the main sources of medieval and modern history (especially those whose manuscript originals are in the Public Record Office, the British Museum and other London repositories). . . . The Committee may admit to use of the Institute any teacher of history in the University, and his research students; also teachers and research students from other universities, and other historians and archivists engaged in research."[11]

It is claimed that one of the main advantages of this type of organisation is that duplication of research material is avoided, and to a very large extent this result has been achieved in the case of this Institute. The presence of both the Institute and the University Library in the same block of buildings has made possible a close co-operation between the two libraries, and this is being extended, with the completion of the University Library's new Periodicals Room above the Institute, to the transfer of some periodicals from the Institute to the new stack and special access for Institute readers to this and other material.

Most of the other institutes since established have followed the pattern and policy of the Institute of Historical Research. The **Institute of Archaeology** (opened in 1937, but not receiving financial assistance from the University until 1945 and now housed in commodious new premises) has a library of over 13,000 volumes, comprising a large collection of works on general archaeological subjects covering especially Europe, Africa and Asia, and more limited sections on allied subjects. Periodicals constitute an important feature of the collection, but in this library it is the non-book material that adds greatly to its strength – collections of archaeological photographs, including a series of air-photographs of the Near East, of archaeological and general maps, and of over 10,000 lantern slides illustrative of excavations on prehistoric, Roman and Dark-Ages sites in Great Britain and of monuments and relics from the same period, also of the archaeology of Europe and Asia as well as of aspects of technology, geology and palaeontology relevant to archaeology. With such specialised material there is little danger of unnecessary duplication in other libraries. With the periodicals the danger does exist, and steps have been taken to rationalise the holdings of, for example, the local and county archaeological and historical journals between the Institute of Historical Research, the University Library and the Institute of Archaeology. In the case of archaeological reports the existence of several copies in the University, one of which cannot be borrowed, is welcomed by staff and students: and this consideration of the needs of reference and loan copies is often a valid reason for duplication in different libraries with different functions and policies.

The **Institute of Advanced Legal Studies** (1948) has amassed a collection of over 53,000 items in ten years. This library comes within the purview of the chapter on *Law Libraries*. It is only necessary here to note that most of the material being collected – the Nuffield Library of Commonwealth Law and the United States holdings, for example – has enriched the resources of the University in fields that would not otherwise be covered. The duplication of United Kingdom material is of positive value, since the law reports, statutes and other basic works are in constant demand.

The **Institute of Commonwealth Studies** "was established in 1949 to promote advanced study of the Commonwealth. Its field of interest is primarily, but not exclusively, that of the social sciences. . . . The library is designed to meet the twofold purpose of supporting the work done in the Institute's seminars, and of giving guidance to students, especially from overseas, on other resources. For the first purpose it is building up a select collection of primary materials, on Commonwealth relations, race relations and demography within the Commonwealth, and political, economic and social development, particularly in the tropical territories. . . . For the second purpose, a strong bibliographical section is being built up by the acquisition of bibliographies, indexes to periodical literature, guides and indexes to government publications and parliamentary papers of the United Kingdom and Commonwealth countries, and similar aids to research. A bibliography of bibliographies in the library and a register of theses in United Kingdom universities are maintained."[12]

Institutes in such specialised fields can fit naturally into the pattern of library provision in the University. The case of the Institutes of Classical Studies (1953) and Germanic Languages and Literatures (1950) is more complex. The **Institute of Classical Studies** is housed in the same building as the Institute of Archaeology, and its library is complementary to that of the Hellenic and Roman Societies, which shares the same premises. This joint library of over 35,000 volumes, including 250 sets of periodicals, was in large measure ready-made for the Institute. Similarly the Priebsch collection, comprising first and early editions of German Classical and Romantic writers, which forms a separate unit of the library of the **Institute of Germanic Languages and Literatures,** has provided a base on which the library can build,[13] but the line of demarcation between the material appropriate to these institutes and to the University Library and the libraries of the colleges, where the tradition of providing strong collections in classical and Germanic studies is of long establishment, is a difficult one to draw. There would seem to be need for further clarification of the overall policy of the University in these fields.

There remain to be considered two institute libraries of a special character. The first of these is the library of the **Institute of Education** which began life in 1902 as the London Day Training College, a teacher training college established by the London County Council. Its director had the title and status of Professor of Education in the University. In 1932 the L.C.C. transferred the College to the University. It has the responsibility of training graduate teachers, and differs from other Institutes of Education in that it is also the Department of Education of London University. Hence the library has a dual responsibility – that of supplying student material for a one-year Certificate of Education course and research material for Diplomas, Associateships and higher degrees. This Institute also has much wider functions than those of any other of the Postgraduate Institutions, since, although very much concerned with research in education, it is also the Area Training Organisation for a large part of the Home Counties, and is thus responsible for the training of all teachers in this area, and for the promotion of further studies among teachers practising in the area. The constituent Teachers' Training Colleges (thirty-four in number) make their own library provision for students, and the Institute Library serves mainly the needs of staff and postgraduate students. The stock totals over 60,000 books and 20,000 pamphlets and there are 600 periodicals currently received. The library has a general collection reflecting the needs of the teaching departments and is particularly strong in Psychology of Education, Comparative Education and Education in Commonwealth Countries. For many years it was gravely handicapped by lack of space, but at the end of 1958 it moved into new, albeit still temporary, quarters. The library now has one large reading room with six small carrels and another room housing archive material, such as Local Education Authority papers. It also has a reference library of Research and Comparative Education, access to which is restricted to staff and research students. Being in close proximity to the University Library, it has a policy of co-operation in the acquisition of material in the history of education.

The last of the institutes to be considered is the **Warburg Institute** which differs from all others in its origin and function. It began as the private library of Professor A. M. Warburg (1866–1929) in Hamburg. His field of work may be briefly defined as the history of the classical tradition, but his "ideas proved to be so fertile that Warburg's library, originally collected merely for his own studies, grew to be a centre for scholars of various descriptions; anthropologists, theologians and historians of religion, medievalists, psychologists, folklorists, philologists and antiquaries not only found the books they needed for their special researches but found them arranged in such a manner as to suggest certain interactions with and relations to other subjects."[14]

The Institute was founded in Hamburg, but with the advent to power of the Nazis was faced with destruction. It sought refuge with its library in London in 1934, but although the University had been active in assisting the transfer, it was not until 1944 that the Warburg Institute was incorporated in the University. It now provides facilities for research "on the symbolism of the religions, arts and literatures of the Mediterranean civilisations. The library (about 100,000 books and offprints, and 900 runs of periodicals) is arranged in four main sections covering the fields of History of Religion, Early Science and Philosophy, History of Literature and Learning, History of Art, and History of Social Forms; and it allows open access to the shelves. The photographic collection (about 230,000) contains material for the history and iconography of classical art in post-classical times, in particular for the tradition of astrological and mythological illustrations."[15]

With such a history and such a special character, it is difficult to place the Warburg Institute Library in the pattern of libraries of the University. It is obvious that it is a research library of great importance for scholars not only within the University but from all parts of the world, but it is also obvious that its stock (apart from the superb photographic collections) must to some extent overlap with and duplicate material available elsewhere in the University. The justification of this duplication lies in the special arrangement of the materials in juxtaposition with the very extensive holdings of foreign material not to be found elsewhere. "The scholar who is expected to penetrate into the borderlands of his special subject must find the new territory ready surveyed for him by the able planning of an expert."[16] In 1958 the Institute moved to its new premises in the University precinct which provide excellent deployment of its specialised and specially arranged resources.

The libraries of the Postgraduate Medical School of London, of the London School of Hygiene and Tropical Medicine, and of the thirteen Postgraduate Medical Institutes are designed to serve the same purpose in relation to medical research and teaching in the University as the institutes already described in relation to other subjects. Since they fall within the scope of the chapter on *Medical Libraries*, there is no need to deal with them further.

THE LIBRARIES OF INSTITUTIONS WITH RECOGNISED TEACHERS

The libraries of the fourth and final category of University institutions – the Institutions with recognised teachers – do not properly belong to this survey, since they are not supported by University funds and are not designed primarily to serve the needs of University staff and students as such. It is worth observing, however, that the libraries of the colleges of technology are receiving greater attention than previously as a result of the increased government grants for technological education; that the libraries of John Innes Horticultural Institution and Rothamsted Experimental Station perform important functions in relation to horticultural and agricultural research; and that the libraries of the Royal College of Music and the Royal Academy of Music contain collections of great value in musicological studies.

CO-ORDINATION AND CO-OPERATION

The question that naturally arises in considering the large and complicated network of libraries at present serving the University is what degree of co-ordination and co-operation exists for the rational planning of these resources and their maximum exploitation. It has already been stated that all the libraries of the University are independent of one another to the extent that each is under the control of the governing body of its own college – and in the case of the University Library the Senate. But to a large extent these governing bodies have an inter-locking membership – many members of the Senate are members of the governing bodies of colleges and also on the councils of the institutes. This means that those who are responsible for library policies are aware of the needs not only of the individual institution, but also of the University as a whole.

At the administrative and routine level, there are many examples of schemes of co-operation and informal consultation, some of which have already been mentioned. One further one may be mentioned – the agreed distribution of responsibility for the collection of specialised law periodicals between the libraries of the London School of Economics, University College, the School of Oriental and African Studies and the Institute of Advanced Legal Studies – with the University Library maintaining a general collection for reference and student needs.

The librarians, however, have in recent years become increasingly aware of the need for closer consultation, more detailed discussion and fuller information amongst themselves. This has led to the establishment of the Standing Conference of Librarians of Libraries of the University of London, which holds periodic meetings and has appointed a number of sub-committees to investigate and report on various aspects of co-operation.

One of the most obvious fields for investigation is that of union catalogues. This is a subject that has been frequently mooted in the past; but desirable as a general union catalogue clearly is in some ways, it has been felt that the value would probably not be commensurate with the immense effort involved. A number of union lists of periodicals in special subjects have already been produced, and the present sub-committee is considering other projects of a similarly limited, and therefore manageable nature, such as the compilation of a directory of special collections. There have been so far two tangible results of the work of the Standing Conference. One of these is the production of a news bulletin giving information on developments, plans, staff and so on in the libraries – information which previously has been surprisingly slow in disseminating itself. The other is participation in the planning of a new repository library.

Almost all the libraries here described complain of present lack of space or at least look ahead to the need for extension. This is not simply the librarian's battle-cry learnt by rote and repeated by reflex action. The need for space is real and is the natural concomitant of the growth of the University and the Colleges themselves, which in its turn is dictated by the increase in the numbers of university students. In many libraries plans for extension or for new and additional building are in progress. These are essential to meet the seating requirements of library readers. They are necessary, also, to house the growing stocks. But an additional solution to the latter problem is being sought in a repository library, which is in process of erection at Egham in the grounds of Royal Holloway College, that is some twenty-two miles from the University site in Bloomsbury. This repository library is intended for the use of all libraries of the University. The initial construction will be for 250,000 volumes, but the building is capable of extension to house at least two million volumes. It is primarily intended as a book store, but there will be a small reading room for the consultation of books on the premises. A Committee of Management will be established to administer the repository, but so far the details of administration have not been elaborated. It seems likely that it will be possible for libraries of the University either to earmark space for reserve stock exclusively for their own use, or to send books to be placed in a general reserve, from which the books can be borrowed by any library of the University. Such a general reserve would require some cataloguing and processing procedures at the repository itself. Whatever measures are finally adopted, it is clear the inception of the repository can mark an important stage in the development of long-term co-ordination of the stocks of the libraries of the University.

It is to be hoped that this brief survey provides some clarification of the picture of these libraries, not merely by listing and describing them, but by showing them in their evolution and development. The picture that emerges is of a vast organism in the process of growth. Nothing is inflexible, but the direction of future growth is dependent on what has gone before. All librarians are only too well aware of the extent to which even within their own libraries they have to live and compromise with the past as well as plan for the future. If at any given moment the structure appears over-rigid and the needs appear to have outgrown the forms, it is comforting to reflect on the changing pattern of the last hundred years, and to recall that in little over a century the wealth of the University embodied in its books has grown from a negligible figure to the impressive total of over three million volumes.

NOTES AND REFERENCES

[1] The teaching of science in Westfield College will be developed in 1961, with the erection of the new Science Building.

[2] This collection originally included many items of Oriental and Slavonic interest. These were later transferred to the School of Oriental and African Studies and the School of Slavonic and East European Studies.

[3] Preface to the Catalogue of R. C. Trevelyan Memorial Library, 1959.

[4] University of London Calendar, 1958–59. 401.

5 Calendar of the School of Oriental and African Studies, 1958–59. Part X. The Library. 138–142.

6 Report of the Interdepartmental Commission of Enquiry on Oriental Slavonic, East European and African Studies. London, H.M.S.O., 1947.

7 Details of the many other special collections and major additions to the library will be found in the Calendar of the School, and its resources on South Asia and the Far East are further detailed in *The Journal of Asian Studies*, XVII, 1957, 183–188. For a description of the important manuscript holdings of the library, see PEARSON, J. D. Oriental Manuscript Collections in the Libraries of Great Britain and Ireland. London, Royal Asiatic Society, 1954, pp. 13–16.

8 Prospectus of the School of Slavonic and East European Studies, 1958–59.

9 Calendar of The Imperial College of Science and Technology, 1958–59. 80.

10 LOGAN, Sir D. W. *op. cit* 28.

11 Calendar of the University of London, 1958–59. 367. The use now made of the Institute library by teachers and post graduate students from other universities, both in Britain and overseas, is very extensive.

12 Calendar of University of London, 1958–59. 360.

13 The Institute has recently acquired part of the library of the late Professor Friedrich Gundolf, including many manuscripts of his own writings and files of his correspondence with members of the Stefan George circle.

14 BING, C. The Warburg Institute. *Lib. Assn. Rec.* 4th Series 1 (8) 1934, 262–266.

15 Calendar of the University of London, 1958–59, 369.

16 BING, C. *op. cit.*

CHAPTER XVI

THE LONDON LIBRARY

By the late C. J. Purnell

BEFORE 1841 there was no general library in London from which the more serious and learned books could be borrowed. There were subscription libraries for fiction and light literature as well as a few small institutional libraries and Dr. Williams's Library which was largely theological. A 'London Library' had been established in 1785 in Ludgate Street with rules similar to those of the present London Library, and a printed catalogue was issued in 1786. In 1801 it was moved to Hatton Gardens and a little later it was amalgamated with the Westminster Library in Jermyn Street, but nothing seems to be known of the fate of this library.

On 18th May, 1832, Thomas Carlyle wrote in his journal: "What a sad want I am in of libraries, of books to gather facts from! Why is there not a Majesty's library in every county town? There is a Majesty's gaol and gallows in every one."

In 1839 busy with his preparatory work on Cromwell he began to feel more acutely the need of such a library and enlisted the help of his friends in furthering the project of starting one. Most energetic among these was William Dougal Christie, a Cambridge scholar of 24 and barrister, who acted as Joint Honorary Secretary till the library was established. Christie was later M.P. for Weymouth and envoy to Brazil. He died in 1874.

The story of their efforts is told in *Carlyle and the London Library, an account of its foundation: with unpublished letters of Thomas Carlyle*, edited by Frederic Harrison in 1907, and in *Carlyle and the London Library*, by Simon Nowell-Smith (*English libraries, 1800–1850*. Lewis, 1958, pp. 59 *seqq.*). Prominent among their activities was the public meeting, presided over by Lord Eliot, of "Friends to the establishment of a Library from which books may be had by subscribers at their homes" held on 24th June, 1840, at which Carlyle made (apart from addresses and lectures) his one and only speech.

The whole speech is worth reading. Here are a few extracts:

"A book is a kind of thing that requires a man to be self-collected. He must be alone with it. A good book is the purest essence of a human soul. How could a man take it into a crowd, with bustle of all sorts going on around him? The good of a book is not the facts that can be got out of it, but the kind of resonance that it awakens in our own minds. A book may strike out of us a thousand things, may make us know a thousand things which it does not know itself. For this purpose I decidedly say, that no man can read a book well, with the bustle of three or four hundred people about him. Even forgetting the mere facts which a book contains, a man can do more with it in his own apartment, in the solitude of one night, than in a week in such a place as the British Museum.

"London has more men and intellect waiting to be developed than any place in the world ever had assembled. Yet there is no place on the civilised earth so ill-supplied with materials for reading for those who are not rich. I have read an account of a Public Library in Iceland, which the King of Denmark founded there. There is not a peasant in Iceland that cannot bring home books to his hut, better than men can in London. Positively it is a kind of disgrace to us, which we ought to assemble and put an end to with all convenient despatch. The founding of a Library is one of the greatest things we can do with regard to results. It is one of the quietest of things; but, there is nothing that I know of at bottom more important. Every one able to read a good book becomes a wiser man. He becomes a similar centre of light and order, and just insight into the things around him.

"A collection of good books contains all the nobleness and wisdom of the world before us. Every heroic and victorious soul has left his stamp upon it. A collection of books is the best of all Universities; for the University only teaches us how to read the book: you must go to the book itself for what it is. I call it a church also – which every devout soul may enter – a church but with no quarrelling, no church-rates . . ."

The remainder of the sentence was drowned in cheers and laughter, in the midst of which Mr. Carlyle sat down.

The chairman and speakers at the meeting were nominated as members of the committee to draw up rules and organise the library and at their first meeting, held at 450A West Strand in July 1840, the following attended: Carlyle, Gladstone, Lord Lyttelton, G. Cornewall Lewis, Monkton Milnes, Philip Pusey and George Venables.

Subsequently meetings were held at 57 and later at 49 Pall Mall.

At the meeting held on 28th November, 1840, it was resolved to open the library on 1st May, 1841, afterwards altered to the 3rd, and a circular was issued calling in promised subscriptions and stating the opinion of the committee that "the establishment of the library will be a great benefit to all residents in London . . . to all followers of literature and science who cannot study with comfort and advantage in a public room . . . and to all families both in London and the country who, needing more books than they can afford to purchase, have now no other resource than the comparatively meagre one of circulating libraries".

On 27th January, 1841, Carlyle proposed J. G. Cochrane as librarian and he was duly elected and acted until 1852.

In the meantime, Christie, inspired by Carlyle, had issued in 1841 a pamphlet with the title *Explanation of the scheme of the London Library*. In this he gave a short survey of the libraries of other countries and emphasised the need for, and usefulness of, the proposed establishment in London of a library which should contain books in all departments of literature and philosophy, and in all languages. "Its chief distinguishing feature will be the privilege enjoyed by subscribers of having books at their homes both in London and in the country." He hinted at a total membership of 5,000, a total not reached until 1944.

Christie ended with the words, "a Lending Library, worthy of the City and of the Nation, to aid and bless learners and teachers alike, strengthening with strong food or soothing with soft medicines the souls of the many, guiding and lightening the labours of those who build up the nation's wisdom and the nation's fame. . . . May it be given to me to see the plant which we have planted and whose young growth we have watched and watered become, by the nation's care, a mighty tree flourishing and bringing forth fruit, growing ever and strengthening, scattering bounties innumerable, standing through future ages, green and strong, a blessing and a glory to the land."

These lengthy quotations from the initial proceedings of the library's promoters are given as they explain the ideals proposed for the library. These ideals were again set forth by Lord Balfour who, presiding at the library's annual meeting on 14th June, 1906, said: "The London Library did not pretend to rival or, indeed, to occupy any portion of the field which was so well occupied by the ordinary lending libraries. The work done by the latter was important and valuable, but it was not the work of their institution nor was it a work with which they could with advantage compete.

"The London Library existed for all those who desired to have at their command the literature of all ages and countries, to have it accessible and to have it in a shape in which they could use it, not merely in that building, but in their own homes.

"He was informed that, so far as foreign literature was concerned there was really no institution in the country in which the best foreign works were so well represented. That their institution carried out the purposes for which it was brought into existence was conclusively shown by the character of the books which were taken out, and which certainly proved that they were not merely turned to the purpose of spending an idle hour agreeably, but that the resources of the library were used in the most important works of historic, scientific and philosophical research."

Three months were devoted to the selection and purchase of books and on 3rd May, 1841, the library was opened. It began in two rooms at 49 Pall Mall rented at £150 a year; with a collection of 3,000 books and a membership of about 500. Original members paid an entrance fee of £6 and an annual subscription of £2. Later the entrance fee was reduced and the annual subscription raised, firstly to £3 then to £3 3s., in 1926 to £4 4s, in 1952 to £6 6s. and in 1958 to £10 10s.

The Earl of Clarendon was the library's first President and remained so until his death in 1870 when Carlyle was elected, to be succeeded by Lord Houghton (1881), Lord Tennyson (1885), Sir Leslie Stephen (1893), Earl Balfour (1904), the Rt. Hon. H. A. L. Fisher (1930), the Earl of Ilchester (1940), T. S. Eliot (1952). The Prince Consort consented to be Patron of the library which has continued under royal patronage ever since.

By 1845 the two rooms were inadequate and the library was moved to its present position, 12 (now numbered 14) St. James's Square, then known as Beauchamp House, at first on a lease with the Royal Statistical Society as sub-tenant and later as owner of the freehold. Gladstone's advice is said to have decided the committee in 1879 to make the purchase for £21,000. The property included stables with exit at No. 7 Duke Street and a house known as No. 9 Duke Street. Beauchamp House soon became overcrowded with books, although the shelves reached from floor to ceiling, and Hagberg Wright, on his appointment as librarian in 1893, saw the necessity of rebuilding. Donations were invited and a loan raised with the result that by 1897 the premises were transformed into a well-equipped library with a long entrance hall, reading room and bookstacks in which ladders were no longer needed.

An additional book store of seven floors designed to hold 180,000 volumes was built on No. 7 Duke Street in 1922 and No. 9 Duke Street was rebuilt and incorporated in the northern extension which was completed in 1934. This new building took in adjoining property in Mason's Yard and provided an addition to the reading room, a new committee room, staff rooms and six floors of bookstacks.

The library owns the freehold of all this property as well as of No. 8 Duke Street which was acquired in 1913 to make possible by removal of basements and 'ancient lights' the building of the stack on part of No. 7. To enable these properties to be purchased and the buildings to be erected, members contributed generously from time to time to donation funds, and sums were reserved from the library's yearly revenue. Mortgage debentures which were also issued have now all been redeemed.

It was the extension in Mason's Yard that was hit by a high-explosive bomb during the night of 23rd February, 1944. The bomb exploded on contact, but even so it wrecked the top four floors of the latest bookstacks and the blast did extensive damage to other parts of the library which had to be closed for four months while books were salvaged and rearranged. Otherwise the library functioned throughout the war, a selection of the scarcest books only being evacuated. The wrecked store has been rebuilt. The oldest periodicals which were on the top floor suffered most damage, especially those with titles beginning with letters in the second half of the alphabet. There were also heavy losses in theological books and in biographies of persons with names beginning with letters from G to J and from S to Z. About 16,000 volumes were either destroyed or too badly damaged to be worth binding.

ADMINISTRATION

At its foundation the library was governed by a President, four Vice-Presidents, three Trustees and a Committee of twenty-four elected from among the members of the library. In 1934 the King was graciously pleased to accede to the committee's request for a Royal Charter. This made no difference to the library's policy or rules except that Trustees were no longer necessary and the number of Vice-Presidents was increased to not more than seven. The Charter gave the library a status which it had hitherto not possessed.

The books in the library have been carefully selected over the years with the help of a long succession of learned and critical students and, as Mr. Frederic Harrison said in 1911, "I believe it now contains all the volumes which a general reader, or even a special student ordinarily has in use."

In the past there have worked on the committee and laboured to build up its store of books such eminent historians as Thomas Carlyle, George Grote, H. Hallam, T. B. Macaulay, J. A. Froude, Earl Stanhope, Sir James Stephen, W. H. Lecky, J. Cotter Morison, Sir Adolphus Ward, Goldwin Smith, Viscount Bryce, H. A. L. Fisher, Sir Herbert Richmond.

Such men of science as Alfred R. Wallace, Professor Huxley, Professor Clifford, Sir J. Lubbock, Herbert Spencer, Sir Francis Galton, St. George Mivart, G. J. Romanes, Sir Archibald Geikie, Sir Arthur Keith, Sir Frederick Treves.

Such critics as John Forster, Arthur Helps, Lord Houghton, Henry Reeve, G. H. Lewes, J. J. Jusserand, Mark Pattison, W. Courthope, Andrew Lang, Dr. W. Smith, Sir Sidney Lee, Sir Edmund Gosse.

Such divines as Bishop Wilberforce, Archbishop Trench, Dean Stanley, Dean Bradley, Frederick Maurice, Dean Milman, Archdeacon Cheetham, Dr. Vaughan, Bishop Thirlwell, Dean Wace, Dean Inge.

Such eminent writers as W. M. Thackeray, Walter Besant, Charles Kingsley, Bunsen, Spedding, Tennyson, Richard Hutton, Leslie Stephen, George Meredith, Dame Rose Macaulay.

The General Committee now meet five times a year. Members of the library meet once a year to pass the annual report and to elect members of committee, etc. The chair is usually taken by the President, or in his absence by a Vice-President, who is supported by members of committee. Many interesting speeches on these occasions have been made by eminent statesmen, historians, critics and others. Among Vice-Presidents who took the chair have been the Duke of Northumberland (1919), the Marquess Curzon of Kedleston (1923), Viscount Ullswater (1927), Viscount Haldane (1928).

A special meeting was held on 5th December, 1898, for the ceremony of the opening of the new building, when Lord Wolseley took the chair and Leslie Stephen, as President, declared the building open. A similar meeting took place on 13th April, 1934, when the new wing was formally opened by the Marquess of Crewe, speeches also being made by the Rt. Hon. H. A. L. Fisher, Earl Baldwin, and the Earl of Ilchester.

The anticipated celebration of the library's centenary to be held in 1941 was prevented by the war but special mention was made at the annual meeting on 6th July by the President and Dr. G. M. Trevelyan, and *The Times Literary Supplement*, 3rd May, 1941, devoted a whole page to an article on the library by the late Harold Child.

The instructions of the committee are carried out by the secretary who is also the librarian, and the following have been appointed to this office: J. G. Cochrane in 1841, William Bodham Donne in 1852, Robert Harrison in 1857, C. T. Hagberg Wright (Knighted in 1934) in 1893, C. J. Purnell (formerly sub-librarian) in 1940, Simon Nowell-Smith in 1950 and Stanley Gillam (formerly sub-librarian) in 1956.

Donne's appointment was strongly supported by Carlyle against Gladstone's nomination of J. P. Lacaita. Carlyle took little part in the management of the library after his appointment and when, in 1870, he accepted election as President he did so on the specific understanding that he must never be asked to preside. Wright's appointment in 1893 was a most fortunate one for the library and after his death in 1940 the following tribute was written of him: "It is certainly no exaggeration to say that the library as it is today is the creation of Sir Charles Hagberg Wright." He lived up to Carlyle's ideal expressed in 1840. "He will be as a wise servant, watchful, diligent, discerning what is what, incessantly endeavouring, *rough-hewing* all things for us, and under the guise of a wise servant, *ruling* while he actually serves."

In 1924 the committee inaugurated a non-contributory staff super-annuation scheme. The fund has been built up by generous gifts from members of the library and by sums set aside annually by the library. It is administered by the Public Trustee.

In addition to the books selected from time to time by the committee, the collection has been enriched by the purchase of books required by members working on some special subject. Many uncommon books difficult to procure nowadays are in consequence to be found on the library's shelves and Hagberg Wright's special interest in Russia and her literature has resulted in the library having one of the best Russian collections in England.

The library is specially strong in books on philosophy, history, literature (English and foreign), topography, archaeology and art, while theology is well represented. Only general books on science are purchased, but natural history is not neglected and the library has some fine books such as Gould's *Birds of Great Britain* (presented by the late P. A. Cohen) and Mathew's *Birds of Australia*. Among out of the way collections is that of literary and historical letters and documents printed by Italian scholars as gifts on marriages of friends and known as 'Per Nozze'. The library also possesses many valuable sets of periodicals and publications of learned societies such as the *Jahrbuch der Preussischen Kunstsammlungen*, the *Jahrbuch der Kunsthistorischen Sammlungen zu Wien*, publications of the Literarischer Verein in Stuttgart and of the Roxburghe Club, to give a few examples.

The largest addition to the library made by purchase was that of the Allan Library bought in 1920. Though largely theological, this contains many historical works and is rich in contemporary Reformation tracts and early editions of the Bible and includes also about seventy incunabula. Between 1911 and 1919 about £800 was expended at the various sales of the Huth Library.

Gifts and bequests of books and money have been numerous. The Prince Consort, shortly after the foundation of the library, gave various books including *Antiquités mexicaines*, 2 vols. folio. Napoleon III, who used the library while living in nearby King Street, presented volumes of the monumental *Histoire générale de Paris*.

Mr. John Chorley, in 1854, gave many rare Spanish plays and arranged a series of similar dramas purchased by the library a year later.

John Stuart Mill gave many philosophical works and Mrs. Mackay 6,000 volumes, chiefly philosophical and theological, used by her husband Robert William Mackay while writing his *Progress of the intellect*. Mrs. Edwin Edwards, in 1883, presented some 400 books written by foreigners about England – these volumes form the bulk of a collection labelled on the shelves *Foreign Impressions of England*.

The executors of Sir Leslie Stephen presented the books which he had used while writing his *History of English thought in the 18th century*, Austin Dobson shortly before his death gave his set of Hogarth prints and his family subsequently added books relating to the same period, Sir Sidney Lee bequeathed early sixteenth-century editions of Italian poets, and Sir Edmund Gosse gave a hundred or so Scandinavian books used for his *Studies in the literature of Northern Europe*.

The bequests of F. C. Conybeare's Armenian Library and of Sir Ernest Wallis Budge's Ethiopic books and the gift by the late Alfred E. Hippesley of his collection of Chinese histories, etc., added considerably to the library's Oriental section.

The library owes to the late Mr. P. A. Cohen the possession of a Fourth Folio Shakespeare, and a magnificent copy of the Kelmscott Chaucer bound at the Doves Press bindery, as well as the facsimile of the Ellesmere Chaucer and many valuable books with coloured plates such as Ackermann's *Microcosm of London* and Pyne's *History of the*

Royal Residences, the purchase of which the library could not have afforded.

The late Mr. John F. Baddeley gave during his lifetime much valuable material, largely in Russian, for the history of the Caucasus and Mongolia and bequeathed the remainder of his collections to the library. He also gave a large collection of portraits and prints of London formed by his mother, Mrs. Fraser Baddeley, which are shelved in special cases in the Art Room.

Mr. Henry Yates Thompson, a trustee of the library for many years, in addition to many other books and money gifts, presented a copy of the Aldine Theocritus, 1495, adorned by an illuminated border and pastoral scene attributed to Dürer. The volume belonged to Pirckheimer and contains his book-plate designed by Dürer. Mrs. Thompson later bequeathed a selection from her husband's library of books mostly connected with illuminated manuscripts to the value of £500, and an additional £1,000 was given through the generosity of the executors. Lord Riddell left £5,000 and his collection of books to the library, and more recently Mrs. J. W. Mackail gave from her husband's library such books as were not already possessed. Mr. Edward Herm-Allen bequeathed his very extensive collection of editions of Omar Khayyam and the works of Edward Fitzgerald, and about 1,400 volumes from the library at Marlborough House were received from the executors of the late Queen Mary, who had accepted honorary membership shortly before her last illness.

The library does not buy manuscripts, but a few have been presented from time to time, including an illuminated Ethiopic Life of St. George bequeathed by Wallis Budge, John Mill's Commonplace books and Charles Reade's collection of cuttings and notes used as material for his novels.

The largest single legacy ever received was that of Major William Prevost which amounted to over £16,000 and enabled the committee to proceed with the building extension of 1933-34. Other large bequests not mentioned above were those of J. R. Solly (£2,950) and Mrs. H. B. Charlton (£7,160). In 1957 the library received £10,000 from an anonymous donor.

The library receives no outside assistance of any sort. It has been built up to its present size and importance entirely from the members' subscriptions, donations and bequests. The present bookstock is estimated at about three-quarters of a million.

For the annual subscription of ten guineas, members living in the

London postal district may borrow up to ten volumes at a time; those in the country fifteen. These, provided they are not required by other members and are re-entered regularly, may be kept indefinitely. Students and scholars who are unable to afford the full subscription can be helped by the Carlyle Trust, which was set up in 1952 principally for the purpose of making the resources of the library available to those to whom membership is invaluable but whose incomes are insufficient to meet the cost.

ARRANGEMENT OF BOOKS

When Hagberg Wright came from the National Library of Ireland, of which he was sub-librarian and which he helped to re-classify according to Dewey, he decided not to adopt this system for the London Library.

Instead he arranged the books in large groups such as History, Literature, Religion, Science, Topography, etc., each of which occupied separate floors of bookstacks. These he subdivided into smaller divisions which are arranged alphabetically under their author's names or the word under which they appear in the Author Catalogue. This is ticked on the title-page and the subject division is written on the back of the title-page and entered in the marked copy of the catalogue or on the tops of the cards. The following are examples of shelf-markings: H. Assyria for History, subdivision Assyria. S. Birds for Science, subdivision Birds.

By this method members of the staff and readers can find most books without looking them up in the catalogue, and the books can be shifted when necessary without alteration in the catalogue.

Dictionaries and encyclopaedias are arranged alphabetically under their subjects in the reading room where the current numbers of periodicals, annuals, etc., are also kept. Bound volumes of periodicals and serial publications of societies are shelved in alphabetical order of their titles in the bookstacks. A bound set of *The Times* from 1812 is kept in the basement where are also Parliamentary Papers and a collection of over 3,000 volumes of pamphlets.

CATALOGUES

The first catalogue of the library was printed in 1842 and ran to 140 pages octavo. Supplements were issued in 1843 and 1844 and new editions and further supplements in 1847, 1852, 1856, 1865, 1875 and

1888. Hagberg Wright compiled an entirely new Catalogue in 1903 of 1,626 double-column quarto pages and a new edition brought up to date was issued in 1913–14 in two volumes of 1,400 and 1,340 pages. Supplements were printed in 1920, 1928 and 1953. British Museum practice has been followed with some exceptions but titles of books have been abbreviated for the sake of economy.

A Subject Index arranged alphabetically was issued in 1909 with supplements in 1923, 1938 and 1955. These volumes include much material not found in other indexes and are used extensively in libraries in this country and abroad.

CHAPTER XVII

LEARNED SOCIETY LIBRARIES

By K. D. C. Vernon

Librarian, The Royal Institution of Great Britain

THE libraries of the numerous learned societies in London together contain a vast accumulation of literature ranging over the sciences, fine arts and humanities. Many are highly specialised and some have unrivalled collections in their own subject fields. The societies which these libraries serve have, in many cases, long and honourable histories having contributed greatly to learning and culture and, in a typically English manner, they are proud that they have contributed so much without having received any official support from the Government. These societies are voluntary associations of men and women who have come together because they are interested in the aims and objects which the societies serve and they feel that they can pursue those interests better as members of a society, rather than as individuals. The libraries therefore have been collected together for the purpose of serving the objects to which the various societies are dedicated and they do this, for the most part, by serving their members. The libraries, some of which are of great national importance, belong to the members of the societies and are supported by funds which have been and still are provided by the members. Thus, strictly speaking, they are private libraries, but as we shall see, trespassers are not prosecuted for seeking information from them.

Before considering the history, contents and purpose of the more important libraries within this group, it is necessary to define the difference between a learned and a professional society. The difference is, in fact, slight, but in order to explain how the dividing line between this and the subsequent chapter on technical and professional libraries has been chosen, we must attempt a definition.

A learned society, as we understand it in this country, is an association of people with a common interest who wish to pursue that interest corporately. They may or may not all be members of a profession or holders of particular qualifications, but they do all wish to promote the study and development of some branch of learning. They do this by holding meetings and discussions and by issuing publications. People are proposed and elected for membership by the members who support the society by their subscriptions. The Chemical Society is an example.

A professional society is an association of the members of one profession who qualify for membership by passing examinations organised by the society and these qualifications entitle them to pursue their professions. The society watches over the interests of the profession and speaks and acts for the profession with the authority of its members. In all other ways professional societies are similar to learned societies. The Royal Institute of British Architects is, for example, the main professional society for architects as the Library Association is for librarians. Broadly speaking, institutes and institutions are professional bodies, societies are not; but there are many exceptions.

This is the dividing line which has been used to decide, somewhat arbitrarily, whether a library will be described in this chapter or in the second half of the subsequent chapter. The administration, financing and running of the two types of libraries are, however, almost identical, although every learned and professional society has its own bye-laws and an individuality which it jealously guards.

The libraries of learned societies all exist as departments of the institution which they serve and whether they are of national importance, such as the library of the Royal Society of London, or merely small jumbled collections of books, the council or governing body of the society has complete control over them. The librarians are responsible to their chief executive officers, with a library committee, composed of members of the society, which is responsible for advising the council or governing body on matters of library policy and administration. The council decides on the allotment of funds to the library from the society's resources and this decision determines the level of service which can be offered by the library. The members of the society are the main body of users and they are able to borrow books and periodicals; but any bona fide scholars are also admitted on application and the libraries, for the most part, co-operate informally with each other and with other types of libraries through the various library co-operation schemes which are in existence. Thus, the service they give reaches out far beyond the immediate membership and the objects of the societies are being followed by this kind of service.

London is particularly fortunate in the large number of learned societies which are situated there. In this chapter no attempt will be made to give a comprehensive picture of the many societies and their libraries; instead, it is proposed to consider briefly a few groups of libraries which are linked either by similar subject interests or by physical location and by this sample to indicate the immense resources of this whole group of libraries. The largest number of societies are concerned with the sciences – physical and biological; so we will begin looking in on their libraries by considering those situated in Burlington House, Piccadilly. In this veritable seat of learning for the sciences and arts there are the Royal Society, the Chemical Society, the Geological Society, the Linnean Society, the Royal Astronomical Society, the Society of Antiquaries and of course the Royal Academy, each with its own library. The first Burlington House was erected about 1664. It was rebuilt early in the eighteenth century and subsequently came into the possession of the Government. In 1867 the Royal Academy was granted a lease of the house on the condition that additions should be made to it to conform with the buildings which the Government proposed to erect round the courtyard to the south for certain learned societies. These societies had all been in existence for a considerable time in various places in London and latterly in Somerset House, but it was thought to be advantageous to bring them together in one central locality. Thus they moved into Burlington House in the 1870s.

The **Royal Society,** founded in 1660 for improving natural knowledge, is the oldest and most eminent learned society in the country. Its earliest members numbered among their ranks Newton, Hooke, Boyle, Sir Christopher Wren and Halley, for example, and for three hundred years the Fellows of the Royal Society have led the way in scientific research in this country. To be elected a Fellow is one of the highest honours which a scientist can attain. The library was started very soon after the Society was founded and Hooke, who was the curator of experiments, used to purchase books regularly for the library. It continued to grow by gifts and purchases and now contains about 150,000 volumes and receives currently some 450 periodicals. From the earliest days it became customary for the Fellows of the Society to present copies of books which they had written and as the Fellows have always been the leading scientists in their various fields, the library has acquired a fine collection of the most notable books on all branches of science. It is especially strong in early scientific works and possesses about fifty incunabula.

As would be expected, the periodicals and serial publications form the largest part of the library and it has always been the policy to collect especially the publications of learned societies and academies from all over the world. Many of these publications are complete sets dating back to the foundation of the society or academy concerned and it is probable that no other library in Europe, at least, possesses such a fine collection of this class of scientific literature. The publications have mostly been received in exchange for the famous *Proceedings* or *Philosophical Transactions* of the Royal Society.

The library is also rich in archives and manuscripts. Among these are the manuscripts of the first two books of Newton's *Principia*, Boyle's letters and papers, the scientific correspondence of Sir John Herschel, the Society's own minute books and correspondence which, together with many other letters and manuscripts of leading scientists, make the collection immensely important in the history of science. The whole collection has recently been catalogued and arranged so that all the manuscripts may now be studied to better effect.

The Royal Society's library is indeed of great importance and its large gracious rooms are worthy both of the collection which they hold and of our premier scientific society which has done so much to expand and maintain the best traditions of British science during three centuries.

The **Chemical Society** was founded in 1841 for the general advancement of chemistry and is the oldest chemical society in the world. Its primary purposes are to foster original research in chemistry and to facilitate the discussion and dissemination of new knowledge in all branches of the science. Its *Journal* and other publications are of prime importance to chemists. The library is now the best chemical library in this country, containing over 50,000 volumes and receiving more than 500 current periodicals. This great collection of periodicals, many of which are complete sets, concerned with all branches of chemistry and allied subjects forms the bulk of the library and records the growth and expansion of man's knowledge in this important field of science where the recording of information is so vital for subsequent use and application.

The library serves not only the Chemical Society and its members, but also all the members of eight other societies concerned with chemistry which together form the Chemical Council. They all contribute to the upkeep of the library and thus avoid the duplication of effort and expenditure which would have been inevitable had each society formed a library of its own. The library has recently been reorganised and its facilities improved and the books are now classified by the U.D.C. Books and periodicals are available on loan and extensive use is made of photocopying. The library is well used by chemists throughout the country and plays an important part in the service of this vital branch of science.

The libraries of the **Royal Astronomical Society** and the **Geological Society** are the most important collections of literature in this country in the fields of astronomy and geology. The library of the Royal Astronomical Society, which was founded in 1820 with Sir William Herschel as its first President, contains some 10,000 volumes; it receives currently 200 periodicals concerned with astronomy and geophysics and maintains a collection of photographs and slides of celestial objects. The library of the Geological Society is very much larger containing about 100,000 volumes including some 500 current periodicals on geology and related subjects. The Society was founded in 1807 by a group of thirteen scientists who dined together at the Freemasons' Tavern on 13th November in that year for the purpose of forming a society to serve the science of geology. The group included G. B. Greenough, who became the first President of the Geological Society, Humphry Davy, William Allen, James Laird and William Babington.

The **Society of Antiquaries** was founded in 1707 by Humphrey Wanley, librarian to the Earl of Oxford, for the study of antiquity and the history of former times. It is now our second oldest society. The library, containing about 100,000 volumes, is concerned with all aspects of archaeological and antiquarian research and is the premier library of its kind in this country. It is an invaluable collection including many historic manuscripts and several incunabula.

The **Linnean Society** stands next to the Royal Astronomical Society in the west wing of Burlington House. This society was founded in 1788 by J. E. Smith and others for "the cultivation of the science of natural history in all its branches"; it almost collapsed between 1848 and 1858, but survived its financial difficulties and now has a fine record of service to science. The famous paper on natural selection by Darwin and Wallace was read before the Society in 1858.

The library was originally started by gifts of books presented to it and now contains 70,000 volumes including Linnaeus' own library of 1,600 books, many of which are annotated by him. The bulk of the collection consists of periodicals and publications of learned societies, in which it is immensely strong. Some 600 periodicals on natural history are currently received and botany especially is one of the main subjects in the library. It lends extensively through the National Central Library.

The last of the fine libraries in Burlington House is that of the **Royal Academy.** The library was started soon after the formation of the Academy in 1768 and so naturally possesses a good collection of eighteenth- and nineteenth-century books on the fine arts. Its catalogues of the Academy exhibitions, its archives and its collection of prints and drawings are of great value to students and historians of art. Like most art libraries it possesses a high proportion of large folio volumes which were produced at a time when publishers were able to do full justice to art and architectural illustrations. The policy of the library is that it should be a working collection on painting, sculpture and architecture for members and students of the Academy and is intended for reference purposes only.

In Albemarle Street, a short way from Burlington House, there is the **Royal Institution of Great Britain.** This famous society has as its objects "the promotion of science and the diffusion and extension of useful knowledge". Founded in 1799 by Benjamin Thompson, Count Rumford, the Institution has since that date pursued its objects with notable success by the twin method of research carried out in its laboratories and by lectures which have become famous not only for their high standard of exposition but also for the scientific demonstrations which illustrate them. The high quality of these lectures has been maintained since 1801 when Humphry Davy came to work at the Institution. Davy, Faraday, Tyndall, Dewar, Sir William Bragg and other notable scientists have in succession been the resident professor in the Institution and have all carried out their great research work in its laboratories. Probably no other learned society has such a remarkable record of scientific research.

The library was started soon after the foundation of the Institution and has grown steadily by means of gifts and purchases until today it contains some 60,000 volumes and receives 450 current periodicals on all branches of science. The library has recently been reorganised into two main divisions – the Old Library, which contains all works published up to the middle of the nineteenth century and which includes many rare books on science and other subjects; and the Modern Library containing books published since that time. The Old Library is now a model of what a learned society's library must have been like in the mid-nineteenth century, being arranged in the order of its old printed catalogue which was published in 1857. The Modern Library is classified by the Bliss Bibliographic Classification.

The library is very strong in its holdings of scientific periodicals, many of which are complete back to volume one. Although it is a very general scientific library, it is stronger in the physical sciences and is now building up its collection on the history of science. It also contains the invaluable manuscripts of Davy, Faraday, Tyndall and Dewar.

In addition to the Burlington House libraries and the Royal Institution, the physical sciences are also well served by two other smaller but more specialised libraries. The library of the **Physical Society**, founded in 1874 and recently amalgamated with the Institute of Physics, is strong in its collection of periodicals concerned with all aspects of physics and has a useful collection of some 2,000 books covering the same field. The **Royal Meteorological Society** has an important library of books, periodicals, photographs and lantern slides on meteorology, geophysics and allied subjects.

The next group of libraries is concerned with the biological sciences. In addition to the Linnean Society, there are the **Royal Agricultural Society**, the **Royal Entomological Society**, the **Royal Horticultural Society**, the **Royal Microscopical Society** and the **Zoological Society**. All these societies possess libraries varying in size from about 10,000 volumes in the library of the Royal Agricultural Society to 90,000 in the Zoological Society. Each library is important in its own field and all are particularly strong in historical works and in their collection of periodicals, because all these societies are well over one hundred years old.

Detailed attention cannot be given here to each society in this group, but the library of the **Zoological Society** is of prime importance. This famous society was founded in 1826 by Sir Stamford Raffles and Sir Humphry Davy for "the advancement of zoology and animal physiology, and for the introduction of new and curious subjects of the animal kingdom". It maintains the famous 'zoos' at Regent's Park and Whipsnade. The library, which was started in 1836, is most comprehensive for zoological literature and receives currently some 700 periodicals. It includes a fine collection of animal photographs and original paintings of mammals and birds. In addition to its other great services to zoology, the Society also publishes the *Zoological Record* which is a comprehensive annual bibliography of zoological literature.

Geography is catered for by the fine library of the **Royal Geographical Society** which contains about 100,000 volumes including many rare works of historical importance, and a remarkable collection of maps and charts, photographs and lantern slides. The Society was founded in 1830 for "the advancement of geographical knowledge by bringing together all interested in geography in its widest interpretation; assisting intending travellers with advice and the loan of scientific instruments; maintaining a collection of books and maps; and by diffusing information through lectures and periodical publications". These objects have been successfully pursued and the library is the leading collection on geography in this country.

The catalogue of subjects which are nobly served by our learned societies goes on. Anthropology, history, sociology and literature, for instance, all have their own societies and some of these have libraries. Engineering in particular has some magnificent libraries which are described in the following chapter, but the library of the **Royal Aeronautical Society** deserves mention here because it contains one of the finest collections of historical aeronautical books and prints in the world. The Society was founded as early as 1866 and the library has been in existence since that date. Some 200 periodicals are currently received, and collections of photographs and slides relating to aeronautical science are maintained. And finally the **Royal Society of Arts,** which was founded in 1754 by an obscure drawing master named William Shipley for the encouragement of arts, manufactures and commerce. After the Royal Society and the Society of Antiquaries it is the next oldest learned society in this country and still remains as one of the few unspecialised societies always ready to provide a forum for the discussion of important subjects within its wide scope of interest. Its work in many fields – technical, scientific, industrial, commercial and artistic – has been of great benefit to this country during the past two hundred years. The library contains about 10,000 volumes on a wide range of subjects, but especially on industrial art and design and on exhibitions. Its collections of letters and manuscripts are very important sources for historians of science, technology and the fine arts. The library receives about 250 current periodicals.

Enough has been said to show the immense scope of the many fine libraries maintained by our learned societies. These libraries, although they are intended primarily for the members of the societies, co-operate informally with one another and with other libraries through the National Central Library or through Aslib and admit bona fide inquirers who make suitable application. Their holdings of periodicals are immense; their historical books and manuscripts are a wonderful inheritance and a rich source of study for scholars; and their stocks of books and ancillary material are maintained in the service of science and culture in all its aspects. Some of the societies which own these fine libraries have been passing through difficult times and have not been able to provide the modern library services which they would desire, because they have not got sufficient money; others provide excellent service. But the members of all the various societies have at hand the literature which they need for their studies and they do get personal service from their librarians. Membership of most of these societies is not difficult to obtain if the person applying is seriously interested in the subject with which a particular society is concerned. Most learned societies do not require any particular qualifications of their members.

The work of these societies has contributed greatly to the increase of knowledge and the well-being of the community. From the publication of Newton's *Principia* in 1687 to the organisation of the International Geophysical Year in 1957–58, the Royal Society has led the way. Faraday at the Royal Institution opened the door to the vast development of the electrical industry by his discovery of electro-magnetic induction in 1831. The idea of the Great Exhibition of 1851, which did so much to encourage British industry, originated at the Royal Society of Arts. The Linnean Society provided the platform for announcing Darwin's and Wallace's theory of the origin of species. Today, in the lovely and gracious rooms at Burlington House, in the fine old house of the Royal Institution, in the charming Adam home of the Royal Society of Arts and in other less well-known places, the libraries of our learned societies are providing literature which is helping people to inquire into and to pursue lines of research and work which are still benefiting this country greatly. And these societies have always been voluntarily supported by men and women who consider the objects of the learned societies to be important. The results which they have achieved and still are achieving speak for themselves.

NOTES AND REFERENCES

General information on the history and development of learned and professional societies is not well documented. The following are useful studies:

BECKER, B. H. Scientific London. London, 1874.

BRITISH ASSOCIATION FOR THE ADVANCEMENT OF SCIENCE. London and the advancement of science. British Association, 1931.

COHEN, JOHN, and others. Natural history of learned and scientific societies. *Nature*, 1954, 173, 328–333.

McKIE, DOUGLAS. Scientific societies to the end of the eighteenth century. *Philosoph. Mag.*, 1948, Commemoration No., 133–143.

ORNSTEIN, M. The role of scientific societies in the seventeenth century. University of Chicago P., 1928.

Several of the published histories of science describe the development of the learned societies, e.g. MASON, S. F. A history of the sciences. Routledge, 1953.

Many societies have published their own histories and most of these include chapters or sections on their libraries. Some of these histories tell fascinating stories about the personalities and notable events connected with the history and development of our learned societies, e.g. histories of The Royal Society, Royal Society of Arts, Royal Academy, Royal Geographical Society, Linnean Society and others.

The libraries are dealt with more specifically in the following:

RICHARDSON, H. C. The working of the library of a learned society. *Lib. Assn. Rec.* 52 (11) 1950, 419–422.

THORNTON, JOHN L., and TULLY, R. I. J. Scientific books, libraries and collectors. Library Association, 1954.

VERNON, K. D. C. Libraries of learned societies and professional bodies (Chapter 9 in Five years work in librarianship 1950–55. Library Association, 1958).

VERNON, K. D. C. Lovely libraries: the libraries and work of some learned societies. Library Association. *Proc. of Annual Conference* 1956.

The following handbooks are useful for giving details of the work and objects of learned societies, including information about hours of opening, scope and facilities available in the various libraries:

Aslib directory: a guide to sources of information in Great Britain and Ireland. 2 vols. Aslib, 1957.

BRITISH ASSOCIATION FOR THE ADVANCEMENT OF SCIENCE. Directory of natural history and other field study societies in Great Britain. British Association, 1959.

HARROD, L. M., *comp.* The libraries of Greater London. Bell, 1951.

Scientific and learned societies of Great Britain. 59th edition. Allen & Unwin, 1958.

Chapter XVIII

TECHNICAL AND PROFESSIONAL LIBRARIES

By E. R. McColvin
Librarian, The Polytechnic

A DISTINCT group of libraries which have close affinities to those of both the university colleges and learned societies is that consisting of the technical colleges and professional institutions. Besides the mutual interest of these institutions in education, in seeing that the engineer, the architect or the banker, for example, has the opportunity to obtain the necessary qualifications to achieve success in his chosen profession, the growth and development of both these groups presents a chapter in the history of the public interest in science and engineering throughout the nineteenth century to the present day.

The early years of the nineteenth century were an awakening period in education. University College was founded in 1826 and King's College two years later. In 1833 elementary education was first assisted by the government grants. There was, too, a lively interest in scientific lecturing. Among the centres for this in London were the Royal Institution (see page 247) and the Royal Polytechnic Institution noted later. The Great Exhibition of 1851 led to the formation of the Science and Art Department, South Kensington in 1853.

Turning to the beginnings and growth of the Mechanics' Institutes, it was against this awakening in education, industry, and politics that the movement started. With the advent of the industrial revolution the old system of apprenticeship, whereby the master working with his apprentices gave them a complete knowledge of the particular craft, disintegrated. Apprenticeship, where it remained, was narrower in scope and less individual in character. The large-scale use of machinery and the beginning of the factory meant that the worker did not have the same opportunity of understanding what he was producing. Too often he was concerned with only a part of the processes involved. The increase in the numbers employed naturally made for a great dilution of skilled labour. The need for giving the young worker in industry some knowledge of the basic rules of science on which industry was working was soon recognised and very early in the nineteenth century began the formation of the Mechanics' Institutes. These institutions varied greatly in size but their aim to give the young worker an opportunity to improve his education, a place to meet for discussion and recreation and basic library facilities, was admirable. It is estimated that in 1850 there were 610 institutions in England. Only forty-five of these had over 500 members. The London Mechanics' Institute, founded in 1823, was started by George Birkbcck who, while Professor of Natural Philosophy at the Glasgow Institution, had begun the movement by giving some instruction to the mechanics making his apparatus.

The movement however declined, largely because of the lack of basic education without which progress in technical education was impossible. It is remembered today as an early attempt to bring knowledge to the ordinary man in the street. Two important educational institutions, Birkbeck College, founded from the London Mechanics' Institute and the College of Advanced Technology, Manchester, starting from the Manchester Mechanics' Institute, are living mementos of the movement.

In London the most important group of Technical Colleges are called Polytechnics. These include London's three 'colleges of advanced technology' (Battersea, Chelsea and Northampton). Before considering the beginnings of the movement it may be of interest to note certain characteristics common to all these institutions. Firstly, thcy came into existence during the latter half of the nineteenth century and thus have traditions stretching back many years. Secondly, each of these bodies has its own legal identity as a self-governing college. They rank as 'aided institutions' and they have received, for many years, valuable support from the London County Council. Thirdly, almost all Polytechnics do a considerable amount of university and advanced work. Fourthly, the Polytechnics have always had a liberal attitude on education and, by the very variety of subjects covered, present to the student a broad outlook. Lastly, these institutions have encouraged athletics and social work.

The Polytechnics owe their inception to Quintin Hogg. Quintin Hogg began his work for youth in London in 1865 and in 1879 his institution was in Long Acre. In 1882 it moved to Regent Street. The premises in Regent Street formerly belonged to the Royal Polytechnic Institution and it was Quintin Hogg's own feeling that 'The Polytechnic' was an appropriate name for the type of institution he was developing. The name was subsequently used when similar institutions were set up in various parts of London on the model of 'The Polytechnic'. The earlier Institution, the Royal Polytechnic Institution, is worthy of remembrance. It was founded by Sir George Cayley, one of the pioneers of aeronautics, in 1838 for research work in and the teaching of engineering and science and for the display of scientific models, manufacturing processes, etc. A Royal Charter was granted in 1839.

From the earliest days **The Polytechnic** has had a library. In the beginning this consisted of a circulating library which, besides containing a representative collection of scientific and technical literature of the period, was strong in English literature and history. A printed catalogue was issued. Besides this were departmental libraries. With the opening of the new library in 1930 and the gradual centralisation of the bookstock, the library has become especially strong in economics, the social sciences, science and engineering, architecture, and literature, both English and foreign. The stock now consists of over 42,000 volumes, of which over 30,000 are available for home reading. The number of scientific and technical periodicals now taken is 365. These holdings are noted in the Science Museum catalogue, in the card index kept at the Education Library, London County Council, and certain sections have been included in *The British union-catalogue of periodicals* and in the recent *Union list of periodicals on mathematics and allied subjects in London libraries* issued by the University of London.

Besides the main Reference Library there are two departmental reference libraries, covering architecture and commerce, economics and sociology. An additional reference library will be incorporated in the extension which it is hoped to start building in the next few years.

The Polytechnic Library has always appreciated the value of co-operation and it has been an outlier of the National Central Library since 1935. Finally, mention must be made of the many links such a library has with industry. Among these are direct representation on the Board of Governors and on the Advisory Committees attached to each department; by personal contact with individual firms; through full-time and part-time members of the teaching staff and, of course, through past and present students, many of whom come for day release and part time from industry.

A *Guide to the library* is available and special reading lists on a variety of subjects such as *mathematics and physics, chemistry, biology and zoology, economics, engineering* and *modern foreign literature*.

The success of Quintin Hogg's work was evidence of the demand for scientific and technical education. This was recognised by the Government by the passing of The Technical Instruction Act of 1889 which allowed local authorities to levy rates for technical education. Through this assistance and that of the City Parochial Foundation, the Polytechnic movement grew rapidly. Woolwich Polytechnic was founded in 1891, the Borough Polytechnic in 1892, Battersea Polytechnic in 1894, Chelsea Polytechnic in 1895, the Northern Polytechnic and the Northampton Polytechnic in 1896. The North Western Polytechnic planned in this period was not opened until 1929. The following notes on the libraries of certain of these will be useful.

The present library of the **Borough Polytechnic** was established in January 1956, the previous library (dating from *c.* 1900) having been demolished by bombing in 1942. Very little of the stock from the old library was salvaged and transferred to the present one. In the years 1942–56 the departments built up individual libraries, most of which have gradually been transferred to the Central Library. The library has shelf accommodation for 10,000 volumes, plus storage space for an additional 4,000 volumes. Seating accommodation is thirty-eight. It is expected that a reading room will be added during 1959. Up to the middle of 1959 the stock has reached over 7,000 books; about 1,200 back volumes of periodicals unbound; 200 current periodical subscriptions; and about 1,500 pamphlets. The bulk of the stock is in the field of science and technology, though there is a growing collection of books on the humanities. The main subjects included are mathematics, physics (including nuclear energy), chemistry, biology, botany and zoology, medicine (including nursing and dental mechanics), mechanical and electrical engineering, catering and cooking (including food technology and bakery), industrial management, chemical engineering and paint technology and plastics. About one-quarter of the books are for reference only, the rest may be borrowed by staff and students, or by other libraries through the National Central Library. The library also borrows through N.C.L., the Science Library and many other sources. It has a Dagmar microfilm reader and will shortly have a photocopying machine.

The original building of the library of the **Battersea College of Technology** was given by Edwin Tate, first Chairman of the Governing Body, in 1910. The stock consists of 14,000 volumes, and 200 current periodicals are taken. The collection is strong in mechanical, civil and electrical engineering, chemistry and physics. It has a microfilm reader.

The library of **Chelsea College of Science and Technology** contains approximately 10,000 books and pamphlets, which are mainly specialised in accordance with subjects taught in the College. There are books of standard reference, foreign languages, music, and sports, and also many years of university and professional past examination papers. The art collection is comprehensive. Many scientific periodicals and journals of leading British, American, and European societies are taken and bound. There are many good runs of bound scientific publications. There is an open access system and books are classified on shelves according to subject. A dictionary card catalogue is provided.

The **Northern Polytechnic** situated in Islington now serves a very wide area and ranks as a major regional collection. The library was first centralised about 1918, having a former existence as departmental collections. It is a joint library serving the Northern Polytechnic and the National College of Rubber Technology. Post-war reorganisation of the library saw the removal of the historic musical instruments to increase seating capacity to eighty. This is now inadequate and a new library is planned for the new extension and the floor area will be doubled (5,000 sq. ft.). Despite drastic revision the stock is now 16,000 books, 4,000 volumes of English and foreign periodicals appropriate to the curriculum and research interest and 40,000 architectural cuttings. A complete set of *Beilstein* is maintained. A private collection of books on the organ is also housed in the library and is made available through the National Central Library. Periodical holdings are entered in *The British union-catalogue of periodicals* and the forthcoming fourth edition of the *World list* will include current holdings. The library obtains photocopies for tuition and research purposes, and a microfilm reader is available in the library. For several years the library has been an approved practice centre for student librarians from University College and the North Western Polytechnic.

The Skinners' Library of the **Northampton College of Advanced Technology** was opened in 1956. There is seating for 125 readers and shelving for about 10,000 volumes. The present stock is 6,000 books and 2,000 bound volumes of journals, and in addition 150 periodicals are kept for periods of from one to ten years according to requirements. Although the library is primarily for reference only, limited borrowing is allowed for lecturers and final-year students. The stock is mainly of technical books. A small section, 'liberal studies', is being developed for general lending purposes.

The **North Western Polytechnic** Library contains about 9,000 volumes and takes 160 current periodicals. There is seating for sixty readers and this will be increased to one hundred. Among the main subjects covered are printing, librarianship, bibliography, banking, economics, economic history, history, British constitution, accounting, management, company secretaryship, transport, French, German, English literature, Latin, Greek, chemistry, physics, mathematics, child care and advertising. The library has a microfilm reader, a microcard reader and a document copier. The North Western Polytechnic has a particular interest to all librarians because of the excellent School of Librarianship built up in the institution since the Second World War.

Two libraries not Polytechnics must be mentioned. Firstly, that of **Sir John Cass College** which owes its foundation to a bequest of Sir John Cass in 1718. The institute was reopened under a new scheme of the Chantry Commissioners in 1902. The College, which is near The Mint, specialises in pure science, metallurgy, and arts and crafts. The stock of the library is over 10,000 volumes and 160 periodicals are taken. There are many long sequences of journals. The library has a translation service for research workers and facilities for photocopying as well as a microfilm reader.

Secondly, the **City of London College** which was one of the pioneer foundations in London education. It owes its beginnings to an appeal by the Bishop of London in 1848 for the formation of evening classes for young men in London. The Metropolitan Evening Classes were thus started at various centres including Crosby Hall, and large numbers attended. In 1861 these classes were reconstituted as the City of London College and for the next thirty years the work flourished. With the recognition of the importance of technical education, the College received assistance from the Charity Commissioners in 1891 and in 1894 from the London County Council. In 1904 the College started full-time tuition in commercial subjects and it is for this work that it is noted today. The library, started in the Crosby Hall days, was destroyed in the blitz of 1942. The present library contains 10,000 volumes, and 125 periodicals are taken currently.

The libraries of professional associations form an important group of London libraries. Many of these fulfil the functions of a learned society in their own field. Although primarily maintained to supply the needs of their members, most of them are willing to assist the general public by the answering of inquiries by letter or by the lending of books through the Science Museum or the National Central Library.

The Institution of Civil Engineers is the oldest of the engineering societies, having been founded in 1818. The reference library contains about 73,000 books and about 19,000 tracts, including many that are rare and not contained in other libraries. The collection embraces textbooks of all branches of engineering and the related theoretical and applied sciences. The library also includes the journals of the principal scientific and professional societies and the periodicals published by the technical press at home and abroad. In addition there is an up-to-date separate collection of books, available for loan to members on application by post or in person. A printed catalogue of these books was published in 1935 and there have been two supplements, in 1948 and 1956. Additions to the library are printed in the "News" section of the *Proceedings* of the Institution, which is published every month. Special bequests include the library of the first President, Thomas Telford, and the Horological Library of N. L. Vulliamy. Admission to the library is restricted to members, graduates and students of the Institution.

The Institution of Mechanical Engineers was founded in 1847. The library of the Institution contains some 65,000 publications on mechanical engineering and related subjects, and is housed at the Institution headquarters, at 1 Birdcage Walk, Westminster, S.W.1, in a room in Elizabethan style overlooking St. James's Park. Lists of additions to the library, with annotations, are published each month in the Institution journal, *The Chartered Mechanical Engineer*. In the reading room, which is situated on the floor below the library, are exhibited the current issues of approximately 400 technical periodicals published throughout the world, many of which are subsequently bound for permanent preservation. The facilities provided by the library and reading room are restricted to the use of members of the Institution only.

The Institution of Electrical Engineers was founded in 1871. The library is one of the most extensive on electrical subjects. The reference library consists of approximately 10,000 books on electrical and certain allied subjects likely to be of interest to members. More than 500 periodicals are being currently received, and the files contain over 600 titles. In addition, there is an extensive collection of pamphlets, reports of conferences, British Standards, Electrical Research Association reports and similar published material. Included in the reference library are two famous historical collections: the Ronalds Library and the library of Silvanus Thompson. Each comprises more than 5,000 works, including several rare fourteenth-century manuscripts and valuable early printed books. The Institution has a unique collection of Faraday manuscripts and the library of Oliver Heaviside, together with his original notebooks. There are a considerable number of photographs and lantern slides which may be borrowed by members. A feature of the Institution Library is the bibliographical facility. This is based very largely on a file of over 50,000 cards of *Electrical Engineering Abstracts* since 1947, arranged in subject order by the Universal Decimal Classification. For subjects outside the field covered by *Electrical Engineering Abstracts*, the annual volumes of the *Engineering Index* are used. The lending section of the Institution Library comprises more than 3,600 books, mainly in the English language, which are duplicates of works in the reference library. A new edition of the Lending Library Catalogue will shortly be available, which shows these books under authors and under subjects by Universal Decimal Classification. New books added to the reference or lending sections of the library are recorded in the accessions list published in the *Journal*.

The library of the **Institute of Marine Engineers** contains 2,800 volumes excluding bound volumes of transactions and proceedings. One hundred and three periodicals are taken currently and seventy sets are held. The stock is entered in *The British union-catalogue of periodicals* and *The Aslib directory*. Abstracts are prepared and marine engineering and shipbuilding abstracts are given in the society's monthly *Transactions*.

The joint library of the **Iron and Steel Institute,** founded in 1869, and the **Institute of Metals** has over 30,000 volumes. It covers iron and steel manufacture, treatment and properties, and properties of non-ferrous metals. Seven hundred journals are currently taken. Abstracts are prepared and published in the *Journal of the Iron and Steel Institute*. Microfilm and photostat copies are available.

The Institution of Mining and Metallurgy, founded in 1892, covers the mining of minerals other than coal and the metallurgy of minerals other than iron. The library contains over 20,000 volumes and 250 periodicals are taken currently. Articles in periodicals are indexed and abstracts prepared.

The Institution of Mining Engineers, founded in 1889, covers the mining of coal and iron ore. The library contains over 10,000 volumes and 150 periodicals are taken.

The economic libraries of London include, firstly, that of the **Royal Statistical Society** founded in 1834. The Society covers the very wide fields of the development of statistical theory and methodology, and the application of statistical methods to scientific research and industry, including government. The library contains 80,000 volumes and 4,000 pamphlets and manuscripts; 400 periodicals are taken currently. A list of serial publications received was printed in the *Journal of the Royal Statistical Society, Series A* (1957), 120, 510–526. The library is now an outlier library in the National Central Library scheme. It includes a special collection, the Yule Library, devoted to the history of statistical method and theory.

The **Institute of Actuaries Library,** the formation of which was one of the original objects of the society, contains 10,000 books and manuscripts on actuarial and kindred subjects. It aims at being comprehensive. Additions to the library are given annually in the *Year Book.* Reciprocal arrangements for library reference exist with the Royal Statistical Society, the London School of Economics and Political Science, the London Mathematical Society, the Chartered Insurance Institute and other bodies.

The first insurance institute was founded in 1873 in Manchester. In 1879, the Federation of Insurance Institutes of Great Britain and Ireland, later known as the **Chartered Insurance Institute,** was formed. The library consists of a reference library which aims to give a comprehensive research service to members. Every year an increasing number of inquiries are received and the amount of work entailed is more than that of much larger libraries. There is also a lending library for the use of members from which books are sent by post throughout the country. The library is strong in overseas, United States and continental publications on insurance, including a collection of rare books in German. The publications of the Joint Fire Research Organisation of the F.O.C. and the Department of Scientific and Industrial Research are well represented. The whole forms a complete collection of current literature on fire in so far as it is of interest to fire surveyors.

The library of the **Institute of Chartered Accountants** in England and Wales contains over 19,000 volumes. The Institute has a most valuable collection of early books on book-keeping and accounts, and details are given in the catalogues published in 1903 and 1913.

Mention must be made of the Kheil collection of 1,600 books purchased in 1913, of which only 200 are in the British Museum. A number of important incunabula have been added since. A brief list of books from 1494 to 1650, by H. W. Thomson and B. S. Yamey, has been printed. For the general literature a *Short List of Books* is issued (last edition, 1957) and this is kept up to date by supplements issued every six months.

The **Institute of Bankers** Library was founded in 1879. The reference library is especially strong in long runs of banking, economic and legal periodicals, including parliamentary papers and reports of international bodies. The collection of law reports dates from 1879. The library has a special collection of manuscripts, books and pamphlets on the history of banking in Great Britain. Over 400 serials and periodicals are taken. These are indexed in the subject catalogue which aims to provide a guide to the modern written material on any subject within the scope of the library. There is a lending library for the use of members covering accountancy, banking, economics, finance, law, management and statistics.

The library of the **Royal Institute of British Architects** originated with the Institute in 1834 and is primarily intended for its members and students. In recent years, however, responsible members of the public have been encouraged to use it and a great many do so regularly. It covers besides architecture, building, topography, town and country planning and allied subjects. It contains approximately 60,000 volumes, including many early printed books, some of great value, manuscripts, and about 350 current periodicals. A separate department holds a collection of some 30,000 architectural drawings and water-colours, dating from the sixteenth century to the present day. It is almost certainly the most remarkable single collection of architectural drawings in existence. An author and subject catalogue was published in 1937–38 and subject bibliographies are issued regularly. The *Library Bulletin*, issued quarterly from 1946, gives details of new additions and an index to selected periodicals. There is a special lending library for members. In recent years the R.I.B.A. have organised one-day conferences for representatives of libraries of schools and colleges of architecture, which have proved most valuable.

Among the schools of architecture in London, besides those of The Polytechnic and Northern Polytechnic, which have special architectural libraries, the collection of the **Architectural Association** must be mentioned. This contains about 10,000 books and over 60,000 lantern slides; 100 current periodicals are taken, and ten sets are held.

Finally, mention must be made of the library of the **Royal Photographic Society** which has over 5,000 volumes and takes 150 current periodicals; 750 sets are held. The Society's holdings are noted in *The British union-catalogue of periodicals* and the *World list*.

CHAPTER XIX

INDUSTRIAL LIBRARIES

By D. R. Jamieson
Patent Office Library

FOR the sake of completeness, it is at least defensible to attempt in the context of this book a chapter on the libraries serving the capital's industry. For with industry no longer clinging to a code of narrow trade secrecy, with its heavy investment in research, and its acceptance of the fact that it simply cannot afford not to share its knowledge, no sector of our society is more aware of the value of freely circulating information and exploiting it for all it is worth.

However, any attempt to give an account of these libraries in London – itself the focus of the country's industry – is bedevilled by a number of considerations. Not least of these is the fact, which is symptomatic of the whole topic, that there is no *typical* industrial library. Indeed, the library in industry is a notable example of the definition of a special library as one that exists to serve a group whose activities are directed towards a common purpose. Again, the industrial library is often only a part of a department or unit built up to collect, disseminate and store information and it cannot be considered in isolation.

In scope, size and nature the various elements that make up the complex of London's industry and commerce vary considerably; and this variety is in turn reflected in their libraries and information departments. For our purpose it is necessary to adopt an arbitrary breakdown of the whole field and to identify some of the principal groups.

The private firm is the most recognisable element, yet it is the one that displays most variation in financial strength, in the scope, manner and location of its operations and in the size of its labour force. Many a firm now running an information department with twenty or more staff could trace the department's development from a collection of reference books in the chief engineer's office. This development, though gradual, can usually be seen to have fallen into three stages. At some point the need is felt for some control of the literature that is steadily building up. It may be a question of sheer bulk, or it may be the fact that valuable books and journals are being mislaid because no one is really responsible for them. At this point it is recognised that someone must be put in charge of the firm's literature; space then has to be allocated for the collection and with this the foundation of a library has been laid. After a period the second stage is reached when the ever-increasing volume of material demands a room to itself, the staff has probably increased to a full-time librarian and an assistant who are using business-like techniques for the routing of journals, for the classification and cataloguing, for the control of loans and purchases. Stage three follows when the actual dissemination of literature is attempted: bulletins are compiled and circulated, translations are undertaken, and literature searches engaged upon as a matter of routine.

Numerically the strongest element, the private firms make up our primary group.

Ever since the impact of the First World War demonstrated the shortcomings which had resulted from a long and widespread un-interest in the systematic use of scientific study in the industrial sector, industry has happily bought an increasing stake in research facilities. A government plan for research, urgently evolved in 1915, directed special attention to the need for applied research. One of the principal parts of this plan gave effect to the scheme of Research Associations, established for individual branches of industry. Controlled and partly financed by the firms concerned, the R.A.s were conceived in the well-justified belief that if an industry were responsible for planning and executing its own programme of research, its members would be likely to put the results into practice. From modest beginnings in 1916, there are now over forty of these Research Associations, of which a dozen are in the London area. The R.A.s consequently form another obvious group.

The Development Associations constitute our third group. Fewer in number than the R.A.s, though not entirely divorced from the business of research, their function is largely promotional. It has been acknowledged by many competitor manufacturers and fabricators of products such as copper, cement, timber, zinc, and electric lighting equipment, that they all stand to gain by an organisation devoted to educating and encouraging users and potential customers in the proper and widest application of their products. There now exists a number of these associations, created, controlled and financed exclusively by their member firms.

Considerably greater in number than the Development Associations are the Trade Associations. Their main functions are to represent their members in all matters concerning the legal, commercial and trading interests generally of that section of industry; to act as a channel of communication with other organisations and the Government; to provide information on general questions asked by other industries and the public; and to serve as a clearing-house for commercial information. The size of a trade association and the scope of its activities are largely dictated by the scale and nature of the industry concerned. They vary widely from a secretary working single-handed in one room, to a large departmentalised staff occupying high-rental office accommodation and responsible for numerous publications, a statistical service, for arranging representation in overseas trade fairs and organising industry exhibitions in this country, and handling a heavy traffic of inquiries from press, public and industry generally. Though rarely boasting a conventional library, the trade associations form yet another group since they are frequently a useful – often the sole – source of information concerning particular topics in the area of industry they represent.

The last of these groups – as we define them – consists of the Public Corporations. Successive governments have committed to public control the ownership and operations of a variety of services. In addition to the more obvious pre-war examples – British (formerly Imperial) Overseas Airways and the B.B.C. – the years since 1945 have witnessed a considerable growth of the public sector of industry, with the setting up of such bodies as the National Research Development Corporation (1948), the Colonial Development Corporation (1948), the U.K. Atomic Energy Authority (1954), and the Central Electricity Generating Board (1948). All of the public corporations have established a library, allied to which in a number of cases there has been deliberately provided some form of information service to its immediate customers and to the public at large.

These, then, are our five groups. To do real justice, however, to the many and varied units serving industry in London would require more extensive treatment than is appropriate within the compass of the present book. The following accounts are of libraries which individually are representative of three of these groups; together they indicate

something of the activities and organisation ıl features of industrial
libraries in the capital.

THE FIRM

Compared with other commercial metals such as iron and copper,
aluminium is a very young metal. The discovery of the process which
made large-scale production of aluminium a commercial proposition
dates from as recently as 1886.

The **British Aluminium Company**[1] was founded in 1894. It is the
only company in Britain which actually produces aluminium as well as
fabricating it to the stage known as semi-manufactures, that is the
tubes, sheets, rods, extrusions, plate and wire from which capital and
consumer goods are eventually made. Like others in the industry,
however, the company is obviously interested in these 'end products'
and will help customers who wish to launch a new product in aluminium, perhaps for the first time, with technical advice and design details.
Therefore it can be said that the information required by the company
in its everyday affairs extends from the location and analysis of suitable
ores to the production of the metal, and to the present and potential
uses of the metal.

In order to collect and disseminate this information, the Intelligence
Department was started in about 1924 with a staff of two or three.
Today there is a total of nineteen people engaged in running the
library, producing the Department's bulletins, translating, and ancillary
services. The Department regards itself as very fortunate in that it is
directly answerable to the Managing Director and is not, as in many
cases in industry, subordinate to another department with a consequent
bias in its work. The Intelligence Department is located at the head
office in London and is equally concerned with both commercial and
technical information. There is a smaller library which serves the
immediate interests of the Research Laboratories at Gerrards Cross, in
Buckinghamshire.

The function of the Department is twofold. First, it must ensure that
all information of interest to the company but originating from the
outside world reaches the members of the staff concerned, and,
second, it acts as a focal point for inquiries from the staff at its head
office and research laboratories, its factories and branch offices in this

[1] For this account I am indebted to Miss M. M. Armstrong of the Intelligence
Department, the British Aluminium Company Ltd.

country and overseas. In addition, the branch offices have their own subscriptions to certain journals and a collection of books for their own immediate use.

Apart from the librarian, there is a staff of five in the Department's library, responsible for circulating journals, arranging loans, ordering publications, and classifying, indexing and filing all the material. The library is an outlier of the National Central Library and a member of the Science Library's Supplementary Loans Scheme; it has access to the libraries of all the institutions and professional associations to which the company either directly belongs or to which it has entrée, as well as many other libraries and information sources through normal goodwill channels.

The bookstock in an industrial library forms part only of the total stock of information and may be quite small: in the British Aluminium library there are at present not more than 2,000 books. The main feature, naturally, is as complete a collection as possible of books concerned with the metallurgy, working and uses of aluminium, including historical works such as *De l'aluminium: ses propriétés, sa fabrication et ses applications* (1859) by Henri Sainte-Claire Deville, one of the pioneers of the isolation and production of aluminium. Apart from this, there are books on metallurgy, metal fabrication and allied subjects, chemical analysis and chemical engineering, trade and economic conditions of various countries, economic geology and mining, ore dressing, and on the history and geography of the many countries of interest to the aluminium industry.

There is also a small reference section comprising directories and handbooks of overseas territories and of other industries. One advantage of locating the company's main library in London is that, with such large libraries at Westminster and the Guildhall in the vicinity, one does not have to carry a heavy stock of directories and commercial reference books.

A vital part of the stock in any industrial library is its journal and newspaper collection. British Aluminium takes about 600 current English-language and foreign periodicals as well as some newspapers; in many cases two, and occasionally multiple, copies are taken. These are supplemented by subscription to an international press-cutting service. In some cases journals are obtained by exchange with the Department's technical bulletin. These journals are routed three or four times a day to successive persons on the regular circulation lists, with additional distribution for items of special interest to others of the staff.

About fifty of the more important journals are bound, the remainder being kept for roughly a year, then discarded after items of interest have been extracted and filed by subject.

The policy regarding what to bind, or keep permanently in some form, and what to discard after a period, is very largely determined by the importance to the company of the subject matter of the material. Other factors which are taken into consideration are the accessibility of the material in other – particularly nearby – libraries; rarity value; and, in the case of foreign material, the means by which the supply can be obtained in the first place.

As well as journals there is a considerable stock of pamphlets, trade literature, patents, standards and other specifications.

The mass of material which the Department receives is not simply given house-room. A flow-pattern of examination, dissemination and filing for later retrieval has been evolved to ensure that British Aluminium derives all possible benefit from its investment in information. The daily intake of correspondence, internal company reports and memoranda, published material and that variety known as 'unpublished', is scanned and divided, so far as is practicable, into one of two streams – technical/scientific and commercial/industrial. Suitable items are fed into bulletins which serve each stream. At this point *all* material of company interest – whether or not it has been used for the bulletins – is interpolated into consolidated subject files classified by a 'local' scheme, with analytical file entries providing for items of multiple subject interest. In the majority of cases the material filed will consist of a copy of the abstract as it appeared (in English) in one of the bulletins, accompanied by either the original material abstracted, or a note of its location. The subject files are classified by a local scheme, while 'shelf' material is arranged by the U.D.C.

The Department issues one commercial and two technical abstract bulletins, a list of forthcoming meetings, exhibitions and trade fairs, and a list of new accessions to the library. These are distributed throughout the Company, and the principal technical publication goes outside the Company to over five hundred individuals and organisations who have a particular interest in development and research in non-ferrous metals.

Light Metals Bulletin is issued once a fortnight and each issue contains roughly two hundred abstracts of articles, papers, patents, books, pamphlets, etc., chiefly devoted to all aspects of aluminium, but with selected information on other light metals such as magnesium and titanium. The abstracts are all in English, regardless of the language of the original, and are arranged in subject order with indexes. Consolidated author and patent indexes are issued for each year's issues.

The *Weekly Patent Service*, as its title implies, is a regular summary of the patent situation in those fields of primary and marginal interest to the Company. It draws attention to selected British patent applications, acceptances and publication of complete specifications and also some patent applications laid open to public inspection in Commonwealth and foreign countries.

In covering commercial-industrial information, account has to be taken of the speed with which developments occur, and also of the many-sidedness of the field to be watched. A company as large as British Aluminium will inevitably be concerned with things developing in the legal, social, economic, parliamentary, and financial spheres, both in this country and overseas. To provide a succint and reasonably rapid summary of news originating from this sector, a commercial abstract bulletin is published by Intelligence Department at least twice a week, for circulation exclusively within the Company. Its keynote is readability and brevity. The average number of pages in each issue is five and never more than eight, so that it is possible to scan it all fairly quickly. And to differentiate it from other duplicated papers arriving at the 'in' tray, it carries a brightly coloured banner across the top of the front sheet. The headings are in the form of short descriptive phrases and each abstract is serially numbered. Bibliographical references of the original material are deliberately excluded, in the interests of rapid scanning: if the source of the original is considered to be of particular interest this is mentioned in the body of the abstract. To supplement the bulletin, items considered to be of special urgency will be circulated on arrival direct to the appropriate quarters, but this does not preclude its subsequent record in the next issue and its going automatically on file.

The information sheet covering advance notices of meetings and exhibitions, etc. is published fortnightly, and the library's accessions list monthly. The head of the Department is the Chairman of the Company's Patents Committee, with the Librarian acting as Secretary. Altogether fifteen people are engaged in one way or another on the writing, assembling, typing, reproduction and dispatch of the Department's bulletins, and on patent work.

Three people in Intelligence Department are concerned with translating for both the Department's bulletins and for the Company generally.

Between them these people can cope with all of the major languages and – a fact which is specially important – they have acquired a good knowledge of the commercial and technical aspects of the Company's operations.

A DEVELOPMENT ASSOCIATION

The library of the **Cement and Concrete Association**[1] was formed in 1935, at the time of the establishment of the Association, and it now employs a staff of eight. It is mainly specialist in character, but extends its collection to civil engineering and allied subjects. The library is one of the most comprehensive in its field in this country and contains most of the published literature in the English language on concrete, including a large selection of articles from technical periodicals and other publications. It also contains a representative collection of foreign literature on the subject. A section of books and records devoted to the early history of cement is another of the library's interesting features.

Another part of the library's holdings comprises a comprehensive collection of manufacturers' catalogues on building materials.

A library of approximately 15,000 photographs covers every aspect of concrete work, including structural and architectural concrete work from all parts of the world. These photographs are lent to the press, to authors and students preparing theses, and also for exhibition purposes. In addition, the photographic library holds a large collection of slides and film strips which are available on loan, too.

The information side of the C.A.C.A. library's activities are, of course, of special importance, and the following are some of the methods which have been adopted.

A monthly accessions list is issued to member companies and associated groups, and translations of selected subject material are made. The staff compile bibliographies and carry out literature searches as required. New literature on cement and concrete is abstracted and issued on cards to the Association's area offices outside London, and sets of these cards are also sent to a large European organisation concerned with the promotion of cement and concrete.

Close co-operation is maintained with other libraries, both special and public. The library also maintains close contact with research organisations concerned with buildings, roads and structures throughout the

---

[1] For this account I am indebted to Miss E. V. Marshall, Librarian of the Cement and Concrete Association.

world. In addition to this, local authorities, industrial concerns, architects, engineers, government departments, and universities up and down the country are supplied with scientific and technical information free of charge and without obligation, in the interests of the cement and concrete industry generally.

A RESEARCH ASSOCIATION

The British paper industry has long realised the need for technical information and development,[1] as was shown by the formation of the Technical Section of the British Paper and Board Makers' Association (the industry's trade association) to organise conferences, publish their proceedings, and to run a library. But as the momentum of technical development increased, the need became evident for centralised research activity to help both the smaller firms with no research facilities of their own and also the larger organisations who were realising the need for *co-operative* research in fundamental fields. Accordingly, the **British Paper and Board Industry Research Association** was set up in 1945, its research work being started about 1948 after the establishment of laboratories at Kenley, in Surrey.

Membership of the Association is limited to British firms in the U.K. and the Commonwealth, and in the year 1958–59 membership was made up of 148 Ordinary and eighteen Associate members.

The controlling body is a Council consisting of the leading figures in the industry; two members nominated by the Department of Scientific and Industrial Research are also included. The Council meets four times a year under the chairmanship of a President, who is also the President for the time being of the British Paper and Board Makers' Association and holds office for three years. Day-to-day management is delegated to a Finance and Management Committee.

It is not easy for the layman to appreciate how wide a field must be covered by a research body serving pulp, paper and board manufacturers, if all the needs of the varied membership are to be met. The following are some of the questions with which the staff have to be ready to deal: inquiries relating to raw materials including woods, native and tropical, straw, reeds, bamboo, bagasse, rags, cotton linters, waste paper, synthetic fibres and glass fibres; mechanical and chemical processes used to disintegrate complex raw materials to free the

[1] For this account I am indebted to Miss S. Laemmle, Librarian and Information Officer, British Paper and Board Industry Research Association.

individual fibres useful for paper-making; processes for the mechanical treatment of these fibres to convert them into paper-making stock; processes in common use or in course of development for transforming the thin slurry of fibres into solid paper or board, waste-water treatment, and the machinery to carry out these processes; control instruments, product testing and instruments to carry out these tests. Lastly, there is the very large number of 'auxiliaries' which are introduced either into the stock before web formation or applied to the surface of the forming or finished web: these include mineral pigments for loading, sizing agents to improve water and ink resistance, synthetic resins used as binders in the stock or as coatings, mould proofing agents, softeners, stiffeners, corrosion inhibitors, flame retardants, dimensional stabilisers and anti-static agents.

The Research Association now has a technical and research staff of eighty and a total staff of one hundred. Of necessity, the number of subjects which can find a place in the research programme at any one time is limited. However, the internal arrangements also allow the staff to devote part of their time to finding answers to the problems put forward by members which do not fall within the province of the fundamental or applied research programme. This side of the Association's work is the function of the Technical Enquiry Service, supported by the Information Section and Library.

The need for a library where information already published on many of the questions brought to the R.A. could quickly be located was thus fairly obvious, and the library was set up at a very early stage in the Association's development and has grown with it ever since. To exploit the resources of the library more effectively, an Information Officer was appointed in 1955 and the Information Section and the Library were finally combined in 1956. To run the department efficiently, the head of this section should preferably have scientific training to degree level, experience in applied research work and some knowledge of library work and the mechanics of indexing and classification.

Out of the total R.A. budget, $8\frac{1}{2}$ per cent is at present being allocated to the Information and Library Section, which, however generous in itself, in fact represents a small sum in relation to current prices, especially since the Association's total income is small compared with the resources that large industrial firms can devote to research and allied services. The Section therefore uses the major portion of its share of the budget for buying continuous runs of papers and other general scientific periodicals essential for the work of the different research departments; these runs number about 150 at present. The proportion of books, reports, patents and other documents acquired each year varies, but is indicated by the following figures:

	1957	*1958*	*1959*
Books	105	90	80
Patents	177	84	61
Reports	125	89	51
Standards	150	96	89

In view of the size of the staff, book selection and purchasing policy generally can be decided co-operatively. Any member of the staff may ask for the purchase of a book or a subscription to a new periodical and fortunately its resources permit meeting most of these requests; the final responsibility regarding purchasing policy, however, rests with the Information Officer Librarian. Photocopying plays an important part to fill gaps and to collect information published in the form of short sections and chapters in many different books and reports. As most of the R.A. Technical Reports are confidential – only a few declassified reports and the R.A.'s quarterly bulletin, *What We Are Doing*, being released for unrestricted circulation – few documents can be obtained by exchange.

Publication of the Technical Reports on the work of the various Sections or Research Departments is the responsibility of the Director of Research and his principal research officers. The Information Officer is responsible for the bulletin *What We Are Doing*, and for circulating to members the abstract bulletin *Library Notes*, which is purchased from the Institute of Paper Chemistry, Madison, U.S.A. All publications of permanent value are printed by conventional letterpress methods.

The periodicals received in the library are read by the Information Officer and abstracted, so as to maintain an up-to-the-minute subject and alphabetical index. (But the task of editing and publishing these abstracts could not be attempted with the small staff available, which comprises a second graduate abstractor, a shorthand typist and a filing clerk. Moreover, the abstracts made by the R.A. would probably not appear very much earlier than *Library Notes* do now, so that the duplication of effort would be quite unjustifiable.) After abstracting, all periodicals are circulated, some members of the staff wishing to see certain titles regularly, others simply specifying subjects of special interest.

Documents other than periodicals are similarly abstracted and entries made in an accessions register and in the subject index. The classification system used for subject filing is home-made and combines broad classification with alphabetical sequences, e.g. for raw materials or properties of paper. The books are collected in roughly classified groups on the shelves and carry a shelf mark, but the collection is not large enough to warrant use of U.D.C. or of any other classification system.

The R.A. also maintains a translation service, employing a full-time translator and a considerable amount of outside help. On average about fifty translations are prepared annually. Translations can be commissioned by any member mill or member of staff; copies are made available at a standard cost per sheet and photocopies can also be supplied at a small charge.

Translation exchange agreements have been made with, for instance, the Printing and Allied Trades Research Association, the Institute of Paper Chemistry, the Canadian Pulp and Paper Research Institute and the Commonwealth Forest Products Research Laboratories. Copies of translations obtained in this way can be borrowed on the same basis as other library material. An index of translations of potential interest but not at present held in the library is maintained. Monthly lists giving details of translations completed and initiated by the R.A. are sent to Aslib and the translation exchange members, and a copy of every translation made is sent to the John Crerar Library, Chicago, which is the translation distributing agency in U.S.A.

Loans to members and other outside organisations and to staff in the past year numbered 613 and 1,802 respectively – of these 437 items had to be borrowed from other libraries. A small union catalogue, compiled over the past few years, helps to minimise the delay in obtaining outside loans. The R.A. library is not open to the public as its specific function is to serve the members of its staff and the member mills. Nevertheless, material is lent to other libraries requiring information in our particular subject field, and as far as possible we have tried to establish direct contact with both borrowers and lenders so that mutually beneficial interlending arrangements have often been established.

The type and extent of inquiries to be answered by the Information Office is very wide, ranging from simple factual questions to requests involving intensive subject searches and the compilation of bibliographies. In framing answers, factors such as the size of the inquirer's mill and the level of technical training of his staff have to be kept in mind. It is also fair to say that many inquirers could never be answered were it not for the generous help given by many other information officers and librarians working in research and industrial organisations. At Kenley, the Information Service and Library therefore benefit like all the other Sections of the British Paper and Board Industry Research Association from the many contacts established over the years with other research organisations both in the United Kingdom and abroad.

Chapter XX

ECCLESIASTICAL AND THEOLOGICAL LIBRARIES

By R. P. D. Thomas
Librarian, Dr. Williams's Library

By the nature of things, ecclesiastical or theological libraries make a much less specific group than, say, medical libraries, for when many older libraries were coming into existence, theology was an almost all-pervading interest. By the same token almost any library today, above a certain age or above a certain size, is sure to have, or to have had, large enclaves of theology.

Thus one might start with the British Museum as the largest theological library in London for it doubtless houses more theology than any other London library. But the same could be said of the Museum in respect of other subjects. For obvious reasons, therefore, the Museum cannot be included in this survey, and the same may well be true of some other libraries with holdings of theology not by any means negligible which cannot be included here. Nevertheless, libraries that must be included remain very numerous and to some extent rather heterogeneous. It may well be, too, that some have escaped notice that should have been included.

In considering the libraries to be included it seems natural to begin with those of the Church of England, just as it seems natural to speak of the man of the household before speaking of his wife. After the Church of England one turns to those bodies that have dissented from the Established Church, and with them may best be grouped other bodies, equally counted as dissenting, though perhaps not primarily known for that as a characteristic. To come to Roman Catholic libraries only at this point may seem a little odd but argues no disrespect, for it is perhaps not historically inappropriate, since Roman Catholicism remained illegal in this country much longer than other dissenting bodies. The same may be said of the Jewish libraries that we come to next. After them must be mentioned a number of libraries of special interest in a rather more precise sense, such as the great Bible Society Library and the Missionary Society Libraries.

Founded in 1610 on the basis of Archbishop Bancroft's own collection of books, **Lambeth Palace Library** claims to be the first public library in London, if not in Europe. As such it is now open without restriction to all accredited students. Of its 100,000 volumes the vast majority are treasures from episcopal libraries of the past. In Archbishop Bancroft's Library were some volumes that had descended from Archbishop Cranmer and many more from Archbishop Whitgift. Even more important than its many rare printed volumes is its vast accumulation of manuscripts, very many of them Church of England records.[1] At the time of the Commonwealth the library was given entire by Parliament to the University of Cambridge. It was reclaimed by Archbishop Juxon after the Restoration and became a convenient deposit for records from the previous years of commotion and then in danger of being destroyed. It thus preserves the series of Augmentation Books and office copies of the Parliamentary Survey.[2] In so far as Lambeth is a modern library, its strength lies chiefly in literature supporting its older collections, in medieval and modern church history in England and also on the Continent and overseas because of the many links abroad of the Church of England.

Of special interest for London history is **St. Paul's Cathedral Library,** housed in a room designed for the purpose by Sir Christopher Wren, indeed one of two rooms designed for the purpose though only one was actually so used. The present library dates from what might be called its second founding in 1707, by the purchase of a private library at that date, increased by the bequest a few years later of the library of Henry Compton, Bishop of London. What remained of the old St. Paul's Cathedral Library after a fire in 1561 and depradations during the Reformation was lost in the Great Fire of 1666. Today it is notable for its extensive series of St. Paul's Cross sermons, for tracts on the Plague and Fire of London and many drawings and models bearing on the history of the Cathedral itself. It also possesses many medieval manuscripts listed by the Historical Manuscripts Commission, and amongst more modern manuscripts the theological and other manuscripts of Edmund Gibson, Bishop of London from 1720 to 1748.[3]

Westminster Chapter Library of Westminster Abbey, though it originated in medieval times and was then housed in the north walk of the cloister, has little or nothing of the library of that date now remaining. A new start was made soon after 1574 and the famous William Camden was secured as librarian. Shortly after that, in 1591, the library was moved into its present quarters in part of the old Dorter or Dormitory, where the collection comprises mainly liturgies, bibles, books on canon law, and works of fathers of the church. A notice of the Abbey muniments will be found in the Historical Manuscripts Commission reports. [4]

Sion College Library, founded in 1635, and for many years London's chief, if not only, great library now houses some 100,000 volumes. Once a general library, including classics, contemporary science and even medicine, its main intake, at the present day, of modern literature is in theology and in other subjects of interest to the clergy of the City of London for whom it was founded and by whom it is still chiefly used, though it is used widely by clergy outside London and its resources are available to historians and research workers. From our present point of view the library's main interest is as a repository of past accumulations of theology and controversial literature of the seventeenth and eighteenth centuries, as also of earlier and later times. We may note, for instance, the 357 volumes of pamphlets gathered by Edmund Gibson, Bishop of London; a collection of some 300 volumes of Port Royal interest collected by Mrs. Schimmel Penninck; a collection of 1,000 volumes, many of them of the seventeenth century and of great rarity bequeathed by the Rev. Theodore Budd, and two large collections of nineteenth-century pamphlets gathered by the Rev. J. Russell and by the Rev. William Scott. These and many other similar works are now readily accessible through the catalogues maintained at the library, which owe much of their effectiveness to the munificence of the Pilgrim Trust. [5]

Once regarded as a rival to Sion College Library was the library known as the Dissenters' Library in Red Cross Street, founded under the will of an English Presbyterian divine, Daniel Williams, who died in 1716, and now known as **Dr. Williams's Library,** in Gordon Square. Of its 100,000 volumes far the greater part is the modern collection of theology, church history and philosophy, kept constantly up to date and used by ministers and other scholars of all denominations and of none. The printed catalogue of 1955 lists the modern collection so far as books, serials and periodicals published from 1900 to 1950 are concerned. Earlier volumes must be sought in the library's card catalogue or in earlier printed catalogues, now out of print.

Alongside the modern library is an extensive collection of older literature of interest not only for Nonconformist history (as might be expected from its origins) but also for English Church history in general and for Huguenot literature of the seventeenth century and also in later years for Unitarian history. Like other once general libraries it has its enclaves of older science, classics and medicine. The older library, in so far as it bears upon early Nonconformity and English religious history in general, has recently been thoroughly re-catalogued with the help of the Pilgrim and Hibbert Trusts.

The library's manuscript collections are mainly of interest for the history of Dissent and include the Richard Baxter manuscripts, certain contemporary records of those opposed to the Elizabethan Church settlement and certain eighteenth-century lists of Dissenting congregations.[6]

A number of Denominational or Denominational Historical Society libraries are located in London.

The one most clearly defined by its title is the excellently tended library of the **Society of Friends**, in Friends' House, Euston Road. An up-to-date dictionary catalogue is maintained on the premises, but a very fair idea of the contents of the library may be derived from Joseph Smith's *A descriptive catalogue of Friends' books*, two volumes, 1867, on the assumption that few books listed there will not be found in the library.[7]

The **Congregational Library,** housed at Memorial Hall, Farringdon, is wider in its scope than would necessarily follow from its name; it is rich in Nonconformist literature generally, of the seventeenth and later centuries. The printed *Catalogue of the Congregational Library,* two volumes, 1895–1920, is an excellent, if no longer complete, guide to the contents of the library with its many rare pamphlets. Additional and very valuable help may be derived from the manuscript folio catalogues, kept at the library, of anonymous literature and of manuscript material. The library also has a full card catalogue. Until shortly before the last war, the library functioned also as a modern library, but war-time dislocation brought to an end the intake of modern books, and it is only recently that the library has become once more accessible with the books restored to their proper shelves.

At Baptist Church House in Southampton Row is maintained the **Baptist Union Library.** Though not a very large library, nor as important as other Baptist libraries in the county (e.g., that of the Baptist Missionary Society to be mentioned later, that of the Baptist College, Bristol and that at Regent's Park College, now in Oxford, once in London) it has a considerable collection of Baptist literature, with strong sections in hymnology and missionary literature. A fuller knowledge of its contents may be derived from *A catalogue of the Baptist Union Library*, 1915.

All the libraries so far mentioned survived the last war with no more than varying degrees of administrative dislocation, but we now come to the **W. B. Shaw Library,** the library of the Presbyterian Historical Society of England, whose contents had to be rescued from the headquarters of the Presbyterian Church of England in Tavistock Place in 1945. With the rebuilding of the headquarters in 1957 the library has returned from temporary exile to its original home and is once again in full working order. Besides the archives of the Church and very considerable collections of news-cuttings and photographs, the library has a large collection of general Dissenting literature of the seventeenth and later centuries.

Yet another Historical Society Library, that of the **Wesley Historical Society,** is housed in London, at 49 City Road, London, E.C.1. As such, it came into being in April 1959, but the nucleus of the collection is the large library of Wesleyana bequeathed to the Society by the late Rev. F. F. Bretherton. A catalogue of the library is promised. [8]

An important library of recent origin of somewhat similar character, though not a denominational library, is the **Evangelical Library,** founded in the present century by Mr. Geoffrey Williams. Said to number 100,000 volumes, a large proportion of items are works of early Puritans and of later Evangelical writers. Others, forming the modern library, are recent works of Evangelical importance.

Although theological college libraries for the most part fall rather outside our present scope because mainly intended as working libraries for staff and students, there are two which have special claims for inclusion.

One is the library of **New College** on the Finchley Road. Besides its working library providing for the normal needs of a Congregational theological college, it has very notable collections of historic divinity. These have been inherited, in the main from eighteenth-century Dissenting Academies, notably from Philip Doddridge's Northampton Academy and its successors and from the second Hoxton Academy and its successors. The College also has collections of manuscripts drawn from the same surroundings, including the originals of many of the letters in the five printed volumes of Doddridge correspondence as also neat volumes of students' lecture notes from some of the early academies. [9]

The other theological college, rich in Dissenting literature of former days, is **Richmond College** in Richmond, Surrey, where two collections have come together in the same library. Of one collection, originally the private library of the Rev. Thomas Jackson, a catalogue running to some 290 pages (altogether some five or six thousand titles) was printed in the third quarter of the last century. The other, similar, collection, perhaps more general but nearly as numerous, has no printed catalogue but is accessible through the library's card catalogue. In addition there are also parts of the libraries of John and Charles Wesley and of John Fletcher of Madeley.[10]

Of Roman Catholic libraries in London the oldest is that at the **London Oratory,** Brompton Road, Kensington. It is not a library open to the public, but its interest to the research worker lies in its extensive collection of the literature of English Roman Catholics from the sixteenth century onwards. It is also important for its large collection of Jansenist literature and includes a collection of some 10,000 volumes of the library of John Henry Newman's curate, David Lewis.

Of like interest for the history of Roman Catholicism in England since the Reformation are the archives stored in the Archbishop's House with the **Westminster Cathedral Library.** Some part of these have been calendared by the Historical Manuscripts Commission.[11] But a more up-to-date and reliable calendar of forty-eight bound volumes of manuscripts dating from 1532 to 1793 is available on microfilm, while other considerable collections of manuscripts are in process of being calendared and may be made similarly available later. The library itself consists mainly of recusant and seventeenth-century Roman Catholic books and includes a run of something like a thousand of the seventeenth century with a particularly important group dating from 1686 to 1688.

At the presbytery of the Farm Street Church (114 Mount Street) are housed the libraries of the **Society of Jesus in London.** One of these, known as the Writers' Library, supports the literary work of the Jesuit Fathers. This library was disorganised during the war but it is now being brought into order again. The other, which we may call the Mount Street Library, was established in the middle of the last century. Both contain much older valuable literature. In connection with these, but maintained in a room readily accessible to research workers, is the collection of books gathered by Joseph Gillow, the Roman Catholic historian, when working upon his *Literary and biographical history, or bibliographical dictionary of English Catholics* [1885–1902]. Another library, the St. Joseph's Library, a subscription library, open to the public, is housed at 31 Farm Street. Containing some 15,000 volumes it is mainly a library of modern works primarily of Roman Catholic interest.

Similar in scope to the St. Joseph's Library is the **Catholic Central Library,** founded in 1914, and later taken over by the Catholic Truth Society. Its collection of some 24,000 volumes consists of modern works, both Catholic and non-Catholic, many of them in foreign languages, especially French. It has also a collection of older pamphlets and other works. The library is maintained out of subscriptions and has a printed catalogue (now out of print) of works down to 1938. Since then there have been a number of supplements.

The greatest library of Hebraica and Judaica, ancient and modern, in London (outside the British Museum) is the **Jews' College Library,** founded in 1855 and now in Montague Place, W.1. Special collections include the Zunz collection of more than a thousand pamphlets dealing mainly with the history of the Jews and their emancipation, the Blumenthal collection of Rabbinics, the Löwy collection of some 9,000 volumes of Orientalia and the Mayerowitsch Music Library. A very considerable accession, numbering near 10,000 volumes, came to the library after the war, being books pillaged by the Nazis from Jewish homes in Europe and now ownerless. There is also an important collection of manuscripts of which a catalogue has been published.[12]

Mention may be made here of the **Jewish Free Reading Room and Institute,** in Adler House, Adler Street, E.1, and of the **Wiener Library,** 4 Devonshire Street, W.1. Both are Jewish libraries, but neither is concerned to any great extent with theology. The former maintains a small library intended for students of modern Hebrew as well as for general readers interested in Jewish literature; about half the books are in Yiddish, the rest being in English and other languages. The latter, the Wiener Library, is almost wholly concerned with the repercussions of the Nazi persecution of the Jews.

When we come to libraries concerned with the great Eastern religions, it is probably true to say that the most important collections are to be found in libraries not by any means primarily theological, notably the **India Office Library** at India House and the library of the **School of Oriental and African Studies** in the University of London. In addition there is the library of the **Buddhist Society** (58 Eccleston Square, S.W.1) with its rapidly expanding collection of some 3,500 volumes. A library at the **Islamic Cultural Centre** may also be mentioned.

As has already been said, with a subject that was a major pre-occupation of almost every century but our own, most libraries of old foundation will harbour considerable enclaves of theology. For instance, older law libraries and medical libraries may most of them be fruitfully searched for stray volumes (and sometimes numerous collections) of theology, just as old ecclesiastical libraries will often be found to possess astonishing riches in medicine and in classical literature. Sometimes, too, specific theological collections have been housed in larger and more general libraries. As an example may be mentioned the library (including a long run of contemporary pamphlets) gathered during his lifetime by Beilby Porteus (1731–1808), Bishop of London, which was formerly at Fulham Palace and is now deposited in the University of London Library.[13] Another example is the library of the **Huguenot Society of London** which is now housed in the library of University College. Similarly what appears to be the only surviving parochial library in London, that of **St. Leonard, Shoreditch**, consisting at one time of 870 books, will now be found in Shoreditch Central Library in Pitfield Street.[14]

Amongst general libraries which nevertheless have a special interest in theology must be remembered the four Metropolitan borough libraries, which under the Metropolitan Special Collections Scheme, inaugurated in 1948, give special attention to departments of theology. These are Hammersmith (Natural Religion, Deism, etc. – Dewey classification 200–219), Deptford (Bible, Christian Theology – Dewey 220–259), Fulham (Christian Polity, Institutions and Denominations – Dewey 260–289) and Westminster (Non-Christian Religions – Dewey 290–299). One might also add Hampstead (Philosophy – Dewey 100–199) and Battersea (Occult – Dewey 133–135). It is the intention of the Scheme that these libraries should not only gather in from other Metropolitan libraries their redundant stock of theology no longer wanted for current purposes, but should undertake also to purchase all British published theology, costing 12s. 6d. and over, within their special field. Doubtless some of them extend their purchasing range rather more widely.

From the more general we come to the more special in a somewhat more specialised sense, viz. the Missionary Society Libraries, and including with them, for convenience as well as for a certain similarity of outlook, the great Bible Society Library. It is worth remembering, however, that some of these libraries have older books of wider theological interest.

The **Bible House Library** of the British and Foreign Bible Society is a very specialised collection of Bibles in English and in many other languages and contains about 22,000 volumes. In 1903–11 the Society published its *Historical catalogue of printed Bibles.* This furnishes a catalogue of the library so far as printed Bibles and commentaries containing the text are concerned. But it also does something more for it includes entries (in brackets) of some important editions not possessed by the library, thus constituting virtually a bibliography. At the present time a new edition of the catalogue is in preparation.

The library of the **S.P.G.**, the Society for the Propagation of the Gospel (15 Tufton Street, Westminster), with its more than 20,000 volumes and because of the long history of the Society since 1701, is important for the development of Anglican missions. It has also a small collection of theology, a children's library, a collection of grammars and dictionaries of many Oriental and African languages, and many early travel books.[15]

The **Church Missionary Society** (6 Salisbury Square, E.C.4) in addition to books on Christian missions has a small collection of Puritan literature. It has also books on Moslem and Buddhist subjects which are added to regularly. Amongst its possessions are the diary and letters of Alexander Mackay and letters and papers of Henry Martyn and of Francis Ridley Havergal.[16]

The **London Missionary Society** has a library of some 10,000 volumes, for the most part connected with the Society's work in the South Seas, Papua, India, China, Africa and the West Indies. It has also manuscript records of official correspondence.[17]

The **Baptist Missionary Society Library** (93 Gloucester Place, W.1) was seriously damaged during the war, but the greater part of the older books and archives survived and are now in the process of being recatalogued. The main strength of the library lies in its relation to the work of the Society in India, Ceylon and Africa, and in books and translations published since the formation of the Society in 1792. But in the nature of things it has gathered a considerable amount of other Dissenting literature of the eighteenth and later centuries. The archives of the Society are of first importance for missionary history and for the history of the countries where the Society has been most active. In so far as it is a modern library it is intended for internal use.[18]

With these we must end this brief survey of theological and ecclesiastical libraries in London. There is no doubt that the list could be extended to include other libraries. It could also be extended in another way. Most of the older libraries have become the repositories of small but very specialised collections, for example, of the letters or books of a certain man or movement. To a very slight extent some indication has been given of some of these. But it is only an indication; perhaps its very slightness should be entered as a warning that they could be multiplied many times over until a fat volume would result, constituting an index to the records of the great and of the not-so-great in London libraries. The outcome, if successful, would be valuable, but the mind boggles at the thought of what the work of making any such compilation would mean. Certainly it is no part of the present scheme to go into detail, and the best excuse for having mentioned the little that has been mentioned is to hint at the wealth of London's theological libraries.

NOTES AND REFERENCES

[1] TODD, H. J. Catalogue of the archiepiscopal manuscripts in the library of Lambeth Palace, 1812, gives a useful account (with index) of some part of the collection.

[2] OATES, J. C. T. The libraries of Cambridge, 1570–1700, in WORMALD, F., and WRIGHT, C. E., eds. The English library before 1700. Athlone P., 1958, 223–225.

[3] ROYAL COMMISSION ON HISTORICAL MANUSCRIPTS. Ninth report, Pt. i, 1–72. See also CLARK, J. W. Care of books. C.U.P., 1901, 282–284.

[4] ROYAL COMMISSION ON HISTORICAL MANUSCRIPTS. Fourth report, Pt. i, 171–199. See also ROBINSON, J. A., and JAMES, M. R. The manuscripts of Westminster Abbey. C.U.P., 1909.

[5] PEARCE, E. H. Sion College and library. C.U.P., 1913.

[6] JONES, S. K. Dr. Williams and his library. Dr. Williams's Trust, 1948 – A short account of the charity and library established under the will of the late Rev. Daniel Williams, D.D. Dr. Williams's Trust, 1917.

[7] LITTLEBOY, A. L. A history of the Friends' reference library. Friends' Hist. Soc., 1921.

[8] *Proceedings of the Wesley Historical Society*, 32, 1959, p. 12 and p. 38.

[9] Other such sets of lecture notes will be found at the Congregational Library and at Dr. Williams's Library.

[10] SMITH, C. R. The Richmond Wesleyana, in CUMBERS, F. H., ed. Richmond College, 1843–1943. Epworth, 1944, 52–54.

[11] ROYAL COMMISSION ON HISTORICAL MANUSCRIPTS. Fifth report, Pt. i, 463–476.

[12] HYAMSON, A. M. Jews' College, London, 1855–1955. Jews' College, 1956. *Bulletin of the Association of British Theological and Philosophical Libraries,*

No. 8 (March 1959), 7–10. Descriptive catalogue of the Hebrew manuscripts of the Montefiori Library, compiled by Hartwig Hirschfeld,
1904.

[13] *Lib. Assn. Rec.* 61 (6) 1959, 156–158.

[14] CHURCH OF ENGLAND. CENTRAL COUNCIL FOR THE CARE OF CHURCHES. The
parochial libraries of the Church of England. Church Information Bd.,
1959, 87. (It is a pity that the other parochial libraries mentioned there,
at St. Botolph, Aldgate; St. George the Martyr, Bloomsbury; and at
St. Martin-in-the-Fields have not been preserved.)

[15] THOMPSON, H. P. Into all lands: the history of the Society for the Propagation of the Gospel in Foreign Parts, 1701–1950. S.P.G., 1951.

[16] STOCK, E. The history of the Church Missionary Society, 4 vols. C.M.S.,
1899–1916.

[17] GOODALL, N. A history of the London Missionary Society, 1895–1945.
O.U.P., 1954.

[18] COX, F. A. A history of the Baptist Missionary Society from 1792 to 1842.
2 vols. Houlston, 1842. (This may be supplemented by LORD, F. T.
Achievement. Carey P., 1942.)

CHAPTER XXI

THE LAW LIBRARIES

By A. R. Hewitt

Revised by J. P. Beaven
Deputy Librarian, Hon. Society of the Middle Temple

THE principal law libraries of London for the use of the legal profession are those of the four Inns of Court, namely, the Inner Temple, the Middle Temple, Lincoln's Inn and Gray's Inn; the Bar Library in the Royal Courts of Justice and the Law Society's Library. The functions and purpose of these libraries are to provide lawyers with the literature and material necessary to enable them to prepare and conduct cases in the Courts, to advise clients, to pursue research and, generally, to further the administration of Justice. Each of these libraries is open to members of the institution of which it is a part and the public are not admitted. In exceptional cases, however, non-members may be permitted to consult works which are not obtainable elsewhere. The library of each Inn of Court is for the use of its own members, i.e. benchers, barristers and students, but members of other Inns are, of course, allowed access to books not available in their own library. The Bar Library in the Law Courts is for the use of members of all the Inns, whilst the Law Society's Library is for the exclusive use of solicitors and their clerks.

A major law library designed primarily for education and research was established in 1947 in the University of London Institute of Advanced Legal Studies in Russell Square.

Very substantial legal collections form a part of the British Museum Library and of the British Library of Political and Economic Science at the London School of Economics, the latter being particularly rich in international law and in European law. Smaller but important legal collections are to be found in the library of the University of London and in those of a number of its colleges, apart from the London School of Economics, notably at University College, the School of Oriental and African Studies, and King's College. The Royal Institute of International Affairs at Chatham House also has a collection of works on international law. The Royal Empire Society, now the Royal Commonwealth Society, has a particularly good collection of Commonwealth law, but it suffered severely from enemy action during the war, as did the legal section of the British Museum Library. Other representative legal collections are in the libraries of the House of Commons and House of Lords; and in those of several Government Offices and Departments, particularly the Foreign Office, the Colonial Office, the Treasury Solicitor's Department and the Commonwealth Relations Office, which houses the well-known former India Office Library. Some of the larger Metropolitan public libraries, such as Westminster and the Guildhall Library, have established useful sections, but since the introduction of the co-operative specialisation scheme, the principal public legal library is that of the Borough of Hammersmith, with about 10,000 law books. Many of these general libraries are more particularly described in other chapters of this work.

FOUNDATION OF THE LIBRARIES

The Inns of Court are of great antiquity. The date of their foundation is unknown but they were certainly functioning in the fifteenth century. Their history, tradition and place in the life of the nation is too well known to need further description in a paper of this nature and it is proposed, therefore, to speak only of their libraries.

It is difficult to state with any degree of exactitude when the libraries of the Inns were founded. In the Inner Temple Records the first reference to a library appears in a minute dated 29th June, 1506, when two members of the Inn were "assigned a chamber newly made under the Library" and it may be assumed, therefore, that the library was certainly in existence before the end of the fifteenth century.

Information concerning the foundation of the library of the Middle Temple is scanty. The earliest reference occurs in a manuscript (preserved in the British Museum) ascribed to the reign of Henry VIII which states "they now have no library" and that "they had a simple library, in which were not many bookes besides the law and that library by meanes that it stood allways open and that the learners had not each of them a key unto it, it was at the last robbed of all the bookes in it". The library was re-founded in 1641 when Robert Ashley, a member of the Society, died and bequeathed his collection of books and the sum of £300 to the Inn.

The Records of Lincoln's Inn are the earliest of any of the Inns of Court (commencing as they do in 1422) and a library is first mentioned on the 13th July, 1475, when the sum of 30s. was paid to a Roger Townshend "pro bibliotheca". In 1505 John Nethersale, a member of the Society, bequeathed 40 marks partly towards rebuilding the library and partly for the singing of a mass for his soul. It is only fair to acknowledge the claim of Lincoln's Inn to possession of the oldest library.

The earliest mention of Gray's Inn in the Records of the Society is dated 1568 but a library existed some years before that date as is evidenced by the will, dated 7th July, 1555, of a Robert Chaloner who left his books to a cousin, Robert Nowell, and a sum of money so that "he maie by cheines therewith and fasten so manye of them in the Librarye at Grauisin as he shall think convenyente".

The Bar Library was established in 1883 and the Library of the Law Society in 1828.

THE LIBRARIES AND EARLY EDUCATION

Although the Records of the Inns of Court contain many references to their libraries, little information is available as to the legal works possessed by the Societies. Legal literature was scanty until the dawn of the seventeenth century and it is known that the contents of the libraries consisted mainly of works on philosophy, theology, canon law, mathematics, algebra, medicine and witchcraft. The possession of works of this nature reflects the type of education afforded by the Inns which was not, by any means, confined to the study and practice of the law. The Inns were, in fact, regarded as universities, law being the principal faculty. Sir John Fortescue in his *De laudibus legum angliae* (written c. 1470), giving an account of the part played by the Inns of Court and Chancery in the life of England in his time, says:

"And to speake uprightly ther is in these greater Innes, yea and in the lesser to, besides the study of the laws as it were an university or schoole of all commendable qualities requisite for Noblemen. There they learn to sing and to exercise themselves in all kinde of harmony. There also they practice dauncing and other Noblemen's pastimes as they use to doe which are brought up in the King's house. On the working daies most of them apply themselves to the studie of the lawe. And on the holy daies to the studie of Holy Scripture; and out of the time of Devine Service to the reading of Chronicles. For there indeede are vertues studied and vices exiled. So that, for the endowment of virtue and abandoning of vice, Knights and Barons, with other States and Noblemen of the Realme place their children in those Innes, though they desire not to have them learned in the Lawes, nor to live by the practice thereof, but onely upon their Fathers Allowance."

INNER TEMPLE

The Inner Temple Library has, on several occasions, suffered damage by fire. One building was burned down during the Great Fire of 1666 and another blown up in 1678 to prevent the spread of another fire in the Temple. What damage to, or loss of, books was sustained during the Great Fire does not seem to have been known but on the occasion of the fire of 1678 the books were removed before the explosion. It was again destroyed by fire in 1941 due to enemy action. On that occasion more than half the contents, namely the general library other than law, amounting to approximately 45,000 volumes, had been sent to the country but a tragic loss was the destruction of a large proportion of its legal collection of some 45,000 volumes.

The Inn's general collection is one of which the Society may feel proud. It consists chiefly of works on genealogy and heraldry, county histories and biographies and includes a fine collection of works of the poets, essayists and dramatists. Its most famous possession is the Petyt manuscripts, which, happily, were saved from destruction. William Petyt, a former Keeper of the Records of the Tower, who died in 1707, left his manuscripts and books, together with the sum of £150 towards a new library building, to the Society. These manuscripts consist of original letters of Kings and Queens of England, diplomatists, foreign agents and other distinguished persons.

Its legal collection, before destruction, was of a high order, including, naturally, law reports, statutes, abridgments, periodicals and textbooks. By means of gift and purchase this has been substantially made good, and the notable collection of Commonwealth law, in particular, restored to its former standing. The library, like those of the Middle Temple and Lincoln's Inn, now numbers over 90,000 volumes.

After the war the library was accommodated temporarily in Nos. 1 and 2, King's Bench Walk, but a worthy new library in English oak has now been provided to the design of Mr. T. W. Sutcliffe, on the former site in King's Bench Walk, where it overlooks Church Court. It has been planned to offer to readers a wide variety of study rooms of different size and situation. It was opened on 21st April, 1958, by the Treasurer, Sir Patrick Spens.

MIDDLE TEMPLE

Although the Middle Temple Library building was badly damaged during the war and rendered unusable, almost its entire collection of books was, happily, saved. The old building in the Garden was blasted on five occasions and it was at last found necessary to demolish it. The majority of the books had been removed to the country in 1941 where they remained until 1946 when a new temporary library was opened by Her Majesty the Queen in November of that year.

As previously mentioned, a writer in the reign of Henry VIII lamented the fact that, because the library "stood allways open" it was robbed of all its books, an unfortunate state of affairs which continued until 1641 when the library was re-founded. In that year died Robert Ashley, a member of the Inn, who bequeathed his own library and a sum of £300 to the Inn, describing it as "this noble Society of the Middle Temple in which I have spent so many years of my life". A catalogue of his books was prepared but unfortunately it no longer exists. Fifty-six volumes may still, however, be identified as belonging to Ashley. At an early date the Society came into possession of a substantial portion of the library of John Donne, poet, Dean of St. Paul's, and Preacher to Lincoln's Inn; of which fifty-nine volumes are still identifiable, bearing his signature and motto.

Very little expenditure was allowed for the purchase of books in the early days but the library was fortunate in receiving several substantial benefactions of both books and money. Unfortunately the offer of the John Selden Library, numbering about 8,000 volumes, was refused as it was found that the accommodation required was more extensive than the Society could afford. Selden's Library had previously been offered to both the Inner Temple and Lincoln's Inn and refused also on the grounds of lack of accommodation. It ultimately found a home in the Bodleian.

The library has been housed in many places in the Inn throughout its history. Ashley's books were first placed under lock and key in one of the Parliament Chambers but this arrangement, naturally, proved very unsatisfactory and in 1650 a set of chambers was fitted up as a library. In 1824 the books were moved to the New Parliament Chamber which was fitted up to serve also as a library. Owing to the rapid expansion of the library this accommodation did not serve long, in spite of the erection of a gallery in the chamber and the incorporation of three store rooms below. In 1854 the foundations were laid for an entirely new building in the Garden to include two floors of professional chambers. The new library was opened on October 31st, 1861 by H.M. King Edward VII, then Prince of Wales. In due time the chambers were absorbed into the library but even that encroachment did not solve the problem of space which was becoming acute by the time of the outbreak of the late war. As previously mentioned, the building was rendered unsafe by enemy action and a temporary library was erected over a static water tank on the site of Nos. 2 and 3 Brick Court, which had been demolished early in the war. Following the restoration of the destroyed chambers in the Inn, a magnificent new library building, in five storeys, was erected in Middle Temple Lane, to the design of Sir Edward Maufe, and was opened on 7th November, 1958 by Her Majesty the Queen Mother, a Bencher of the Inn. The bookcases and furniture on the main floor, and on the gallery floor, housing the Commonwealth collection and Students' Library, are entirely in mahogany. The top floor, comprising the American Library, is furnished in oak. The library has thus returned almost to its site in earlier centuries.

The Middle Temple Library is rich in works on English law and is very well supplied with Scottish, Irish and Commonwealth law. It contains a good collection of books on international and Roman-Dutch law and its American Library, to which reference will be made again later, is still the most representative in Europe. In 1954 a generous gift of some 550 volumes from the United States Government, and formally presented by the Ambassador, filled in certain deficiencies in the library. In 1955 the Baron Ver Heyden de Lancey presented to the library nearly 1,000 volumes, many of great value, on English and French literature, art, history, travel, social history, biography, manners and customs, and various of the fine arts. It forms a link with the early and less pressing days when the libraries of the Inns of Court were repositories of books on general culture. General literature, topography and genealogy were already well-covered fields. The total number of volumes in the library is now over 90,000.

LINCOLN'S INN

Lincoln's Inn enjoys the distinction of possessing the oldest law library but, like the other Inns of Court, little of value is known about its early history. The building to which John Nethersale contributed in 1505 was completed in the year 1508 but its site is unknown. As the library grew, it moved about the Inn and it is known to have been housed in rooms in Stone Buildings and Old Square. The present building was opened in 1845 and extended in 1872. It consists of one large main reading and reference room with others below and adjacent which have been absorbed into the library from time to time. As in the case of most libraries of today, space available is inadequate and a few years ago the Society was compelled to dispose of a collection of French and English literature numbering some 5,000 volumes. The time is not far distant when the problem must be faced of still further accommodation in addition to the present building.

The early growth of the library was slow. During the first 100 years few books were added and in 1608 an order was made by the Council that new Masters of the Bench should contribute a sum of 20s. and that every new barrister should contribute a sum of 13s. 4d. towards the purchase and presentation of books until it reached the high standard it enjoys today. It contains not only a fine legal collection but also a representative library of historical, topographical and biographical works. The Inn is justly proud of its manuscripts. It possesses the Hale, Melmoth, Hill and Maynard collections which, together with others, number some 1,000 volumes. Sir Mathew Hale was a renowned lawyer and legal writer and was Lord Chief Justice in 1671. His manuscripts, together with those of Sir John Maynard, who was a King's Serjeant and a Judge in the reign of Charles II, are of great historical and intrinsic value. The library also possesses a collection of over 2,000 early historical tracts and pamphlets.

The library has been enriched over a period of many years by the generosity of members. It has long held a remarkable collection of Parish Registers, which is still currently maintained. A notable feature of the legal library is the collection of Private Acts not printed by the King's Printer, relating principally to inclosures and estates, and printed at the expense of the parties concerned, dating from 1727 to 1838 and numbering 149 volumes. A collection of forty volumes of Road Acts from 1754 to 1796 is particularly valuable. This, in addition to a full holding of legislation, public and private, issued by the King's Printer, and of bound Parliamentary Papers dating from the beginning of the nineteenth century.

Happily, Lincoln's Inn Library escaped damage during the war (except for the loss of its stained glass windows) and its collection, now numbering over 90,000 volumes, remains unimpared.

GRAY'S INN

The library of Gray's Inn today reflects more than any of the Inns of Court libraries the losses of the late war. During one of the incendiary bomb attacks on London, on 10th May, 1941, the entire library was destroyed by fire. The items saved from destruction were few: all the illuminated manuscripts, a few of the chained books (including Ralegh's *History of the World*, Coke's *Institutes* and Coke on Littleton), some classics and a number of volumes of Baconiana. The rest, general literature and law, were burned. Since the destruction, a collection of law reports, statutes, legal textbooks, etc., together with a few classics, has been obtained by gift and purchase amounting to about 27,000 volumes in all. The library was indebted to his late Majesty King George VI for a gift of statutes covering the period from Magna Carta to 1941. The loss of an extensive collection of Roman, Roman-Dutch and Civil Law has been minimised by a collection of Roman-Dutch Law presented by Dr. Robert Warden Lee. Since 1946 the library has acquired by gift a distinguished collection of some 1,600 volumes of general French literature of the Louis XIV and Louis XVI periods.

After being housed for a time in a prefabricated building in the Garden, the library is now accommodated in an appropriate new building to the design of Sir Edward Maufe, on the old site in South Square. It was opened on 11th December, 1958 by the Prime Minister, the Rt. Hon. Harold Macmillan.

Before its destruction Gray's Inn Library had occupied the site since 1788, enlargements having been made in 1840, and 1884. Prior to this the library, dating from the sixteenth century, was sited in Gray's Inn Square. On 18th July, 1929 the great Holker Library designed by Sir Edwin Cooper was opened by the Rt. Hon. Stanley Baldwin, as the result of a bequest in 1926 from the late Lord Justice Holker. Before destruction it possessed approximately 35,000 and included a good working law library and a representative collection of general literature.

THE SUPREME COURT LIBRARIES

The Bar Library in the Royal Courts of Justice was founded in 1883 jointly by the four Inns of Court and was originally intended as a reference library for members of the Bar of all the Inns having business in the Courts. It is now regarded, however, as the library of the Royal Courts of Justice in spite of the fact that it is maintained by the Bar for the Bar. It is managed by a joint committee of eight members, two from each Inn, and the cost of books, binding and salaries is met by the Inns in equal proportions. Other expenses (lighting, heating, etc.) are borne by the Treasury. It contains some 35,000 volumes almost entirely dealing with law and its function is to provide the practising barrister with the reference books necessary for the proper presentation of his cases in Court.

In addition to the Bar Library there are several smaller libraries throughout the Law Courts which are housed in the various courts. The largest of these are in the Appeal Courts and the Lord Chief Justice's Court. The control and supervision of these libraries is exercised by the librarian of the Bar Library but the expense of maintenance is borne entirely by the Treasury.

Finally, there is the Probate Library, also housed in the Courts, which, like the others, is controlled by the librarian of the Bar Library. It is a subscription library and the subscribers (who are members of the Bar) are entitled to borrow books therefrom. It was formerly known as the Chancery Library and was established in 1831 at Westminster where the Courts of Law then sat, until 1883 when it moved to the Law Courts in the Strand.

THE LAW SOCIETY

The Law Society's Library is of comparatively recent foundation. In June 1828 a member of the Society named Thomas Metcalfe presented a set of the *Statutes-at-large* and round this single gift has developed the splendid library possessed by the Society today. Donations of books and money for the purchase of books have been received from judges, barristers and members of the Society so that, in spite of the fact that it was founded so many years after the libraries of the Inns of Court, it now ranks as one of the great law libraries.

It possesses a fine collection of statutes, law reports and legal textbooks. In addition to the law collection the library is rich in almost complete sets of Directories, Court Guides, Army and Navy lists, Law lists and University and other Calendars. There is a complete set of the *London gazette* from its commencement in 1665 and of *The Times* newspaper (except for the year 1815). It also possesses a fine collection of Private Acts of Parliament dating from 1700, Parliamentary Papers and Appeal Cases in the House of Lords since 1700 and in the Privy Council since 1854. A noteworthy collection is the Mendham Library which was formerly the property of the Rev. Joseph Mendham, a scholar of some standing, which was presented to the Society in 1870. It consists of historical and theological works, books and pamphlets on theological controversy, editions of the Old and New Testaments and liturgies. It is now, however, more of antiquarian than of practical value.

The library, which contains approximately 77,000 volumes, is for the use of members and their clerks but the Council may admit other fit and proper persons to use the library on such terms and conditions as they may lay down. The Society also maintains a students' library at the Law Society's School of Law, Lancaster Gate, London.

INSTITUTE OF ADVANCED LEGAL STUDIES

The Institute was established by the University of London in 1947 as part of its post-war development programme. Its building in Russell Square was opened by the then Lord Chancellor, Viscount Jowitt, in June 1948. Since then, the foundations for a legal research library have been laid and over 60,000 books have been acquired.

Considerable time was spent, initially, on formulating library policy, and discussions took place with other libraries in the University of London and with certain other authorities. To provide a factual basis for these discussions, a number of surveys were undertaken to ensure that the overall provision of law books in the University should be as systematic as possible. The Institute has published and maintained current information on holdings of various categories of legal literature in libraries in London (and to some extent elsewhere in Britain). These cover legal periodicals, Commonwealth and United States legal literature and publications on air law.

The Institute is hoping to acquire in time a full collection of legal literature for England and Wales, and for other parts of the British Isles. For the Commonwealth, the 'Nuffield Library of Commonwealth Law' (made possible by a grant from the Nuffield Foundation) now contains a comprehensive range of legal literature for all Commonwealth countries except India and Pakistan (which, by agreement, are the special responsibility of the School of Oriental and African Studies).

For the United States, the more important treatises required for research have been acquired. In addition, several series of Law Reports are taken, and the important American Jurisprudence. The main gap in American legal literature filled by the Institute, however, has been in legal periodicals, where well over 100 titles are received. An attempt is being made to obtain earlier volumes not at present acquired.

For the main legal subjects (as distinct from literature on specific countries) provision has been made for literature in Western European languages on jurisprudence, comparative law, Roman law, canon law, public international law and conflict of laws.

For legal systems outside Anglo-American common law, emphasis has been given to countries in Western Europe and to a lesser extent in Latin America, as part of the policy for legal libraries within the University of London.

CONTENTS OF THE LAW LIBRARIES

Space does not permit a detailed description of the contents of the individual libraries which are all of a similar character and it is proposed, therefore, for the benefit of those having little knowledge or experience of law libraries and legal literature, to mention, very briefly and simply, the type of works to be found in such a library.

Further, it is impossible to mention the early printed legal works and classics, a subject which in itself would occupy more space than has been allotted to the whole of this chapter. Each library possesses (or did possess, as the case may be) a fine collection of old statutes, digests, abridgments, reports and textbooks, some of considerable intrinsic value and all of great antiquarian and historical interest.

Statutes. One of the main sources of law is the Statute law enacted by Parliament and a law library must, as a first essential, contain sets of Acts of Parliament (public, local and private), together with the Rules and Orders made under statutory authority and other instruments having the force of law. Statutes of the Realm have been issued by Royal authority from the earliest times, but many collections, revisions, digests and abridgments have been privately issued and are of considerable importance. Various indices to Statutes have also been published but only one of practical value now remains and is issued periodically by H.M. Stationery Office.

Law Reports. Reports of cases heard and determined by the Courts are many in number, amounting to some thousands of volumes. The earliest reports were collected and issued as *Year books* which first appeared in printed form at the commencement of the sixteenth century. Volumes of reports were published either under the name of the judge delivering the judgments or, more frequently, under the name of the 'reporter' compiling the record. Some were, and still are, issued under the title of the subject matter of the cases reported. The commencement of the first 'Official' series of reports in 1865, namely *The law reports*, issued by the Incorporated Council of Law Reporting, really put an end to the individual volumes of reports, although several continued to appear spasmodically for a few years after that date. Various series of reports of cases in all Courts began to appear in the nineteenth century – including the *Law journal reports* (1822), the *Jurist* (1837), the *Law times reports* (1843) and the *Times law reports* (1884), but these have ceased publication in recent years. In addition to the series of general reports, special series have been published from time to time, for example, *Cox's criminal cases* (1843–1941), *Bankruptcy and company cases* (1884–1942), *Reports of patent cases* (1884-), *Knight's local government reports* (1903-), *Lloyd's list law reports* (1919-), to name only a few. The last three series are still current. The past twenty-five years have seen the inauguration of two comprehensive series of reports issued as quickly as possible after the hearing of the cases, viz., the *All-England law reports*, and the *Weekly law reports*. The latter are published by the Incorporated Council of Law Reporting, as are the new *Reports of restrictive practices cases*.

Trials and Peerage Claims. Mention must be made of those reports commonly referred to as 'Trials' (both collections and individual cases) and 'Peerage Claims'. Trials are, for the most part, reports of famous criminal cases and some hundreds of volumes have been published in the course of time. Peerage Claims are very numerous and consist of the documents, evidence and judgments in Claims to peerages submitted to, and determined by, the Committee of Privileges of the House of Lords.

Digests. Such a mass of reported cases mentioned would be practically useless without the Digests which give the main points of decided cases, collected together according to their subject matter or under the branch of law they illustrate. The first Digests were of Statute law, or both Statute law and reported Cases, but, apart from an historical interest, the early works are of little practical value today. They have been superseded by the encyclopaedic works now in common use – *Mew's digest* (first published in 1882) and the *English and Empire digest* (which commenced publication in 1919). The several series of reports also have Digests of cases reported in those series – the *Law reports*, the *Weekly law reports*, *Lloyd's list*, the *All-England law reports*, etc. Since the war *Current law* has provided an up-to-date Digest not only of case law, but of statutes, instruments and other references.

Textbooks. The next branch of legal literature to which reference must be made is the textbook, a term which is really self-explanatory. The earliest law books were, of course, in manuscript, usually compiled for the writer's own use and guidance. The beginning of printing saw the beginning of legal textbooks as we know them today, since when they have appeared in ever-increasing numbers on all conceivable branches of law, some good and some bad; some classics and some of mere passing interest.

Legal Periodicals. The first of the great legal periodicals or journals was the *Law magazine*, first published in 1829. Many have appeared and, having served a purpose, have passed away. The chief periodicals of today are the *Justice of the peace* (which commenced publication in 1838-), the *Law times* (1843-), the *Solicitors' journal*, or *Weekly reporter* as it was first called (1857-), the *Law journal* (1866-) and the *Law quarterly review* (1885-). Other current series not of such early date are the *Journal of comparative legislation*, *Law notes*, *Cambridge law journal*, the *Modern law review* and the *Journal of criminal law*.

Encyclopaedias. Legal encyclopaedias are a comparatively modern innovation (if we exclude some of the old Abridgments of Law). The *Encyclopaedia of English law* appeared in 1896 and Halsbury's *Laws of England* in 1907. Others are the *Encyclopaedia of forms and precedents* (1902), the *Encyclopaedia of local government* (1905) and the *Encyclopaedia of court forms* (1937). New editions and supplements have been issued from time to time. They are monumental works in many volumes and are invaluable both in practice and research.

General Literature. In addition to those works which might be described as purely legal in character, a good law library will contain sets of Parliamentary Papers, Calendars of State Papers, Journals and Debates of both Houses of Parliament, the *London gazette*, *The Times* newspaper, a selection of publications of learned societies, calendars and reference books and a representative collection of works on history, biography, travel, topography, medicine, English literature, etc.

Law other than English. So far English law only has been reviewed but a law library must also contain a collection of a similar character relating to Scotland, Ireland, countries of the Commonwealth and the Colonies and the United States of America, with a selection of works on Roman law, Roman-Dutch law, and foreign and international law. It is interesting to recall that, on the occasion of the laying of the foundation stone for the old Middle Temple Library in 1858, Sir Fortunatus Dwarris, the Master Treasurer, said a law library "ought to contain the laws of all ages, and of all the countries, and the laws which govern them; the *legum leges*. Next, the most important, that it should show the application of those laws in the thousands and tens of thousands of adjudged cases, reported from all the Courts."

Scotland and Ireland. Scotland, Northern Ireland and the Republic of Ireland have distinct systems of law with their own statutes, reports, digests, encyclopaedias, periodicals and textbooks. The number of volumes involved is not, fortunately, so great as that in England but the statutes and reports, with a selection of textbooks, periodicals, etc., must be available in an English law library.

Commonwealth Law. The Commonwealth sections of the library can be very extensive and, broadly speaking, each country, state, province and colony has its own series of statutes or ordinances and reports, totalling many thousands of volumes. Colonial legislation alone is considerable as every territory is obliged, under Colonial Office Regulations, to supply copies of its laws and ordinances to the four Inns of Court, the Bar Library and the Law Society, among other institutions. Commonwealth countries also send copies of their statutes and other legislation to those libraries as a matter of courtesy.

India is prolific in the publication of laws and reports, copies of which are also delivered to the libraries previously mentioned.

In addition to statutes and reports, a selection of textbooks, digests and periodicals must also be available.

American Law. The basis of American law is the English Common law and there is, as a result, a close affinity between the English and American legal systems. The sources of law of both nations are constantly referred to in the Courts and in the literature of the two countries. It is essential, therefore, that a representative collection of American law books should be available in this country. A number of the law libraries have attempted in some measure to meet this need but the Middle Temple Library has until recently been the only library to provide such literature to any great extent. The developments of the Institute of Advanced Legal Studies in the American field are described above in the particulars relating to that Library. The Middle Temple's collection of case-law is complete, containing as it does reports of cases in the several States of the Union and in the Federal Courts, both individual State reports and the reports issued in the 'National Reporter System'. It also contains the *American digest*, an enormous work occupying seventy feet of shelving; the *Corpus juris* and the *Corpus juris secundum*, an encyclopaedic work totalling to date over 200 volumes; a selection of the more important legal periodicals; the *United States code annotated;* the *Restatement of the law;* the *American law reports annotated; Shepard's citations; Words and phrases;* the *Uniform laws annotated;* the Federal Statutes and a good selections of textbooks. In an effort to reduce expenditure an arrangement was made between the Bar Library and the Middle Temple whereby the Bar Library subscribed to the Codes of Laws of the individual States and the Middle Temple to the 'National Reporter System', but the State Laws in the Bar Library are no longer up to date. Reference to the important donation to the Middle Temple Library in 1954 by the United States Government is made above.

OTHER LEGAL COLLECTIONS

Considerations of space have limited this survey to the principal law libraries but it is desirable to refer briefly to certain other legal collections in London, although a number of the smaller collections have been mentioned in the opening paragraphs of this chapter.

The Central Criminal Court, Old Bailey, contains a small reference library for practitioners of approximately 1,500 volumes on criminal law. It also possesses a valuable set (with a few gaps) of the Old Bailey Sessions Papers from 1777 to 1913. The Bar Mess has a few hundred volumes for its own use.

The field of international law and relations is well served by the library of the former Grotius Society (now incorporated in the British Institute of International and Comparative Law), which possesses some 2,000 volumes on the subject. It is housed at No. 1, Temple Gardens.

The Hardwicke Society, one of the legal debating societies, has an outstanding collection of Trials and works on advocates and advocacy, numbering some 1,200 volumes. The library is for the use of all members of the Hardwicke Society and is housed in the Middle Temple Barristers' Common Room.

CHAPTER XXII

MEDICAL LIBRARIES

By W. R. Le Fanu

Librarian, Royal College of Surgeons of England

WHEN the previous edition of *The Libraries of London* appeared, the medical libraries were still being reorganised in the aftermath of war. The succeeding twelve years have seen a great development of their activity. London has become in these years the centre of postgraduate medical training, attracting from all over the world young doctors who are seeking advanced qualifications. Far more fundamental medical research is now pursued in London than ever before, while the undergraduate medical schools have been infused with new vigour and enterprise through the help of the University Grants Committee. This lively movement of scientific medicine has been reflected and supported by the medical libraries. The Medical Section of the Library Association, founded in 1947, has been busy throughout the period and has brought the staffs of the medical libraries into mutual contact, through meetings, weekend conferences, and practical publications. During the centenary celebrations of the Library Association in 1950, the Medical Section's meeting was warmly supported by leading medical men, who also gave active encouragement to the highly successful International Congress of Medical Librarianship, the first of its kind, which was organised by the librarians of the larger London medical libraries in 1953.

Fifty years ago the general sense of the medical profession looked for efficiency through the amalgamation of the smaller libraries into one general medical library. This movement resulted in forming the great library of the Royal Society of Medicine, still the chief medical library in the Commonwealth and one of the busiest libraries of any kind in London. Today it is seen that the highly specialised groups of workers in the very numerous centres of research and teaching, which have grown up since 1945, each require a well-organised special library close at hand. This trend began between the wars with the foundation of the libraries of the Medical Research Council, the London School of

Hygiene and Tropical Medicine, and the Postgraduate Medical School at Hammersmith, each of which is geared to the potential demand of a particular class of medical workers. Since the last war the British Postgraduate Medical Federation has promoted the growth of a series of University Institutes each devoted to a special branch of medicine and connected with the leading hospital of that specialty. The libraries of these research and postgraduate-teaching institutes are the most notable addition to the family of medical libraries in London. Together they provide the current specialised medical literature on a scale not attempted hitherto.

The success of the Medical Section of the Library Association has proved the unity underlying these diverse and independent medical libraries. The Library Association published lately a *Directory of medical libraries in the British Isles* which shows that there are sixty-nine medical libraries in London with fifty smaller hospital libraries. This is approximately half the total number of medical libraries in the country. The larger medical libraries of London were also described in the *Proceedings* of the Congress of 1953. It would be impossible as well as unnecessary to describe them all; I shall therefore mention only the larger libraries and those which have made some specially interesting contribution to library activities in the past decade.

The **Royal Society of Medicine** was formed in 1907 by amalgamating a number of smaller libraries with those of the Royal Medico-Chirurgical Society, the Ophthalmological Society, and the Obstetrical Society. A munificent gift from the Wellcome Foundation in 1953 enabled the Society to enlarge and improve its library facilities. In spite of limited space in the busy centre of the West End, this library performs a national function on a private income. The possibility of its development into a National Medical Library, for which its wealth of books and efficiency of service entitle it, has been mooted in recent years, but for the present it continues as a private subscription library chiefly used by consultants throughout the country though also useful to research workers. Its comprehensive collection of medical periodicals (*Catalogue*, 1938) and its great reference and loan collection cover every aspect of medicine. The Society also owns an important library of historical medical books.

The **British Medical Association's Library** is, again, primarily the private subscription library of the tens of thousands of medical men and women who are members of the Association. It provides an admirable and much used loan service for the practitioner and possesses the most comprehensive collection in the country of modern medical periodicals, acquired in connection with the Association's abstracting service.

The old-established subscription library of Messrs. **H. K. Lewis,** the booksellers in Gower Street, provides modern English and American books. Besides its large personal clientele, it is much used by special libraries for books which they require for only brief reference.

The **British Museum** is little used as a medical library, but in addition to its copyright holding of all British medical publications, it possesses a distinguished range of foreign medical periodicals. For scholars and historians its fund of older medical books is unsurpassed, while its manuscripts of medical interest have never been fully explored. Professor and Mrs. Singer's card catalogue of medical manuscripts is available in the Students' Room of the Department of Manuscripts.

The line between medicine and the biological and biophysical sciences becomes every year less definite. No medical library does as yet – or perhaps ever will – provide the full range of scientific literature likely to be wanted from time to time by its readers. The Science Library's loan service therefore provides an essential adjunct for medical libraries, while it does not itself cover medical literature. Medical scientists equally make use of the Patent Office Library.

The excellent Medical Sciences Library at **University College** has the advantage of intimate contact with the Biological and Physical libraries of the College (see Chapter XIII); named the **Thane Library** in memory of Sir George Thane, professor of anatomy, it provides a first-class collection of anatomical and physiological literature, and plays a leading part in medical library co-operation.

The **University of London Library** (Chapter XII) has, in the years since the war, formed an important medical collection, notable for its large range of periodicals. This is, in part, supported by the British Postgraduate Medical Federation. The collection is largely used in the reading rooms of the University Library but is also available for loan.

The **Medical Research Council Library** at Mill Hill is primarily concerned to provide current literature for the research workers at the National Institute of Medical Research, where the library has its fine premises, and for those in all the research undertakings throughout the country sponsored or aided by the Council. It is notable for its extensive collection of periodicals in the bio-medical sciences, its liberal loan policy, and its efficient information service.

The **Library of the Royal College of Surgeons of England** combines one of the principal historical medical libraries, particularly rich in anatomical books, with a great fund of periodicals, and the modern research library of the College's scientific departments. During the last fifteen years the College has developed its teaching and research activities on a very large scale, and now promotes postgraduate education through the Institute of Basic Medical Sciences (anatomy, surgical pathology, and applied physiology) affiliated to the University. There are also departments of ophthalmology, dental research, and anaesthesia.

The **London School of Hygiene and Tropical Medicine** supports the most extensive specialised medical library among the postgraduate schools of the University. Its collections cover all aspects of public health and tropical medicine and general medicine in tropical countries. Particularly notable are its holdings of official reports and periodicals from the Commonwealth and colonial countries. Its pre-eminence is largely due to the life-work of an outstanding librarian, Cyril Barnard, who was tragically killed in a street accident when he was about to retire in 1959. Barnard played a leading part in the library profession, and is known all over the world for his *Medical Classification*.

The medical library of the **British Council** is active in diffusing knowledge of current British medicine to foreign countries and to foreign visitors. Its monthly *British Medical Booklist* is an invaluable guide to new publications. This library files a large number of unusual foreign periodicals, and is generous in placing these in appropriate reference libraries when it no longer requires them for current use.

Some of the special libraries follow the same policy of transferring to larger libraries the general periodicals which they do not require to keep indefinitely. Some steps towards rationalising their holdings in accord with their current interests have been made by specialised libraries, particularly within the 'London group' of the co-operating larger medical libraries. The postgraduate institutes and the undergraduate schools similarly co-operate in their respective groups. The Wellcome Historical Medical Library organises, on behalf of the Medical Section of the Library Association, an active and efficient exchange pool for periodicals and book duplicates. This pool is widely used by some hundreds of libraries through the Commonwealth and abroad.

Discussions among the principal medical libraries on the problem of combined storage were called in recent years by the British Medical Association, but unfortunately proved abortive. Dr. F. N. L. Poynter, Librarian of the Wellcome Historical Medical Library, has made a practical and generous contribution to this pressing problem by offering hospitality, with his Trustees' approval, to certain other medical libraries in the new stack of the Wellcome Foundation.

Additions and improvements have been made to many library buildings, but no strikingly original contribution to library architecture has appeared among the medical libraries. An interesting and successful innovation is the renting of a floor in a neighbouring office block to provide adequate space for the expanding library of the Charing Cross Hospital Medical School.

Medical literature is represented among the fields of interest selected by the Metropolitan Borough Libraries' Subject Specialisation Scheme. This subject was allotted in 1949 to the Marylebone Public Library which has formed a valuable medical collection, the first in this country to be freely available, with only minor restrictions, to the general public.

There are several old-established but active libraries for the professions allied to medicine: no list of London's medical libraries would be complete which did not include those, for instance, of the **British Dental Association,** the **Pharmaceutical Society,** the **Royal College of Nursing,** the **Royal College of Veterinary Surgeons,** and the **Royal Veterinary College.**

The famous and ancient library of the **Royal College of Physicians** has been reorganised since the end of the war, and now plays an active part in the study of medical history, with a bias towards medical biography. Exhibitions of historical interest are regularly arranged, for which typescript catalogues with valuable annotations are prepared. A more ambitious exhibition of medical records was arranged by the College Library in connection with the British Records Association in the autumn of 1958 and proved most stimulating.

The **Medical Society of London** possesses a valuable historical library, unfortunately little known. The **Society of Apothecaries** has dispersed its interesting small library, transferring its botanical books to the **Chelsea Physic Garden.**

The medico-historical collections at the British Museum have already been mentioned. They are almost rivalled by the vast **Wellcome Historical Medical Library,** which comprises nearly a quarter of a million volumes of original texts and modern books of reference and historical research, including an outstanding collection of medical and scientific incunabula, 100,000 autograph letters, and a considerable Oriental section. The contributions of this active library to current library affairs have already been mentioned in connection with the exchange of duplicates and co-operative storage. It also publishes a periodical index of *Current work in the history of medicine.*

Much has been done in the past ten years to provide an adequate library service for the medical profession in London, and indeed for the many medical men and women throughout the country and the Commonwealth who also look to London. This has been achieved through the growth of a spirit of liberal co-operation among a very large number of independent libraries of varying scope. A shortcoming which cannot readily be remedied is the lack of regular provision of medical books in foreign languages; foreign periodicals, on the other hand, are very thoroughly represented.

NOTES AND REFERENCES

BARNARD, C. C. A classification for medical and veterinary libraries. 2nd edition. H. K. Lewis, 1955.

British Medical Booklist. British Council. Monthly, since 1950.

BRITISH RECORDS ASSOCIATION. Catalogue of an exhibition of medical records in the library of the Royal College of Physicians, with an introduction by L. M. Payne. B.R.A., 1958.

Bulletin of the Medical Section of the Library Association. Irregular, since 1948.

Current Work in the History of Medicine. Wellcome Historical Medical Library. Quarterly, since 1954.

LIBRARY ASSOCIATION, MEDICAL SECTION. Directory of medical libraries in the British Isles. Library Association, 1957.

Proceedings of the First International Congress of Medical Librarianship, London, 20–25 July, 1953, ed. by F. N. L. Poynter. *Libri* 3, 1954, especially Notes on some London medical libraries, pages xxiii-xxxi, and POYNTER, F. N. L. A plan for the establishment of combined national depositories and exchange centres for medical periodicals, pages 285–291.

WELLCOME HISTORICAL MEDICAL LIBRARY. A catalogue of incunabula (610 items) by F. N. L. Poynter. O.U.P., 1954.

Chapter XXIII

MUSIC LIBRARIES

By J. H. Davies

B.B.C. Music Librarian

THE principal sources of detailed information on London's music libraries are to be found (*a*) under "Libraries and Collections" in the fifth edition of *Grove's Dictionary of music,* 1954 and (*b*) in the *Aslib directory.* The purpose of this chapter is to supplement the classified data therein by a general description of how the needs of musical scholarship and practical musical activity are currently met by those libraries. The following headings are not mutually exclusive but will serve to focus attention on some main aspects.

SOURCE MATERIAL

The British Museum naturally stands pre-eminent as the national repository of music, both printed and manuscript. Broadly speaking these two classes of music are housed and administered independently by the Music Room and the Department of Manuscripts respectively, though certain manuscripts are to be found located in the Music Room, over and above the latter's holdings of the great collection of Handel manuscripts forming part of the Royal Music Library. The post-war years have added to the Museum's music collections very considerably by the acquisition in 1949 of the Hirsch collection (principally printed music). With the assignment to the nation in 1958 of the Royal Music Library, a point of procedure was changed: it is no longer necessary for the Principal Keeper of Printed Books to obtain the permission of the Queen's Librarian before granting permission to copy or publish works from this collection.

Libraries like that of the Royal Philharmonic Society and the Madrigal Society have deposited their collections on loan to the British Museum, though in the former case, the working library of scores is at the Royal Academy of Music. Because the smaller colleges are essentially teaching institutions, this does not preclude possession of valuable research materials being owned by, e.g., Trinity College of

Music, and Gresham College. Finally there are sizeable reference libraries in London University (Senate House), at Messrs. Novello's, and at Sadler's Wells Theatre (see below).

PERFORMANCE

Among the London libraries primarily geared for musical performance, the B.B.C.'s music libraries are by far the largest, since they have to meet all broadcast needs. Its own 'Central Music Library' (not to be confused with the similarly named library at Westminster referred to below) provides orchestral, choral, recital, light music, etc. services to an unparalleled extent, and over the widest conceivable range. A great deal of extra-mural help is given, under certain conditions, but it cannot function as a public lending library. The *International catalogue of rare orchestral materials* (International Association of Music Libraries, 1959) owes much to B.B.C. initiative. Orchestral performance is also served by the domestic libraries of the standing orchestras of London (London Philharmonic Orchestra, London Symphony Orchestra, Royal Philharmonic Orchestra, Philharmonia, etc.) supported (for copyright works) by the hire libraries of London music publishers. Some of the latter, such as Boosey & Hawkes, and Chappell's, covering many subsidiary firms, are very extensive indeed. At least two firms (Messrs. J. & W. Chester Ltd. and Goodwin & Tabb Ltd.) maintain general hire libraries of repertory music as well as their own copyrights, the former also having an extensive chamber-music subscription library. Yet further libraries, besides the rate-supported ones (Metropolitan boroughs, boroughs and county councils in the area) concerned with performance are those of the teaching institutions (see below), the Central Music Library, Westminster (now virtually incorporated with the Westminster Public Library service and handling directly the Metropolitan inter-loans of music), the National Federation of Music Societies (which has an orchestral and chamber-music library and a national index of members' choral holdings) and the L.C.C.'s Music Department Library which serves its school orchestras. The teaching institutions all have their orchestral libraries, too, e.g. that at the Royal Academy of Music, which includes the Henry Wood Library.

NATIONAL PROPAGANDA

For facilitating performance of their own music, a number of nations have, since the war, established lending libraries and information services. Headed by those of the British Council, these include the Polish Cultural Institute, the Society for Cultural Relations with Russia, and the United States Information Service. Some continental composers' societies, such as Donemus (for Holland) and Nordiska (for Scandinavia) use London publishers (Lengnick, etc.) as their official agents. Material of this kind is usually sold or lent or hired in photo-copied form, to special order.

RECORDED MATERIAL

The B.B.C., with its separate Gramophone and Recorded Pro-grammes Libraries, both of immense scope, lead the field here, as in the sphere of 'live' music, and their activities are similarly limited to broadcast use. Their rare foreign recordings, together with much ethno-music on disc or tape, form a vast corpus of material, much of it unique, which will form the research material of the future. The British Institute of Recorded Sound (1951-) is already justifying its claim to be the national archive in this field, and is now able, under certain conditions, to dub research material from the B.B.C. archives. A growing proportion of the rate-supported libraries now maintain separate gramophone lending libraries, and the number of music librarians wholly occupied in administering these and the music stocks is slowly increasing. Boroughs like Westminster, Marylebone, Fulham, Holborn, Croydon and Lambeth employ separate staff on such duties, and a number of them publish catalogues or lists of records and scores.

SPECIALISED SERVICES

Even within the musical field some libraries are rigid specialists. Sadler's Wells Theatre now houses the Novello reference library of vocal scores, latterly supplemented by the late Professor Edward Dent's operatic library including many of his translations. The working library of the Royal Opera House is more or less limited to repertory needs, but there is an archive of nineteenth-century materials dating from Colonel Mapleson's days. The library of the English Folk Dance and Song Society is of prime importance, both for books, illustrations and records in that field. It has recently been re-named the Vaughan Williams Memorial Library, and houses that master's own library of folk-song material. The National Library for the Blind maintains a library of over 40,000 pieces of Braille music, serving about 100 readers and 250 brailled works of musical literature.

Bulk service to choirs and orchestras, in so far as this is organised in London, emanates from the firms and institutions mentioned earlier under 'performance'. There is no direct equivalent of the municipal subscription services offered by the Manchester and Liverpool Public Libraries.

PROFESSIONAL ORGANISATION

The Library Association grants specialist certificates in the Literature and Librarianship of Music as part of its normal examination syllabus. Oral training for this is now in the hands of the North-Western Polytechnic. All other aspects of current professional work are centred in the London-based United Kingdom Branch of the International Association of Music Libraries which holds regular meetings and occasional conferences, and which generally attempts to link metropolitan, national, and international activity.

CATALOGUES AND INDEXES

B.B.C. Music Library
> Composer and title catalogues: Orchestral, choral, songs, chamber music. 1956– [Duplicated for internal use only]

B.B.C. Recorded Programmes Permanent Library
> Index of incidental music recordings. 1957–
> Folk and national music recordings. 1958–

British Catalogue of Music [quarterly and annually]. 1957–

British Museum
> Catalogue of printed music 1487–1800. 2 vols. and suppts. 1912–40
> Catalogue of the King's Music Library. 3 vols. 1927–29
> Catalogue of manuscript music. 3 vols. 1906–09
> Current accessions [annual]. 1884–
> Katalog der Musikbibliothek Paul Hirsch. 4 vols. 1928–47
> Music in the Hirsch library (B.M. Accessions, Part 53). 1951
> Books in the Hirsch Library (B.M. Accessions, 3rd series, Part 291B). 1959.
> Royal College of Music [Hand-list of MSS. on deposit]

British union catalogue of early music, ed. E. Schnapper. 2 vols. 1957

Central Music Library. List of operas available. 1955

Chester, J. & W., Ltd. Catalogue of chamber music. 1949

Composers' Guild of Great Britain. Catalogue, vol. 1: British orchestral music. 1959

English Folk Dance & Song Society
    A Guide to English folk-song collections by M. Dean-Smith. 1954
    An Index of English song, by E. A. White and M. Dean-Smith.
    1951
Goetz, Angelina. Catalogue [of scores] R.A.M. 1903
Goodwin & Tabb Ltd. Reference catalogue – orchestral material. 1949
International Association of Music Libraries. Radio Commission.
    Catalogue of rare materials. 1959 (Members only)
National Federation of Music Societies
    Catalogue of chamber music. 1955
    Catalogue of choral works, 2nd edition. 1953
Plainsong & Mediaeval Music Society. Catalogue. 1928
Royal College of Music. Catalogue of printed music. 1909
Sacred Harmonic Society. Catalogue. New edition. 1872 (Collection
    deposited in Royal College of Music, 1883)

PRIVATE, ETC., MUSIC COLLECTIONS

A list of the principal collections, formerly independent and now to be found, complete or in part, in London libraries.

B.B.C.	= British Broadcasting Corporation
B.M.	= British Museum
C.M.L.	= Central Music Library
[1]E.F.D.S.S.	= English Folk Dance and Song Society
R.A.M.	= Royal Academy of Music
R.C.M.	= Royal College of Music
T.C.M.	= Trinity College of Music

Present location

Barry, C. A.	R.A.M.
Benson, L.	R.C.M.
Blom, Eric	C.M.L.
Blunt, Janet (folk material)	E.F.D.S.S.
Bonavia, F.	B.B.C.
Borghese, Antonio	B.M.
Boult, Sir Adrian (orchestral parts)	B.B.C.
(orchestral scores)	Liverpool University
Bridge, Sir Frederick	T.C.M.
Broadwood, Lucy (folk-song MSS.)	E.F.D.S.S.
Butterworth, George S. K. (folk-song MSS.)	E.F.D.S.S.

[1] For detailed description see *E.F.D.S.S. Journal*, Dec. 1958.

Chapel Royal (MSS.)	B.M.
Chappell, William (folk-song MSS.) . . .	E.F.D.S.S.
Charlotte, Queen, wife of George III . . .	B.M.
Chelle, W. (MS. treatises)	Lambeth Palace
Christie-Moor, Mrs. Winifred (Edwin Evans and Gerald Cooper collections)	C.M.L.
Church House, Westminster (Julian and Mann collections)	B.M.
Concentores Society	Gresham College
Concerts of Ancient Music	R.C.M.
Cooper, Gerald	C.M.L.
Cotton (MSS.)	B.M.
Cross, Percy (orchestral music – the 'Siddell' Library, Manchester)	B.B.C.
Dannreuther, Edward	R.C.M.
Dent, Edward (opera scores)	Sadler's Wells
Dragonetti (operas)	B.M.
Edwards, F. G.	B.M.
Egerton (MSS.)	B.M.
Einstein, A. (Smith College archive: film) . .	B.B.C.
Ella, John	R.C.M.
Elvey, Sir George	University of London
English Bach Society	R.A.M.
Evans, Edwin	C.M.L.
Folk Song Society	E.F.D.S.S.
Fox Strangways, A. H.	B.B.C.
Gardiner, G. B. (folk-songs)	E.F.D.S.S.
Gardiner, H. Balfour (folk-song MSS.) . .	E.F.D.S.S.
Gatty, R. A. (folk-songs)	E.F.D.S.S.
George III, IV	B.M.
Gilchrist, Anne G. (folk material) . . .	E.F.D.S.S.
Goetz, Angelina (full scores)	R.A.M.
Gordon, J. B. (vocal scores)	Sadler's Wells
Grainger, Percy (folk-song MSS.) . . .	E.F.D.S.S.
Grove, Sir George (printed music) . . .	R.C.M.
Hammond, H. E. D. (folk-songs) . . .	E.F.D.S.S.
Harley (MSS.)	B.M.
Hawkins, Sir John (treatises and madrigals) . .	B.M.
Hill, A. F. (early editions: part of collection) . .	B.M.
Hirsch, Paul	B.M.
Julian, J. (hymnology)	B.M.
Kalisch, A. (vocal scores)	R.A.M.

Present location

Kennedy, Peter (folk-song recordings) . . .	E.F.D.S.S.
Kimpton, G. (orchestral music)	R.A.M.
King's Music Library (now Royal Music Library) .	B.M.
Lambert, Constant (orchestral music) . . .	B.B.C.
Landau, Baron Horace de (MSS. and early editions:	
part of collection)	B.M.
Lansdowne (MSS.)	B.M.
Leather, Mrs. E. M. (folk-songs)	E.F.D.S.S.
Littleton, A. H. (early music and treatises) . .	University of London
Lomax, Alan (folk-song recordings) . . .	E.F.D.S.S.
Madrigal Society	B.M.
Mann, A. H. (hymnology)	B.M.
Meyerstein, E. H. W. (autographs: part of collection)	B.M.
Newman, Eldridge (orchestral music) . . .	B.B.C.
Newmarch, Rosa (vocal scores)	Sadler's Wells
Novello & Co. (vocal scores)	Sadler's Wells
Parker, Rev. John (MS. Continental madrigals) .	B.M.
Parry, Sir Charles H. H. (printed music) . . .	R.C.M.
(MSS.)	B.M.
Perabo, E. (MSS.)	B.M.
Pitt, Percy (orchestral music)	B.B.C.
Prendergast, H. (church music)	R.A.M.
Ries, Ferdinand	R.A.M.
Ronald, Sir Landon (orchestral music) . . .	B.B.C.
Royal Music Library (formerly King's Music Library)	B.M.
Royal Philharmonic Society (MSS.) . . .	B.M.
(printed scores and parts)	R.A.M.
Sacred Harmonic Society (printed music) . .	R.C.M.
(MSS.)	B.M.
Scholes, Percy (portion of library, remainder to McGill	
University, Montreal)	C.M.L.
Sharp, Cecil (photo-copies and microfilms of folk	
materials: originals in Clare College, Cambridge) .	B.M. and E.F.D.S.S.
Siddell, F. W. (orchestral music – the Percy Cross	
Library, Manchester)	B.B.C.
Sloane, Sir Hans (MSS.)	B.M.
Smith, J. C. (Handel transcripts)	B.M.
Stanford, Sir Charles (autographs)	R.C.M.
Stevens, R. J. S. (MSS. and printed editions) . .	R.A.M.
Terry, C. S. (Bach collection, ex R.C.M.) . .	Oxford University Faculty of Music
Thomas, A. Goring	R.C.M.

Present location

Vernon, Lord (Italian music)	B.M.
Victoria, Queen	B.M.
Victoria and Albert Museum	R.C.M.
Waley, S. W.	R.C.M.
Westmorland, 11th Earl of	R.A.M.
White, Rev. E. H. (folk-song index) . .	E.F.D.S.S.
Williams, R. Vaughan (folk materials) . .	E.F.D.S.S.
Windsor, J. M.	R.C.M.
Wood, Sir Henry J. (orchestral music) . .	R.A.M.

INDEX

Capital letters indicate subjects or forms of literature described as special or important collections.

317